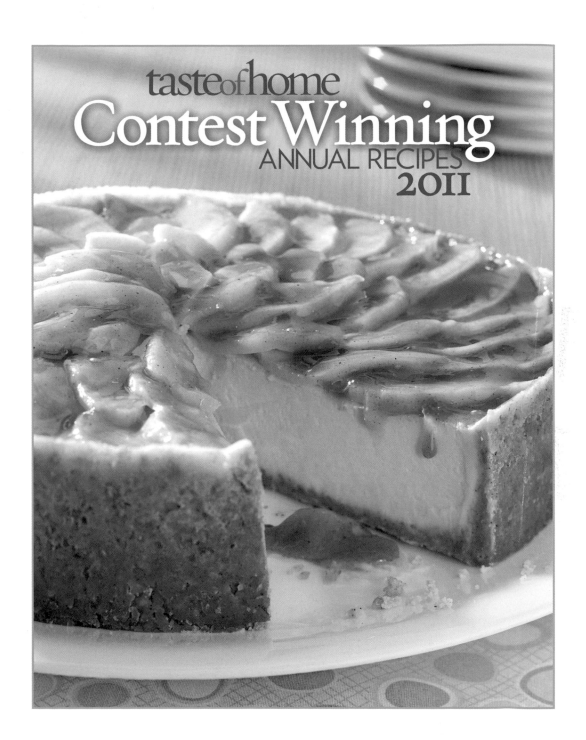

taste of home
Contest Winning
ANNUAL RECIPES
2011

taste of home
Contest Winning
ANNUAL RECIPES
2011

VICE PRESIDENT, EDITOR IN CHIEF: Catherine Cassidy
VICE PRESIDENT, EXECUTIVE EDITOR/BOOKS: Heidi Reuter Lloyd
CREATIVE DIRECTOR: Howard Greenberg
FOOD DIRECTOR: Diane Werner, RD
SENIOR EDITOR/BOOKS: Mark Hagen
EDITOR: Michelle Rozumalski
ASSOCIATE CREATIVE DIRECTOR: Edwin Robles, Jr.
ART DIRECTORS: Gretchen Trautman, Jessie Sharon
CONTENT PRODUCTION SUPERVISOR: Julie Wagner
LAYOUT DESIGNER: Kathy Crawford
PROOFREADER: Linne Bruskewitz
RECIPE TESTING & EDITING: Taste of Home Test Kitchen
FOOD PHOTOGRAPHY: Taste of Home Photo Studio
ADMINISTRATIVE ASSISTANT: Barb Czysz

NORTH AMERICAN CHIEF MARKETING OFFICER: Lisa Karpinski
VICE PRESIDENT/BOOK MARKETING: Dan Fink
CREATIVE DIRECTOR/CREATIVE MARKETING: Jim Palmen

THE READER'S DIGEST ASSOCIATION, INC.
PRESIDENT AND CHIEF EXECUTIVE OFFICER: Mary G. Berner
PRESIDENT, NORTH AMERICAN AFFINITIES: Suzanne M. Grimes

TASTE OF HOME BOOKS
© 2011 REIMAN MEDIA GROUP, LLC
5400 S. 60TH ST., GREENDALE WI 53129
INTERNATIONAL STANDARD BOOK NUMBER (10): 0-89821-874-8
INTERNATIONAL STANDARD BOOK NUMBER (13): 978-0-89821-874-9
INTERNATIONAL STANDARD SERIAL NUMBER: 1548-4157
ALL RIGHTS RESERVED. PRINTED IN U.S.A.

TASTE OF HOME IS A REGISTERED TRADEMARK OF THE READER'S DIGEST ASSOCIATION, INC.

PICTURED ON FRONT COVER:
CINNAMON APPLE CHEESECAKE (P. 210). PHOTOGRAPH BY ROB HAGEN.
FOOD STYLED BY KAITLYN BESASIE. SET STYLED BY DEE DEE JACQ.

FOR OTHER TASTE OF HOME BOOKS AND PRODUCTS, VISIT WWW.SHOPTASTEOFHOME.COM.

TABLE OF CONTENTS

BARBECUE WINGS, PG. 14

SMOKED TURKEY PASTA SALAD, PG. 44

TANGY MEAT SAUCE, PG. 107

ICED CINNAMON CHIP COOKIES, PG. 169

OVER 350
PRIZE-WINNING RECIPES & TIPS!

Every edition of *Contest Winning Annual Recipes* gives you the "best of the best" from *Taste of Home*, the world's #1 food source. With so many top-rated dishes together in one cookbook, it's no wonder this series has become popular with cooks from coast to coast.

You'll find even more favorites in this brand-new eighth edition, *Contest Winning Annual Recipes 2011*. It's packed with more than 350 prize-worthy specialties and expert kitchen tips.

Each standout dish was a contest winner in either *Taste of Home* magazine or one of its sister magazines—*Simple & Delicious, Healthy Cooking, Country* and *Country Woman*. We've included an entire year's worth of winners. It truly is the "cream of the crop!"

Wondering how recipes become tops in a contest? First, home cooks from all around read our request for entries and send in their creations—the must-have dishes family and friends request time and again.

Then our Test Kitchen professionals sort through the many recipes we receive and prepare the most promising ones for our judging panel of experienced food editors. After much sampling (yum!), the judges select a Grand Prize winner and runners-up.

Winners from Dozens of Contests

The recipes in this collection come from more than two dozen different recipe contests, covering a wide variety of foods. So no matter what type of dish you're looking for, you're sure to find it here.

Ten big chapters have everything you need—snacks and beverages; salads; soups and sandwiches; breakfast dishes; main courses; sides, breads and condiments; cookies, bars and candy; cakes and pies; and desserts.

For a complete list of chapters, please see the Table of Contents on page 3. Below, we've included a quick summary of the year's worth of contests in this book and the top winner of each:

- **HAM IT UP:** Our judging panel decided the nicest slices came from Stuffed Ham with Raisin Sauce (p. 140), the Grand Prize winner.

- **MARVELOUS MUFFINS:** Berry Cheesecake Muffins (p. 76) were big with our taste-testers, who chose this recipe from over 3,000 entries.

- **READY FOR RHUBARB:** Ripe for the picking came Rhubarb Swirl Cheesecake (p. 226), a scrumptious dessert you'll want to serve all summer long.

- **STICK TO KABOBS:** Fire up for a hot time at your next barbecue with the first-place creation, Chicken and Asparagus Kabobs (p. 104).

- **ABSOLUTELY APPLES:** Chunky Apple Cake (p. 196) harvested high honors as the Grand Prize winner in this bountiful contest.

- **MEAT LOAF AND MEATBALLS:** Need something to satisfy hearty appetites? Rely on Taco Meat Loaves (p. 116) to please even the hungriest at the table.

- **MAIN DISHES FROM MIXES:** Take a shortcut that leads to made-from-scratch taste. Just use a mix to to fix Sausage Spinach Bake (p. 144).

- **MAKE IT IN THE MICROWAVE:** Top-rated Apricot Chicken (p. 100) is so special, everyone will think you spent hours in the kitchen.

- **FUSS-FREE CHICKEN:** For a winner of a dinner, start with a main course of quick-and-easy Smothered Chicken Breasts (p. 112).

- **EASY PICNIC SALADS:** Pack your basket with a refreshing medley everyone will love—first-place Crunchy Romaine Strawberry Salad (p. 36).

COLORFUL BEEF WRAPS, PG. 64

NO-BAKE LIME CHEESECAKE, PG. 222

- **30-MINUTE ENTREES:** Weeknight cooking doesn't get much faster—or more delicious—than Chicken in Lime Butter (p. 108).

- **SIMPLE PARTY STARTERS:** Finger foods are well in hand for time-crunched cooks when they rely on Grilled Jerk Chicken Wings (p. 10).

- **SIMMERING SENSATIONS:** Get your creative juices flowing with distinctive Corsican Chicken (p. 96), a slow-cooked entree the whole family will enjoy.

- **CHIP CHALLENGE:** When it comes to recipes featuring chocolate chips, you just can't beat decadent Chocolate Crunch Ice Cream (p. 218).

- **GELATIN GREATS:** This colorful contest left plenty of wiggle room, but first-place winner Tuxedo Cream Dessert (p. 222) really broke the mold.

- **PERKING UP PORK:** With veggies, apples and a luscious cream sauce, a platter of Country-Style Pork Medallions (p. 132) is guaranteed to please.

- **PEAR-ADISE ON A PLATE:** Orchard-fresh flavor was abundant in Old-Fashioned Pear Dessert (p. 214), chock-full of fresh fruit and autumn appeal.

- **AWESOME APPETIZERS:** Grand Prize-winning Buffalo Wing Poppers (p. 26) will be popular at sports parties, holiday gatherings—any event at all!

- **A LIGHT TAKE ON CAKES:** Watching what you eat? You can still indulge in a luscious dessert when you whip up sweet-tangy Lemon Delight Cake (p. 184).

- **MEATLESS MAINSTAYS:** No one will miss the meat when you make first-place Greek Pizzas (p. 126), topped with tomatoes, spinach and lots of cheese.

- **IT'S A WRAP:** Bundle up fancy appetizers—Veggie Shrimp Egg Rolls (p. 14)—for a get-together and be prepared to hear raves.

- **BRING ON THE BERRIES:** Our judges found a bushel of delight in comforting, oven-baked Berry Nectarine Buckle (p. 206).

- **TANTALIZING TOMATOES:** Terrific Tomato Tarts (p. 18) give you a pizza-like appetizer or side that has fresh-from-the-garden flavor.

- **TRIM DOWN WITH TURKEY:** For a Thanksgiving feast or any time at all, Peppery Grilled Turkey Breast (p. 92) will wow the crowd.

To help you find exactly the kinds of menu items you're searching for, we've included both a General Recipe Index and an Alphabetical Index at the end of this book. (They begin on page 228.)

Whatever celebrated specialties you choose from, with *Contest Winning Annual Recipes 2011*, you can rest assured they're honest-to-goodness winners—and sure to be prized by your family for years to come.

TERRIFIC TOMATO TART, PG. 18

PG. 14

PG. 9

PG. 28

SNACKS & BEVERAGES

Why settle for ordinary, ho-hum munchies from the store when you can serve something really special? Make eyes light up with Buffalo Wing Poppers, Calzone Pinwheels, Caramel Apple Dip and much more.

PG. 23

Rhubarb Cheesecake Smoothies

Prep: 20 min. + cooling

Kathy Specht, Clinton, Montana

We love smoothies and have lots of fun experimenting to create unusual combinations. With the extra-special touch of cream cheese, this refreshing concoction is a yummy way to help use up your bounty of homegrown rhubarb.

- 2 cups diced fresh *or* frozen rhubarb
- 1/4 cup water
- 4 tablespoons honey, *divided*
- 1-1/2 cups vanilla ice cream
- 1 cup milk
- 1 cup frozen sweetened sliced strawberries
- 2 packages (3 ounces *each*) cream cheese, cubed
- 1/2 cup vanilla yogurt
- 1/4 cup confectioners' sugar
- 5 ice cubes

1. In a large saucepan, bring the rhubarb, water and 2 tablespoons honey to a boil. Reduce heat; cover and simmer for 5-10 minutes or until rhubarb is tender. Remove from the heat; cool to room temperature.

2. In a blender, combine the vanilla ice cream, milk, rhubarb mixture, strawberries, cream cheese, vanilla yogurt, confectioners' sugar, ice cubes and remaining honey; cover and process for 1 minute or until smooth. Pour into chilled glasses; serve immediately. **Yield:** 6 servings.

Olive Bruschetta

Prep/Total Time: 30 min.

Linda Austin, Lake Hopatcong, New Jersey

The topping on this convenient and colorful party classic can be made several days ahead of time. In fact, it actually tastes better if prepared in advance so all of the fresh flavors can blend together. Serve this appetizer at room temperature with toasted slices of crusty French bread or your favorite crackers.

- 2 cups grape tomatoes, quartered
- 2 celery ribs, chopped
- 1/2 cup shredded carrot
- 1/4 cup sliced ripe olives
- 1/4 cup sliced pimiento-stuffed olives
- 1/4 cup minced fresh flat-leaf parsley
- 1/4 cup chopped red onion
- 1 teaspoon minced garlic
- 3 tablespoons olive oil
- 2 tablespoons balsamic vinegar
- 1/4 teaspoon salt
- 1/8 teaspoon pepper
- 1 loaf (1 pound) French bread baguette, sliced and toasted

In a large bowl, combine the first eight ingredients. In a small bowl, whisk the oil, vinegar, salt and pepper; pour over vegetables and toss to coat. Serve on toasted baguette slices. **Yield:** 2-1/2 dozen.

Curried Chicken Turnovers

Prep: 40 min. **Bake:** 20 min.

Mary Kisinger, Calgary, Alberta

Guests just can't resist these golden-brown turnovers. Everyone likes the scrumptious curried-chicken filling, and puff pastry makes for an impressive-looking hors d'oeuvre.

- 1/2 cup finely chopped celery
- 1/4 cup finely chopped onion
- 1/4 cup finely chopped carrot
- 2 teaspoons butter
- 1 tablespoon all-purpose flour
- 1-1/2 teaspoons curry powder
- 1/4 teaspoon salt
- 1/2 cup chicken broth
- 1-1/2 cups diced cooked chicken
- 1/4 cup sour cream
- 1/4 cup plain yogurt
- 1 package (17.3 ounces) frozen puff pastry, thawed
- 1 egg yolk
- 1 teaspoon water

1. In a large skillet, saute the celery, onion and carrot in butter for 4-6 minutes or until tender. Stir in the flour, curry powder and salt until blended. Add broth. Bring to a boil; cook and stir for 1 minute or until thickened. Remove from the heat. Stir in the chicken, sour cream and yogurt.

2. On a lightly floured surface, roll each pastry sheet into a 12-in. x 10-in. rectangle. With a floured 3-in. round cookie cutter, cut out 12 circles from each rectangle. Place 2 teaspoons chicken mixture on one side of each circle. Moisten edges with water; fold dough over filling. Press edges with a fork to seal.

3. Place 1 in. apart on a greased baking sheet. In a small bowl, beat egg yolk and water; brush over pastry. Bake at 400° for 17-20 minutes or until golden brown. Serve warm. **Yield:** 2 dozen.

Calzone Pinwheels

Prep/Total Time: 30 min.

Lisa Smith, Bryan, Ohio

Once you try these pint-sized calzones, you may never go back to the large ones! The cute tidbits take advantage of refrigerated crescent rolls—you simply spread on the filling, roll up the dough, cut slices and bake.

- 1/2 cup ricotta cheese
- 1 teaspoon Italian seasoning
- 1/4 teaspoon salt
- 1/2 cup shredded part-skim mozzarella cheese
- 1/2 cup diced pepperoni
- 1/4 cup grated Parmesan cheese
- 1/4 cup chopped fresh mushrooms
- 1/4 cup finely chopped green pepper
- 2 tablespoons finely chopped onion
- 1 package (8 ounces) refrigerated crescent rolls
- 1 jar (14 ounces) pizza sauce, warmed

1. In a small bowl, combine the ricotta cheese, Italian seasoning and salt. Stir in the mozzarella cheese, pepperoni, Parmesan cheese, mushrooms, green pepper and onion. Separate crescent dough into four rectangles; seal perforations.

2. Spread cheese mixture over each rectangle to within 1/4 in. of edges. Roll up jelly-roll style, starting with a short side; pinch seams to seal. Cut each into four slices.

3. Place slices cut side down on greased baking sheets. Bake at 375° for 10-15 minutes or until golden brown. Serve warm with pizza sauce. Refrigerate leftovers. **Yield:** 16 appetizers.

1 package (8 ounces) cream cheese, softened
1/2 cup mayonnaise
1-1/2 teaspoons Dijon mustard
1 can (6 ounces) small shrimp, rinsed and drained
1 can (6 ounces) crabmeat, drained, flaked and cartilage removed
2/3 cup shredded Monterey Jack cheese, *divided*
1/2 cup chopped green onions
1 round loaf (1 pound) sourdough bread
Assorted fresh vegetables

1. In a large bowl, beat the cream cheese, mayonnaise and mustard until smooth. Stir in the shrimp, crab, 1/3 cup Monterey Jack cheese and onions.

2. Cut the top fourth off the loaf of bread; carefully hollow out bottom, leaving a 1/2-in. shell. Cube removed bread; set aside.

3. Spoon seafood mixture into bread shell. Sprinkle with remaining cheese. Wrap tightly in heavy-duty foil and place on a baking sheet.

4. Bake at 350° for 25 minutes. Unwrap; bake 20-25 minutes longer or until cheese is melted and dip is heated through. Serve with vegetables and reserved bread cubes. **Yield:** 2-1/4 cups.

Bread Bowl Seafood Dip

Prep: 15 min. **Bake:** 45 min.

Terry Flewelling, Lacombe, Alberta

Our family has a special hors d'oeuvre supper every Christmas Eve, and this seafood-stuffed dip is a mainstay. I discovered the recipe when a friend of mine prepared it for my daughter's wedding shower. Sourdough bread makes an attractive "bowl" and looks even better surrounded by fresh veggies.

Bowled Over

Bread bowls are a fun and tasty way to serve stews, too. Many bakeries carry small round loaves specifically for this purpose. If you can't find any, look for extra-large crusty buns or firm sourdough rolls instead.

Grilled Jerk Chicken Wings

Prep/Total Time: 30 min.

1/2 cup Caribbean jerk seasoning
18 fresh chicken wingettes (2 to 3 pounds)
2 cups honey barbecue sauce
1/3 cup packed brown sugar
2 teaspoons prepared mustard
1 teaspoon ground ginger

1. Place jerk seasoning in a large resealable plastic bag; add chicken wings, a few at a time, and shake to coat. In a small bowl, combine barbecue sauce, brown sugar, mustard and ginger; set aside.

2. Using long-handled tongs, moisten a paper towel with cooking oil and lightly coat the grill rack. Grill chicken wings, covered, over medium heat or broil 4 in. from the heat for 12-16 minutes, turning occasionally.

3. Brush with sauce. Grill or broil, uncovered, 8-10 minutes longer or until juices run clear, basting and turning several times. **Yield:** 6 servings.

Editor's Note: Caribbean jerk seasoning may be found in the spice aisle of your grocery store.

CAREN ADAMS FONTANA, CALIFORNIA

I've been serving this Caribbean-style appetizer for many years, and it's become a must-have menu item for every get-together I host. The lip-smacking chicken wings are so simple to fix and don't require a lot of ingredients or preparation time. You can also change up the recipe for different crowds by altering the seasoning for a mild or extra-spicy kick.

GRAND PRIZE WINNER

Prosciutto Chicken Kabobs

Prep: 30 min. + marinating Grill: 10 min.

Elaine Sweet, Dallas, Texas

Fresh basil leaves give the prosciutto slices and chicken strips in these grilled wraps wonderful flavor.

3/4 cup five-cheese Italian salad dressing
1/4 cup lime juice
2 teaspoons marinade for chicken
1/2 pound boneless skinless chicken breasts,
    cut into 3-inch x 1/2-inch strips
12 thin slices prosciutto
24 fresh basil leaves

AVOCADO DIP:
2 medium ripe avocados, peeled
1/4 cup minced fresh cilantro
2 green onions, chopped
2 tablespoons lime juice
2 tablespoons mayonnaise
1-1/2 teaspoons prepared horseradish
1 garlic clove, minced
1/4 teaspoon salt

1. In a large resealable plastic bag, combine the Italian salad dressing, lime juice and marinade for chicken; add the chicken. Seal bag and turn to coat; refrigerate for 1 hour.

2. Drain and discard the marinade. Fold prosciutto slices in half; top each with two basil leaves and a chicken strip. Roll up jelly-roll style, starting with a short side. Thread the roll-ups onto metal or soaked wooden skewers.

3. Grill, covered, over medium heat or broil 4 in. from the heat for 5 minutes on each side or until chicken is no longer pink.

4. Meanwhile, in a small bowl, mash the avocados. Stir in the cilantro, onions, lime juice, mayonnaise, horseradish, garlic and salt. Serve with kabobs. **Yield:** 12 appetizers.

Editor's Note: This recipe was tested with Lea & Perrins Marinade for Chicken.

Rosemary Cheese Patties

Prep/Total Time: 25 min.

Judy Armstrong, Prairieville, Louisiana

Everyone in our house loves snacks, so I combined some of our favorite ingredients to create this speedy stovetop recipe. The golden cheese patties seasoned with rosemary, cayenne pepper and garlic can be assembled in advance, then browned in the skillet just before your guests arrive.

1 package (8 ounces) cream cheese, softened
1 cup grated Parmesan cheese
3/4 cup seasoned bread crumbs, *divided*
2 eggs
1-1/2 to 2 teaspoons minced fresh rosemary
1-1/2 teaspoons minced garlic
1/8 to 1/4 teaspoon cayenne pepper
2 tablespoons olive oil
Marinara sauce, warmed, optional

1. In a large bowl, beat the cream cheese, Parmesan cheese, 1/4 cup bread crumbs, eggs, rosemary, garlic and cayenne until blended.

2. Place the remaining crumbs in a shallow bowl. Shape heaping tablespoonfuls of cheese mixture into 1-1/2-in. balls; flatten to 1/2-in. thickness. Coat with bread crumbs.

3. In a large skillet, brown patties in oil in batches over medium heat until golden brown. Drain on paper towels. Serve warm with marinara sauce if desired. **Yield:** 12 servings.

Spicy Pork Baguette Bites

Prep: 20 min. + marinating **Bake:** 30 min.

Virginia Anthony, Jacksonville, Florida

Here's an interesting twist on mini cocktail sandwiches. Lime mayonnaise provides a cool counterpoint to the nicely spiced pork, and toasted baguette slices add crunch.

1 teaspoon paprika
1/2 teaspoon salt
1/2 teaspoon dried oregano
1/2 teaspoon ground cumin
1/4 teaspoon garlic powder
1/4 teaspoon cayenne pepper
1/4 teaspoon pepper
1 pork tenderloin (1 pound)
LIME MAYONNAISE:
1/2 cup mayonnaise
1 tablespoon lime juice
1/2 teaspoon grated lime peel
1 French bread baguette (1 pound), sliced and toasted
Additional grated lime peel, optional

1. In a small bowl, combine the first seven ingredients; rub over the pork tenderloin. Place in a large resealable plastic bag; seal and refrigerate overnight.

2. Place the pork tenderloin on a rack in a foil-lined shallow roasting pan. Bake, uncovered, at 425° for 30-35 minutes or until a meat thermometer reads 160°. Let stand for 5 minutes.

3. Meanwhile, in a small bowl, combine mayonnaise, lime juice and peel. Thinly slice the pork tenderloin; serve on toasted bread with a dollop of lime mayonnaise. Sprinkle with additional lime peel if desired. **Yield:** 20-24 appetizers.

Fontina Asparagus Tart

Prep: 15 min. **Bake:** 20 min.

Heidi Meek, Grand Rapids, Michigan

This elegant vegetable appetizer made with convenient frozen puff pastry, lots of fontina cheese and a splash of lemon is ready for baking in just 15 minutes. But it looks so impressive, your family and friends will think you slaved in the kitchen all day. They'll also be vying for every last tasty slice!

1 pound fresh asparagus, trimmed
1 sheet frozen puff pastry, thawed
1/2 pound fontina cheese, shredded, *divided*
2 tablespoons lemon juice
1 teaspoon grated lemon peel
1 tablespoon olive oil
1/4 teaspoon salt
1/4 teaspoon pepper

1. In a large skillet, bring 1 in. of water to a boil; add asparagus. Cover and cook for 3-5 minutes or just until crisp-tender; drain.

2. On a lightly floured surface, unfold puff pastry. Roll into a 16-in. x 12-in. rectangle; transfer to a parchment paper-lined baking sheet. Bake at 400° for 10 minutes or until golden brown.

3. Sprinkle 1-1/2 cups cheese over pastry. Arrange asparagus on top; sprinkle with remaining cheese. Combine the lemon juice, lemon peel, oil, salt and pepper; sprinkle over top. Bake 10-15 minutes longer or until asparagus is tender and cheese is melted. Slice and serve warm. **Yield:** 24 servings.

Barbecue Wings

Prep/Total Time: 30 min.

Sara Yarrington, Salem, New Hampshire

With a hint of celery seed and hot sauce, these spicy-sweet chicken wings always disappear quickly at get-togethers.

Oil for deep-fat frying
 1 **package (40 ounces) fresh *or* frozen chicken wingettes, thawed**
 1/2 **cup barbecue sauce**
 1 **tablespoon butter**
 1 **teaspoon celery seed**
 1 **teaspoon hot pepper sauce**

1. In an electric skillet or deep-fat fryer, heat the oil to 375°. Fry the chicken wings, a few at a time, for 8 minutes or until golden brown and juices run clear, turning occasionally. Drain the chicken wings on paper towels.

2. In a small microwave-safe bowl, combine the barbecue sauce, butter, celery seed and hot pepper sauce. Cover and microwave on high for 1 minute or until heated through.

3. Place the chicken wings in a large bowl; add prepared sauce and toss to coat. **Yield:** 6 servings.

Veggie Shrimp Egg Rolls

Prep: 45 min. + standing Cook: 10 min./batch

 This recipe includes Nutrition Facts & Diabetic Exchanges.

 2 **teaspoons minced fresh gingerroot**
 1 **garlic clove, minced**
 3 **tablespoons olive oil, *divided***
 1/2 **pound uncooked medium shrimp, peeled, deveined and chopped**
 2 **green onions, finely chopped**
 1 **medium carrot, finely chopped**
 1 **medium sweet red pepper, finely chopped**
 1 **cup canned bean sprouts, rinsed and finely chopped**
 2 **tablespoons water**
 2 **tablespoons reduced-sodium soy sauce**
 38 **wonton wrappers**
APRICOT-MUSTARD DIPPING SAUCE:
 3/4 **cup apricot spreadable fruit**
 1 **tablespoon water**
 1 **tablespoon lime juice**
 1 **tablespoon reduced-sodium soy sauce**
 1-1/2 **teaspoons Dijon mustard**
 1/4 **teaspoon minced fresh gingerroot**

1. In a large skillet, saute the ginger and garlic in 1 tablespoon oil over medium heat for 1 minute. Add the shrimp, green onions, carrot, red pepper, bean sprouts, water and soy sauce; cook and stir for 2-3 minutes or until vegetables are crisp-tender and the shrimp turn pink.

2. Reduce heat to low; cook for 4-5 minutes or until most of the liquid has evaporated. Remove from the heat; let stand for 15 minutes.

3. Place a tablespoonful of shrimp mixture in the center of a wonton wrapper. (Keep the wrappers covered with a damp paper towel until ready to use.) Fold the bottom corner over filling. Fold sides toward the center over filling. Moisten remaining corner with water; roll up tightly to seal.

4. In a large skillet over medium heat, cook the egg rolls, a few at a time, in remaining oil for 5-7 minutes on each side or until golden brown. Drain on paper towels.

5. In a blender, combine the sauce ingredients; cover and process until smooth. Serve with egg rolls. **Yield:** 38 egg rolls.

Nutrition Facts: 2 egg rolls with 1-1/2 teaspoons sauce equals 108 calories, 3 g fat (trace saturated fat), 19 mg cholesterol, 222 mg sodium, 17 g carbohydrate, 1 g fiber, 4 g protein. **Diabetic Exchanges:** 1 starch, 1/2 fat.

CAROLE RESNICK CLEVELAND, OHIO

These Asian-inspired appetizers are sure to be the hit of your next cocktail party. The egg rolls are loaded with chopped shrimp, but you could also try them with cooked crab, lobster or chicken instead. They're so good with the tangy apricot dipping sauce.

GRAND
PRIZE
WINNER

Black Forest Ham Pinwheels

Prep: 20 min. + chilling

Kate Dampier, Quail Valley, California

These popular pinwheels always wow the crowd at Christmas parties and other events. People like the smokiness of the ham and the surprise of the dried cherries.

> 1 package (8 ounces) cream cheese, softened
> 4 teaspoons minced fresh dill
> 1 tablespoon lemon juice
> 2 teaspoons Dijon mustard
> Dash salt and pepper
> 1/2 cup dried cherries, chopped
> 1/4 cup chopped green onions
> 5 flour tortillas (10 inches), room temperature
> 1/2 pound sliced deli Black Forest ham
> 1/2 pound sliced Swiss cheese

1. In a small bowl, beat the cream cheese, dill, lemon juice, mustard, salt and pepper until blended. Stir in dried cherries and onions. Spread over each tortilla; layer with ham and cheese.

2. Roll up tightly; wrap in plastic wrap. Refrigerate for at least 2 hours. Cut into 1/2-in. slices. **Yield:** about 3-1/2 dozen.

Strawberry Banana Smoothies

Prep/Total Time: 5 min.

Christy Adkins, Martinez, Georgia

Frozen fruit makes these frosty thirst-quenchers extra thick and refreshing on a warm summer's day. Best of all, the recipe is a great way to use up that last banana.

> ✔ This recipe includes Nutrition Facts & Diabetic Exchanges.

> 3/4 cup fat-free milk
> 3/4 cup ice cubes, crushed
> 1/2 cup strawberry yogurt
> 1/2 cup frozen unsweetened strawberries
> 1 small firm banana, chopped and frozen
> Sugar substitute equivalent to 1/4 cup sugar

In a blender, combine all of the ingredients; cover and process for 30-45 seconds or until smooth. Stir mixture if necessary. Pour into chilled glasses; serve immediately. **Yield:** 3 servings.

Editor's Note: This recipe was tested with Splenda no-calorie sweetener.

Nutrition Facts: 1 cup equals 110 calories, 1 g fat (trace saturated fat), 3 mg cholesterol, 55 mg sodium, 23 g carbohydrate, 1 g fiber, 4 g protein. **Diabetic Exchanges:** 1/2 fruit, 1/2 reduced-fat milk.

Cran-Apple Salsa

Prep/Total Time: 15 min.

Jody Bauer, Balaton, Minnesota

Here's a snack-time twist on the usual cranberry relish served at holiday dinners. The salsa packs a sweet-tart blend of fresh flavors, goes together in a mere 15 minutes and has beautiful ruby-red color. Just add tortilla chips and enjoy!

 This recipe includes Nutrition Facts & Diabetic Exchange.

1 package (12 ounces) fresh *or* frozen cranberries, thawed
3 medium apples, cut into wedges
1 medium sweet red pepper, cut into pieces
1 small red onion, chopped
1/2 cup sugar
1/3 cup unsweetened apple juice
3 tablespoons minced fresh cilantro
2 tablespoons chopped jalapeno pepper
1 teaspoon grated lime peel
Tortilla chips

1. In a food processor, process the cranberries, apples, sweet red pepper and red onion in batches until coarsely pureed.

2. Transfer to a serving bowl. Stir in the sugar, apple juice, cilantro, jalapeno and lime peel. Refrigerate until serving. Serve with tortilla chips. **Yield:** 5 cups.

Editor's Note: When cutting hot peppers, disposable gloves are recommended. Avoid touching your face.

Nutrition Facts: 1/4 cup (calculated without chips) equals 45 calories, trace fat (trace saturated fat), 0 cholesterol, 1 mg sodium, 12 g carbohydrate, 1 g fiber, trace protein. **Diabetic Exchange:** 1 fruit.

Fresh Advice

Fresh cranberries are in season from early fall through December. When buying, look for packages with shiny, bright red (light or dark) cranberries. Avoid berries that are bruised, shriveled or have brown spots.

Festive Baked Brie

Prep/Total Time: 30 min.

Genny Derer, Madison, Wisconsin

This rich, smooth Brie cheese is reminiscent of fondue. With a topping of sun-dried tomatoes, herbs and caramelized onions, it's a real showstopper on an appetizer buffet.

1 large onion, halved and thinly sliced
2 tablespoons butter
2 tablespoons olive oil
1/2 cup oil-packed sun-dried tomatoes, drained and chopped
1/4 cup minced fresh parsley
2 tablespoons minced fresh basil
Dash pepper
1 round (8 ounces) Brie cheese
Assorted crackers

1. In a large skillet over medium heat, cook onion in butter and oil for 15-20 minutes or until golden brown, stirring frequently; set aside.

2. In a small bowl, combine the tomatoes, parsley, basil and pepper. Remove rind from the top of the Brie; place Brie in an ungreased ovenproof serving dish. Top with tomato mixture and onion mixture.

3. Bake, uncovered, at 400° for 10-12 minutes or until cheese is softened. Serve warm with crackers. **Yield:** 6-8 servings.

1 cup water
2 tablespoons butter
1/2 teaspoon salt
1/8 teaspoon cayenne pepper
1 cup all-purpose flour
4 eggs
1-1/4 cups shredded Gruyere *or* Swiss cheese
1 tablespoon Dijon mustard
1/4 cup grated Parmesan cheese

1. In a large saucepan, bring water, butter, salt and cayenne to a boil. Add flour all at once and stir until a smooth ball forms. Remove from the heat; let stand for 5 minutes. Add eggs, one at a time, beating well after each addition. Continue beating until mixture is smooth and shiny. Stir in Gruyere and mustard.

2. Drop by rounded teaspoonfuls 2 in. apart onto greased baking sheets. Sprinkle with Parmesan cheese. Bake at 425° for 15-20 minutes or until golden brown. Serve warm or cold. **Yield:** 4 dozen.

Cheese Puffs

Prep: 15 min. **Bake:** 15 min./batch

Jamie Wetter, Boscobel, Wisconsin

Looking through one of my mom's old cookbooks, I discovered this recipe and thought of updating it by adding cayenne pepper and Dijon mustard. The tender puffs bake to a golden brown and prove irresistible on an appetizer table.

A Good Egg

You can check the freshness of an uncooked egg by placing it in a glass of cold water. If the egg is fresh, it will remain on the bottom of the glass. If the egg floats to the surface of the water, it is not fresh and should not be used.

Terrific Tomato Tart

Prep: 15 min. **Bake:** 20 min.

 This recipe includes Nutrition Facts & Diabetic Exchanges.

12 sheets phyllo dough (14 inches x 9 inches)
2 tablespoons olive oil
2 tablespoons dry bread crumbs
2 tablespoons prepared pesto
3/4 cup crumbled feta cheese, *divided*
1 medium tomato, cut into 1/4-inch slices
1 large yellow tomato, cut into 1/4-inch slices
1/4 teaspoon pepper
5 to 6 fresh basil leaves, thinly sliced

1. Place one sheet of phyllo dough on a baking sheet lined with parchment paper; brush dough with 1/2 teaspoon oil and sprinkle with 1/2 teaspoon bread crumbs. (Keep the remaining phyllo covered with plastic wrap and a damp towel to prevent it from drying out.) Repeat layers, being careful to brush oil all the way to edges.

2. Fold each side 3/4 in. toward center to form a rim. Spread with pesto and sprinkle with half of the feta cheese. Alternately arrange the red and yellow tomato slices over the cheese. Sprinkle with pepper and remaining feta.

3. Bake at 400° for 20-25 minutes or until the crust is golden brown and crispy. Cool on a wire rack for 5 minutes. Remove parchment paper before cutting. Garnish with basil. **Yield:** 8 servings.

Nutrition Facts: 1 piece equals 135 calories, 7 g fat (2 g saturated fat), 7 mg cholesterol, 221 mg sodium, 13 g carbohydrate, 1 g fiber, 5 g protein. **Diabetic Exchanges:** 1-1/2 fat, 1 starch.

DIANE HALFERTY CORPUS CHRISTI, TEXAS

These warm squares look fabulous and taste just as good. Colorful fresh tomatoes, feta cheese and prepared pesto perfectly complement the crispy phyllo-dough crust.

GRAND
PRIZE
WINNER

Slow Cooker Mexican Dip

Prep: 15 min. **Cook:** 1-1/2 hours

Heather Courtney, Ames, Iowa

My husband and I really enjoy entertaining, so we take every opportunity to do so. Packed with ground beef, hot Italian sausage, refried beans, rice and cheese, this Southwestern-style dip is always a hit as well as a request. It couldn't be much easier to put together, and using our slow cooker leaves us free to share more quality time with guests.

1-1/2 **pounds ground beef**
   1 **pound bulk hot Italian sausage**
   1 **cup chopped onion**
   1 **package (8.8 ounces) ready-to-serve Spanish rice**
   1 **can (16 ounces) refried beans**
   1 **can (10 ounces) enchilada sauce**
   1 **pound process cheese (Velveeta), cubed**
   1 **package tortilla chip scoops**

1. In a Dutch oven, cook the beef, sausage and onion over medium heat until meat is no longer pink; drain. Heat rice according to package directions.

2. In a 3-qt. slow cooker, combine the meat mixture, rice, beans, enchilada sauce and cheese. Cover and cook on low for 1-1/2 to 2 hours or until the cheese is melted. Serve with tortilla scoops. **Yield:** 8 cups.

Hearty Rye Melts

Prep/Total Time: 30 min.

Melanie Schlaf, Edgewood, Kentucky

When we moved from the Midwest to Kentucky, we were invited to a neighborhood gathering where we sampled this distinctive finger food. We learned that it's traditionally served at Derby Day parties, but the meat-topped bread slices have become a favorite at our house year-round.

1/2 **pound lean ground beef (90% lean)**
1/2 **pound bulk pork sausage**
1-1/2 **teaspoons chili powder**
   8 **ounces process cheese (Velveeta), shredded**
  24 **slices snack rye bread**
Fresh parsley sprigs, stems removed

1. In a large skillet, cook the beef and sausage over medium heat until no longer pink; drain. Add chili powder and cheese; cook and stir until the cheese is melted. Spread a heaping tablespoonful onto each slice of bread. Place on a baking sheet.

2. Bake at 350° for 12-15 minutes or until the edges of bread begin to crisp. Garnish with parsley. Serve warm. **Yield:** 2 dozen.

Parsley Pointer

To keep fresh parsley in the refrigerator for several weeks, wash the entire bunch in warm water, shake off all excess moisture, wrap it in a paper towel and seal it in a plastic bag. For longer storage, remove the paper towel and place the sealed bag in the freezer. Break off and crumble the amount you need for recipes.

Savory Ham Cheesecake

Prep: 35 min. **Bake:** 1 hour + chilling

Shannon Soper, West Bend, Wisconsin

My mother was the best cook I knew—everything she made was special. She liked this beautiful appetizer cheesecake on Sundays after the previous night's ham dinner.

    3 cups oyster crackers, crushed
    1 cup grated Parmesan cheese
1/3 cup butter, melted
FILLING:
    4 packages (8 ounces *each*) cream cheese,
        softened
    4 eggs, lightly beaten
    2 cups finely chopped fully cooked ham
    2 cups (8 ounces) shredded Swiss cheese
1/3 cup minced chives
1/4 cup minced fresh basil
1/4 teaspoon salt
1/4 teaspoon white pepper
Assorted crackers

1. In a large bowl, combine the cracker crumbs, Parmesan cheese and butter. Set aside 1/4 cup crumb mixture for topping. Press remaining crumb mixture onto the bottom and 2 in. up the sides of a greased 9-in. springform pan. Cover and refrigerate for at least 30 minutes.

2. In a large bowl, beat cream cheese until smooth. Add the eggs; beat on low speed just until combined (mixture will be thick). Add the ham, Swiss cheese, chives, basil, salt and pepper; beat just until combined. Pour into the prepared crust. Sprinkle with reserved crumb mixture.

3. Place pan on a baking sheet. Bake at 325° for 60-70 minutes or until the filling is almost set. Turn the oven off. Leave cheesecake in oven with the door ajar for 30 minutes.

4. Cool on a wire rack for 10 minutes. Carefully run a knife around edge of pan to loosen; cool 1 hour longer. Refrigerate overnight. Remove sides of pan. Serve cheesecake chilled or at room temperature with crackers. **Yield:** 24-30 servings.

Warm Crab Dip

Prep/Total Time: 15 min.

Colleen Taliaferro, Woodbine, Maryland

Maryland's Chesapeake Bay is known for crabs, and they're a big favorite of ours. When fresh crabmeat is available, we'll use it in this recipe, but canned works well, too. The creamy dip is wonderful for holidays or any occasion at all.

    1 package (8 ounces) cream cheese, cubed
1/2 cup mayonnaise
    1 tablespoon lemon juice
    2 teaspoons Worcestershire sauce
1/2 teaspoon sherry, optional
    2 cans (6 ounces *each*) lump crabmeat, drained
    1 tablespoon chopped green onion
Assorted crackers *or* baked pita chips

In a large heavy saucepan, heat the cream cheese, mayonnaise, lemon juice, Worcestershire sauce and sherry if desired over low heat, stirring often. Stir in the crab and onion; heat through. Serve warm with crackers. **Yield:** 2-1/4 cups.

Chicken Lettuce Wraps

Prep/Total Time: 25 min.

Kendra Doss, Kansas City, Missouri

Filled with chicken, mushrooms, water chestnuts and carrots, these wraps are both wholesome and yummy. The gingerroot, rice vinegar and teriyaki sauce give them Asian flair.

 This recipe includes Nutrition Facts & Diabetic Exchanges.

1-1/2 **pounds boneless skinless chicken breasts, cubed**
1 **tablespoon plus 1-1/2 teaspoons peanut oil, *divided***
3/4 **cup chopped fresh mushrooms**
1 **can (8 ounces) water chestnuts, drained and diced**
1 **tablespoon minced fresh gingerroot**
2 **tablespoons rice vinegar**
2 **tablespoons reduced-sodium teriyaki sauce**
1 **tablespoon reduced-sodium soy sauce**
1/2 **teaspoon garlic powder**
1/4 **teaspoon crushed red pepper flakes**
1-1/2 **cups shredded carrots**
1/2 **cup julienned green onions**
12 **Bibb or Boston lettuce leaves**
1/3 **cup sliced almonds, toasted**

1. In a large nonstick skillet coated with cooking spray, cook chicken in 1 tablespoon oil for 3 minutes; drain. Add mushrooms, water chestnuts and ginger; cook 4-6 minutes longer or until chicken is no longer pink. Drain and set aside.

2. In a small bowl, whisk the rice vinegar, teriyaki sauce, soy sauce, garlic powder, red pepper flakes and remaining oil. Stir in the carrots, green onions and chicken mixture.

3. Spoon onto lettuce leaves; sprinkle with almonds. If desired, fold sides of lettuce over filling and roll up. **Yield:** 6 servings.

Nutrition Facts: 2 wraps equals 230 calories, 9 g fat (2 g saturated fat), 63 mg cholesterol, 278 mg sodium, 12 g carbohydrate, 3 g fiber, 26 g protein. **Diabetic Exchanges:** 3 very lean meat, 2 vegetable, 1 fat.

Turkey Wonton Cups

Prep: 30 min. **Bake:** 5 min./batch

Barbara Rafferty, Portsmouth, Rhode Island

Convenient wonton wrappers make these cute hors d'oeuvres as fun to make as they are to munch. I tried them at a party and couldn't believe how yummy they were. Ground turkey, cheddar cheese, ranch dressing, green onions and olives are all the ingredients you'll need for the filling.

 This recipe includes Nutrition Facts & Diabetic Exchanges.

48 wonton wrappers
1-1/4 pounds lean ground turkey
2 cups (8 ounces) shredded reduced-fat cheddar cheese
1 cup fat-free ranch salad dressing
1/2 cup chopped green onions
1/4 cup chopped ripe olives

1. Press wonton wrappers into miniature muffin cups coated with cooking spray. (Keep wrappers covered with a damp paper towel until ready to bake.) Bake at 375° for 5 minutes or until lightly browned. Cool for 2 minutes before removing from pans to wire racks.

2. In a large nonstick skillet coated with cooking spray, cook the turkey over medium heat until no longer pink; drain. In a large bowl, combine the turkey, cheese, ranch dressing, onions and olives. Spoon by rounded tablespoonfuls into wonton cups.

3. Place cups on an ungreased baking sheet. Bake at 375° for 5-6 minutes or until heated through. Serve warm. **Yield:** 4 dozen.

Nutrition Facts: 2 wonton cups equals 154 calories, 7 g fat (3 g saturated fat), 34 mg cholesterol, 366 mg sodium, 14 g carbohydrate, trace fiber, 11 g protein. **Diabetic Exchanges:** 1 starch, 1 lean meat, 1/2 fat.

Fruit and Caramel Brie

Prep/Total Time: 15 min.

Tracy Schuhmacher, Penfield, New York

Brie is one of my favorite cheeses, and this sweet-savory recipe is party-special but surprisingly easy to throw together.

1 round (8 ounces) Brie cheese, rind removed
1/3 cup caramel ice cream topping
1/4 cup dried cranberries
1/4 cup chopped dried apples
1/4 cup chopped walnuts
1 loaf (1 pound) French bread baguette, sliced and toasted

Place Brie in a microwave-safe bowl. In a small bowl, combine topping, berries, apples and nuts. Spread over Brie. Microwave, uncovered, on high for 60-90 seconds or until cheese is heated through and slightly melted. Serve with bread. **Yield:** 8 servings.

Editor's Note: This recipe was tested in a 1,100-watt microwave.

Brie in Brief

Named after a region of France, Brie is a soft cows' milk cheese that is pale in color with a grayish-white, edible rind. Brie cheese is perfect for use on cheese platters at parties...or to melt in sandwiches, soups or fondues.

Sugar 'n' Spice Nuts

Prep/Total Time: 30 min.

Joan Klinefelter, Utica, Illinois

My daughters, grandchildren...everyone looks forward to this mouthwatering mix of crunchy nuts, spices and fruit when they're home with us during the holiday season. And tucked in colorful tins, this snack makes a handy last-minute gift idea for busy hostesses or drop-in visitors.

- 1/4 cup packed brown sugar
- 1/2 teaspoon ground cinnamon
- 1/4 teaspoon cayenne pepper
- 1 egg white
- 1 cup salted cashews
- 1 cup pecan halves
- 1 cup dry roasted peanuts
- 1/2 cup dried cranberries

1. In a small bowl, combine brown sugar, cinnamon and cayenne; set aside. In a large bowl, whisk the egg white; add nuts and dried cranberries. Sprinkle with the sugar mixture and toss to coat. Spread in a single layer on a greased baking sheet.

2. Bake at 300° for 18-20 minutes or until golden brown, stirring once. Cool. Store in an airtight container. **Yield:** 3-1/2 cups.

Chicken Enchilada Dip

Prep/Total Time: 20 min.

Leah Davis, Morrow, Ohio

A friend brought this appetizer to our house for a dinner party. Guests loved the Southwestern-style chicken and cheese dip so much, no one had much of an appetite left for supper! My friend graciously shared the recipe, and I've served it many times since—always with rave reviews.

- 2 cups shredded cooked chicken
- 1 can (10-3/4 ounces) condensed cream of chicken soup, undiluted
- 1 cup (4 ounces) shredded cheddar cheese
- 1 can (5 ounces) evaporated milk
- 1/2 cup chopped celery
- 1/3 cup finely chopped onion
- 1 can (4 ounces) chopped green chilies
- 1 envelope taco seasoning

Tortilla chips

In a 2-qt. microwave-safe dish, combine the first eight ingredients. Microwave, uncovered, on high for 4-5 minutes; stir. Microwave, uncovered, 3-4 minutes longer or until heated through. Serve the dip with tortilla chips. **Yield:** 3 cups.

Editor's Note: This recipe was tested in a 1,100-watt microwave.

Greek Salsa

Prep/Total Time: 30 min.

Heidi Mitchell, Cornwall, Prince Edward Island

Color, texture and a fantastic blend of flavors—this salsa has it all. Plus, it's easy to adapt to suit your family.

- 1 tablespoon white balsamic vinegar
- 2 tablespoons olive oil, *divided*
- 2-1/2 teaspoons Greek seasoning, *divided*
- 1 garlic clove, minced
- 1 cup grape tomatoes, quartered
- 3/4 cup chopped cucumber
- 1/2 cup crumbled feta cheese
- 1/2 cup chopped red onion
- 1 can (2-1/4 ounces) sliced ripe olives, drained
- 1 package (12 ounces) whole wheat pita breads

1. In a small bowl, combine white balsamic vinegar, 1 tablespoon oil, 1-1/2 teaspoons Greek seasoning and garlic; set aside.

2. In a large bowl, combine the tomatoes, cucumber, feta cheese, onion and olives. Drizzle with the vinegar mixture and toss to coat. Chill until serving.

3. Cut each pita bread into eight wedges. Place on an ungreased baking sheet. Brush with remaining oil; sprinkle with remaining Greek seasoning. Bake at 400° for 6-8 minutes or until crisp. Serve chips with salsa. **Yield:** 2-3/4 cups salsa and 40 pita chips.

Sized Just Right

The recipe for refreshing Greek Salsa calls for mincing and chopping ingredients. Keep in mind that mincing generally results in pieces no larger than 1/8 inch, and chopping can produce 1/4-inch to 1/2-inch pieces.

1 cup seeded chopped tomatoes
1/2 cup diced zucchini
1/2 cup chopped sweet red pepper
1 small onion, diced
1 tablespoon brown sugar
2 teaspoons lime juice
2 teaspoons cider vinegar
1 teaspoon chopped seeded jalapeno pepper
1 garlic clove, minced
1/2 teaspoon ground cumin
1/8 teaspoon salt
1/8 teaspoon pepper
Tortilla chips

In a small bowl, combine the first 12 ingredients. Cover and refrigerate for 8 hours or overnight. Using a slotted spoon, transfer salsa to a serving bowl. Serve with tortilla chips. **Yield:** 2 cups.

Editor's Note: When cutting hot peppers, disposable gloves are recommended. Avoid touching your face.

Nutrition Facts: 1/2 cup (calculated without tortilla chips) equals 40 calories, trace fat (trace saturated fat), 0 cholesterol, 81 mg sodium, 9 g carbohydrate, 2 g fiber, 1 g protein. **Diabetic Exchange:** 2 vegetable.

Zucchini Tomato Salsa

Prep: 20 min. + chilling

Jennifer Magrey, Sterling, Connecticut

Wondering what to do with all of my garden-grown zucchini, I came up with this colorful salsa that also takes advantage of fresh tomatoes. Try it on tortilla chips, crackers, burgers, baked potatoes…even over cream cheese as a spread.

 This recipe includes Nutrition Facts & Diabetic Exchange.

Simple Seeding

To remove the seeds from a tomato for Zucchini Tomato Salsa or another recipe, cut the tomato in half horizontally and remove the stem. Holding a tomato half over a bowl or sink, scrape out the seeds with a small spoon or squeeze the tomato to force out the seeds. Then chop or slice as directed in the recipe.

Buffalo Wing Poppers

Prep: 20 min. **Bake:** 20 min.

20 jalapeno peppers
1 package (8 ounces) cream cheese, softened
1-1/2 cups (6 ounces) shredded part-skim mozzarella cheese
1 cup diced cooked chicken
1/2 cup blue cheese salad dressing
1/2 cup buffalo wing sauce

1. Cut peppers in half lengthwise, leaving stems intact; discard seeds. In a small bowl, combine the remaining ingredients. Pipe or stuff into pepper halves.

2. Place the stuffed pepper halves in a greased 15-in. x 10-in. x 1-in. baking pan. Bake, uncovered, at 325° for 20 minutes for spicy flavor, 30 minutes for medium and 40 minutes for mild. **Yield:** 40 appetizers.

Editor's Note: When cutting hot peppers, disposable gloves are recommended. Avoid touching your face.

BARBARA NOWAKOWSKI MESA, ARIZONA

The tastes of buffalo wings and pepper poppers pair up in this appealing appetizer. It's sure to disappear fast, so you may want to make a double batch—and have copies of the recipe handy!

GRAND PRIZE WINNER

Chorizo-Queso Egg Rolls

Prep: 45 min. + chilling **Cook:** 5 min./batch

Kari Wheaton, Beloit, Wisconsin

This combination of crisp wontons, tangy sausage and cream cheese is a take-off on my favorite Mexican entree.

   1/2 cup mayonnaise
   1/2 cup sour cream
     2 ounces cream cheese, softened
     2 tablespoons minced fresh cilantro
     1 tablespoon chopped chipotle pepper in adobo sauce
     6 ounces uncooked chorizo or bulk spicy pork sausage
     2 cups crumbled queso fresco
   1/4 cup enchilada sauce
   1/4 cup chopped green chilies
     1 package (12 ounces) wonton wrappers
Oil for frying

1. For dipping sauce, in a small bowl, combine the mayonnaise, sour cream, cream cheese, cilantro and chipotle peppers. Cover and refrigerate until serving.

2. Crumble the chorizo into a large skillet; cook for 6-8 minutes over medium heat or until fully cooked. Drain. Stir in the queso fresco, enchilada sauce and green chilies.

3. Position a wonton wrapper with one point toward you. Place 2 teaspoons of filling in the center. (Keep remaining wrappers covered with a damp paper towel until ready to use.) Fold bottom corner over filling; fold sides toward center over filling. Roll toward the remaining point. Moisten top corner with water; press to seal. Repeat with remaining wrappers and filling.

4. In an electric skillet, heat 1 in. of oil to 375°. Fry egg rolls in batches for 1-2 minutes on each side or until golden brown. Drain on paper towels. Serve warm with dipping sauce. **Yield:** 4 dozen.

Wassail Bowl Punch

Prep: 10 min. **Cook:** 1 hour

Margaret Harms, Jenkins, Kentucky

All ages will enjoy a mug of this heartwarming punch. The blend of spice, fruit and citrus flavors is wonderful! You can assemble it before heading outdoors for winter activities, then sip away the chill when you return.

     4 cups hot brewed tea
     4 cups cranberry juice
     4 cups unsweetened apple juice
     2 cups orange juice
     1 cup sugar
   3/4 cup lemon juice
     3 cinnamon sticks (3 inches)
   12 whole cloves

1. In a 5-qt. slow cooker, combine the first six ingredients. Place cinnamon sticks and cloves on a double thickness of cheesecloth; bring up the corners of the cloth and tie with string to form a bag. Add to slow cooker.

2. Cover and cook on high for 1 hour or until punch begins to boil. Discard spice bag. Serve warm. **Yield:** 3-1/2 quarts.

Caramel Apple Dip

Prep/Total Time: 15 min.

Becky Heiner, West Valley City, Utah

This four-ingredient caramel dip is so simple and scrumptious. People always want to know how long it took to prepare on the stovetop—and are amazed to learn that I made it in the microwave. When I don't have large marshmallows on hand, I simply substitute 2 cups of the miniature kind.

    1 package (14 ounces) caramels
    20 large marshmallows
    1/2 cup butter, melted
    1/3 cup heavy whipping cream
Apple slices

Place caramels in a microwave-safe bowl. Microwave, uncovered, on high for 1 minute. Add marshmallows; microwave for 1 minute or until marshmallows are melted, stirring occasionally. Whisk in butter and cream until combined. Serve with apple slices. Refrigerate leftovers. **Yield:** 2-1/2 cups.

Editor's Note: This recipe was tested in a 1,100-watt microwave.

Meatballs in Plum Sauce

Prep: 50 min. + standing Bake: 30 min.

Mary Poninski, Whittington, Illinois

A lip-smacking sauce featuring plum jam coats these moist, homemade bites beautifully. With a mix of ground beef, pork and veal, they're a meat-lover's dream and guaranteed to tide over hungry guests until dinnertime.

    1/2 cup milk
      1 cup soft bread crumbs
      1 egg, lightly beaten
      1 tablespoon Worcestershire sauce
      1 medium onion, finely chopped
    1/4 teaspoon salt
    1/4 teaspoon pepper
    1/8 teaspoon ground cloves
    1/2 pound lean ground beef
    1/2 pound ground pork
    1/2 pound ground veal
      2 tablespoons canola oil
    1/2 teaspoon beef bouillon granules
    1/2 cup boiling water
      3 tablespoons all-purpose flour
      1 cup plum jam
    1/2 cup chili sauce

1. In a large bowl, pour milk over bread crumbs; let stand for 10 minutes. Add the egg, Worcestershire sauce, onion, salt, pepper and cloves. Crumble beef, pork and veal over mixture and mix well (mixture will be soft). Shape into 1-in. balls.

2. In a large skillet, brown meatballs in oil in batches. Drain on paper towels. Place in a greased 13-in. x 9-in. baking dish.

3. In a small bowl, dissolve the beef bouillon in water. Stir flour into pan drippings until blended; add the bouillon mixture, jam and chili sauce. Bring to a boil; cook and stir for 1-2 minutes or until thickened. Pour over meatballs.

4. Cover and bake at 350° for 30-45 minutes or until the meat is no longer pink and the sauce is bubbly. **Yield:** 10-12 servings.

Flavorful Tomato Juice

Prep: 20 min. **Cook:** 45 min. + chilling

Jeannie Linsavage, Albuquerque, New Mexico

Jalapenos, spicy pepper sauce and horseradish are some of my favorite ingredients, and I knew they'd be the perfect way to spice up a thick, homemade tomato juice. Try this when you have a bounty of garden-fresh produce.

 This recipe includes Nutrition Facts & Diabetic Exchanges.

8 medium tomatoes, chopped
1-1/2 cups water
1 small onion, chopped
3 garlic cloves, minced
1 jalapeno pepper, seeded and chopped
3 tablespoons sugar
3 tablespoons lime juice
2 teaspoons celery seed
1 teaspoon salt
1 teaspoon ground mustard
1 teaspoon prepared horseradish
1/8 teaspoon dried basil
1/8 teaspoon dried parsley flakes
Dash hot pepper sauce

1. In a large saucepan, combine all the ingredients. Bring to a boil. Reduce heat; simmer, uncovered, for 30 minutes or until tomatoes are tender. Cool to room temperature.

2. Transfer mixture to a blender; cover and process until blended. Strain and discard seeds. Return tomato juice to saucepan. Bring to a boil. Reduce heat; simmer, uncovered, for 12-18 minutes or until juice measures 3 cups. Cool. Transfer to a pitcher; cover and refrigerate until chilled. **Yield:** 4 servings.

Editor's Note: When cutting hot peppers, disposable gloves are recommended. Avoid touching your face.

Nutrition Facts: 3/4 cup equals 121 calories, 2 g fat (trace saturated fat), 0 cholesterol, 624 mg sodium, 27 g carbohydrate, 4 g fiber, 3 g protein. **Diabetic Exchanges:** 2 vegetable, 1 starch.

Mini Spinach Frittatas

Prep/Total Time: 30 min.

Nancy Statkevicus, Tucson, Arizona

These delicious miniature frittatas come together in minutes and take less than half an hour to bake. Plus, the recipe doubles easily for a crowd and freezes well, too.

1 cup ricotta cheese
3/4 cup grated Parmesan cheese
2/3 cup chopped fresh mushrooms
1 package (10 ounces) frozen chopped spinach, thawed and squeezed dry
1 egg
1/2 teaspoon dried oregano
1/4 teaspoon salt
1/4 teaspoon pepper
24 slices pepperoni

1. In a small bowl, combine the first eight ingredients. Place a slice of pepperoni in each of 24 greased miniature muffin cups. Fill muffin cups three-fourths full with cheese mixture.

2. Bake at 375° for 20-25 minutes or until completely set. Carefully run a knife around edges of muffin cups to loosen. Serve warm. **Yield:** 2 dozen.

Baked Chicken Nachos

Prep: 20 min. **Bake:** 15 min.

Gail Cawsey, Fawnskin, California

My husband likes this snack so much, he often requests it for dinner! The nachos get fantastic flavor from seasonings and a splash of lime juice. The recipe calls for rotisserie chicken, but you could also use leftover chicken from a meal.

2 medium sweet red peppers, diced
1 medium green pepper, diced
3 teaspoons canola oil, *divided*
1 can (15 ounces) black beans, rinsed and drained
1 teaspoon minced garlic
1 teaspoon dried oregano
1/4 teaspoon ground cumin
2-1/4 cups shredded rotisserie chicken
4-1/2 teaspoons lime juice
1/8 teaspoon salt
1/8 teaspoon pepper
7-1/2 cups tortilla chips
8 ounces pepper Jack cheese, shredded
1/4 cup thinly sliced green onions
1/2 cup minced fresh cilantro
1 cup (8 ounces) sour cream
2 to 3 teaspoons diced pickled jalapeno peppers, optional

1. In a large skillet, saute peppers in 1-1/2 teaspoons oil for 3 minutes or until crisp-tender; transfer to a small bowl. In the same skillet, saute the beans, garlic, oregano and cumin in remaining oil for 3 minutes or until heated through.

2. Meanwhile, combine the chicken, lime juice, salt and pepper. In a greased 13-in. x 9-in. baking dish, layer half of the tortilla chips, pepper mixture, bean mixture, chicken, cheese, green onions and cilantro. Repeat layers.

3. Bake, uncovered, at 350° for 15-20 minutes or until heated through. Serve with sour cream and pickled jalapenos if desired. **Yield:** 16 servings.

PG. 49

PG. 46

PG. 36

SPECIAL SALADS

Confetti Broccoli Slaw for a backyard barbecue…Mixed Greens with French Dressing to round out a weekday meal…Asian Veggie Gelatin for a potluck…these are just some of the specialties you'll find here!

PG. 44

Beef Kabob Spinach Salad

Prep: 10 min. + marinating **Grill:** 10 min.

Gail Reinford, Souderton, Pennsylvania

This easy entree combines marinated, grilled beef with spinach and a creamy homemade dressing. I like to round out the meal with roasted potatoes and fresh-baked rolls.

- 1/4 cup packed brown sugar
- 4 teaspoons white vinegar
- 2 teaspoons chili powder
- 1 teaspoon salt
- 1 teaspoon canola oil
- 1/2 to 1 teaspoon hot pepper sauce
- 2 pounds beef top sirloin steak, cut into 1-inch cubes
- 1 cup (8 ounces) plain yogurt
- 1/3 cup chopped green onions
- 1 garlic clove, minced
- 1 package (10 ounces) fresh baby spinach

1. In a large resealable bag, combine the brown sugar, vinegar, chili powder, salt, oil and hot pepper sauce. Add the beef; seal the bag and turn to coat. Refrigerate for 30 minutes. Meanwhile, in a small bowl, combine the plain yogurt, green onions and garlic; cover and refrigerate until serving.

2. Drain and discard marinade. Thread the beef cubes onto eight metal or soaked wooden skewers. Grill, covered, over medium heat for 4-6 minutes on each side or until meat reaches desired doneness. Serve with spinach and yogurt sauce. **Yield:** 8 servings.

Holiday Tossed Salad

Prep/Total Time: 20 min.

Pat Loeffler, Grafton, Wisconsin

With red color from dried cranberries and unpeeled apples, this festive salad is perfect for a Christmastime feast.

 This recipe includes Nutrition Facts.

- 8 cups torn mixed salad greens
- 2 medium red apples, diced
- 1/2 cup crumbled blue cheese
- 1/3 cup dried cranberries
- 1/3 cup coarsely chopped walnuts, toasted
- 1/4 cup sliced green onions
- 2 tablespoons olive oil
- 2 tablespoons thawed cranberry juice concentrate
- 1 tablespoon white wine vinegar

Dash salt and pepper

In a large salad bowl, combine the salad greens, apples, blue cheese, dried cranberries, walnuts and green onions. In a small bowl, whisk the remaining ingredients. Pour over salad; toss gently to coat. Serve immediately. **Yield:** 6-8 servings.

Nutrition Facts: 1 cup equals 144 calories, 9 g fat (2 g saturated fat), 6 mg cholesterol, 151 mg sodium, 14 g carbohydrate, 3 g fiber, 4 g protein.

Hawaiian Ham Salad

Prep: 15 min. + chilling

Vickie Lowrey, Fallon, Nevada

Plenty of pineapple, ham, macadamia nuts and coconut give this fresh-tasting medley a real taste of the tropics. Sometimes I substitute celery for the water chestnuts.

- 1 can (8 ounces) unsweetened pineapple chunks
- 3 cups cooked brown rice
- 2 cups cubed fully cooked ham
- 1 can (8 ounces) sliced water chestnuts, drained and halved
- 1/4 cup finely chopped red onion
- 1/2 cup plain yogurt
- 1/2 teaspoon salt
- 1 medium apple, chopped
- Lettuce leaves
- 1/3 cup chopped macadamia nuts, toasted
- 1/4 cup flaked coconut, toasted

1. Drain the pineapple, reserving 1 tablespoon juice. In a large bowl, combine the pineapple, rice, ham, water chestnuts and red onion. Cover and refrigerate for at least 2 hours.

2. In a small bowl, combine yogurt, salt and reserved pineapple juice. Pour over ham mixture and toss to coat. Stir in apple.

3. Serve on lettuce-lined plates; sprinkle with the macadamia nuts and coconut. **Yield:** 4 servings.

Buffalo Chicken Lettuce Wraps

Prep/Total Time: 25 min.

Priscilla Gilbert, Indian Harbour Beach, Florida

These homemade buffalo chicken wraps have excellent flavor. Honey and lime juice help tone down the hot wing sauce and create a refreshing zip. Try these for lunch or a light summer meal with a tall glass of ice-cold lemonade.

- 1/3 cup crumbled blue cheese
- 1/4 cup mayonnaise
- 2 tablespoons milk
- 4-1/2 teaspoons lemon juice
- 1 tablespoon minced fresh parsley
- 1 teaspoon Worcestershire sauce
- 1 pound boneless skinless chicken breasts, cubed
- 1 teaspoon salt
- 1 tablespoon canola oil
- 1/4 cup lime juice
- 1/4 cup Louisiana-style hot sauce
- 1/4 cup honey
- 1 small cucumber, halved lengthwise, seeded and thinly sliced
- 1 celery rib, thinly sliced
- 3/4 cup julienned carrots
- 8 Bibb *or* Boston lettuce leaves

1. For dressing, in a small bowl, combine the first six ingredients. Cover and refrigerate until serving.

2. Sprinkle chicken with salt. In a large skillet, cook chicken in oil until no longer pink. Combine the lime juice, hot sauce and honey; pour over chicken. Bring to a boil. Reduce heat; simmer, uncovered, for 2-3 minutes or until heated through. Remove from the heat; stir in the cucumber, celery and carrots.

3. Spoon 1/2 cup chicken mixture onto each lettuce leaf; fold sides over filling and secure with a toothpick. Serve with blue cheese dressing. **Yield:** 8 servings.

Layered Salad Reuben-Style

Prep/Total Time: 30 min.

Amy Smith, Avon, Connecticut

This fun twist on the traditional seven-layer salad is great for large get-togethers. It combines lettuce and tomato with classic Reuben sandwich fixings such as rye bread and Swiss cheese. I buy pastrami in 1/4-inch slices and chop it up at home, but you could also use leftover corned beef.

4-1/2 teaspoons butter, melted
1/8 teaspoon salt
1/8 teaspoon pepper
2 cups cubed rye bread
1 package (16 ounces) ready-to-serve salad greens
2 cups chopped pastrami
1 large tomato, diced
1/2 cup sauerkraut, rinsed and well drained
1/4 cup thinly sliced green onions
1 bottle (8 ounces) Thousand Island salad dressing
3/4 cup shredded Swiss cheese

1. In a small bowl, combine butter, salt and pepper. Add the rye bread cubes and toss to coat.

2. Arrange the rye bread in a single layer in an ungreased 15-in. x 10-in. x 1-in. baking pan. Bake at 400° for 8-10 minutes or until golden brown, stirring occasionally. Cool.

3. In a large salad bowl, layer half the salad greens, pastrami, tomato, sauerkraut, onions and dressing; repeat layers. Sprinkle with prepared croutons and Swiss cheese. **Yield:** 12 servings.

Crunchy Romaine Strawberry Salad

Prep/Total Time: 30 min.

1 package (3 ounces) ramen noodles
1 cup chopped walnuts
1/4 cup butter
1/4 cup sugar
1/4 cup canola oil
2 tablespoons red wine vinegar
1/2 teaspoon soy sauce
8 cups torn romaine
1/2 cup chopped green onions
2 cups fresh strawberries, sliced

1. Discard seasoning packet from ramen noodles or save for another use. Break noodles into small pieces. In a large skillet, cook noodles and walnuts in butter over medium heat for 8-10 minutes or until golden; cool.

2. For dressing, in a small bowl, whisk the sugar, oil, vinegar and soy sauce. Just before serving combine the romaine, onions, strawberries and noodle mixture in a large bowl. Drizzle with dressing and toss gently. **Yield:** 12 servings.

LESLIE LANCASTER ZACHARY, LOUISIANA

With strawberries, ramen noodles, green onions, romaine and walnuts, this impressive mix has been a hit with people of all ages at every gathering we've brought it to. The mouthwatering combination of tastes and textures seems to please every palate.

GRAND
PRIZE
WINNER

Watermelon Tomato Salad

Prep/Total Time: 25 min.

Matthew Denton, Seattle, Washington

Watermelon and tomatoes may seem an unlikely pair, but they make a winning combination in this easy recipe. Dressed with parsley, basil and fresh-squeezed lime, the eye-catching dish gives you a wonderful sample of summer's bounty.

 This recipe includes Nutrition Facts & Diabetic Exchange.

- 10 cups cubed seedless watermelon
- 2 pints yellow grape *or* pear tomatoes
- 1 medium red onion, chopped
- 1/2 cup minced fresh parsley
- 1/2 cup minced fresh basil
- 1/4 cup lime juice

In a large bowl, combine the watermelon, tomatoes and red onion. In a small bowl, combine the parsley, basil and lime juice. Pour over the watermelon mixture and toss to coat. Refrigerate salad until serving. **Yield:** 16-18 servings.

Nutrition Facts: 3/4 cup equals 33 calories, trace fat (trace saturated fat), 0 cholesterol, 7 mg sodium, 10 g carbohydrate, 1 g fiber, 1 g protein. **Diabetic Exchange:** 1/2 fruit.

Orient Express Chicken Salad

Prep: 25 min. + marinating Grill: 10 min.

Sara Dziadosz, Olathe, Kansas

I came up with this one Mother's Day and got rave reviews. The colorful, fresh-tasting entree makes great use of convenience items, including a can of mandarin oranges, packaged greens and a bottle of sesame ginger marinade.

- 4 boneless skinless chicken breast halves (4 ounces *each*)
- 1 cup sesame ginger marinade
- 1/2 cup balsamic vinaigrette
- 2 tablespoons brown sugar
- 1 tablespoon reduced-sodium soy sauce
- 1/2 teaspoon ground ginger
- 1/4 teaspoon crushed red pepper flakes, optional
- 1 package (5 ounces) spring mix salad greens
- 1 cup chow mein noodles
- 1/2 cup sliced green onions
- 1/2 cup shredded Parmesan cheese
- 1/3 cup dried cranberries
- 1 tablespoon sesame seeds, toasted
- 1 can (11 ounces) mandarin oranges, drained
- 1/4 cup slivered almonds, toasted

1. Place the chicken in a large resealable plastic bag; add the marinade. Seal bag and turn to coat; refrigerate for at least 30 minutes. For dressing, in a small bowl, whisk the vinaigrette, brown sugar, soy sauce, ginger and red pepper flakes if desired. Cover and refrigerate until serving.

2. Drain and discard the marinade. Grill the chicken, covered, over indirect medium heat or broil 4 in. from the heat for 5-6 minutes on each side or until a meat thermometer reads 170°.

3. In a large bowl, toss salad greens, noodles, onions, cheese, cranberries and sesame seeds. Divide among four plates. Top with the oranges and almonds. Cut chicken into diagonal slices; arrange over each salad. Serve with dressing. **Yield:** 4 servings.

Sweet Slaw

Prep: 20 min. + chilling

Agnes Ward, Stratford, Ontario

When I was paging through a church cookbook, I discovered this out-of-the-ordinary recipe featuring a hint of pineapple in the dressing. Now it's the only coleslaw I make.

- 2 **cups shredded cabbage**
- 1/4 **cup finely chopped onion**
- 2 **tablespoons shredded carrot**
- 2 **tablespoons finely chopped celery**
- 2 **tablespoons finely chopped green pepper**

DRESSING:
- 1/4 **cup mayonnaise**
- 2 **tablespoons unsweetened crushed pineapple, drained**
- 1 **tablespoon unsweetened pineapple juice**
- 1 **tablespoon cider vinegar**
- 2 **teaspoons sugar**
- 1/4 **teaspoon salt**
- 1/8 **teaspoon pepper**

In a small bowl, combine the cabbage, onion, carrot, celery and green pepper. Combine the dressing ingredients; pour over cabbage mixture and toss to coat. Cover and refrigerate for at least 1 hour before serving. **Yield:** 2 servings.

Surefire Shredding

To shred cabbage by hand for Sweet Slaw or another recipe, start by cutting the cabbage into wedges. Then place the cut side down on a cutting board and use a large, sharp knife to cut the wedges into thin slices.

Grilled Apple Tossed Salad

Prep: 15 min. + marinating **Grill:** 15 min.

Paul Soska, Toledo, Ohio

Grilling the apples adds even more flavor to this salad boasting blue cheese and a homemade balsamic dressing. For a special presentation, I serve it on plates from my great-grandmother.

- 6 **tablespoons olive oil**
- 1/4 **cup orange juice**
- 1/4 **cup white balsamic vinegar**
- 1/4 **cup minced fresh cilantro**
- 2 **tablespoons honey**
- 1/2 **teaspoon salt**
- 1/2 **teaspoon chili sauce**
- 1 **garlic clove, minced**
- 2 **large apples, cut into wedges**
- 1 **package (5 ounces) spring mix salad greens**
- 1 **cup walnut halves**
- 1/2 **cup crumbled blue cheese**

1. For the dressing, in a small bowl, combine the first eight ingredients. Pour 1/4 cup into a large resealable plastic bag; add apples. Seal bag and turn to coat; refrigerate for at least 10 minutes. Cover and refrigerate remaining dressing until serving.

2. Drain apples, reserving marinade for basting. Thread onto six metal or soaked wooden skewers. Grill apples, covered, over medium heat for 6-8 minutes or until golden brown, basting frequently. Turn and grill 6-8 minutes longer or until golden and tender.

3. In a large salad bowl, combine the greens, walnuts and blue cheese. Add apples. Drizzle with reserved dressing and toss to coat. **Yield:** 4 servings.

Pea 'n' Peanut Salad

Prep/Total Time: 15 min.

Laurinda Nelson, Phoenix, Arizona

Even people who say they don't care for peas end up loving this crunchy creation. It won over my kids, too! I love the fact that it's so easy to prepare and makes an interesting alternative to more traditional dishes. A friend gave me the recipe years ago, and I've been enjoying it ever since.

    1 **package (10 ounces) frozen peas, thawed**
    1 **cup dry roasted peanuts**
    1 **cup chopped celery**
    6 **bacon strips, cooked and crumbled**
1/4 **cup chopped red onion**
1/2 **cup mayonnaise**
1/4 **cup prepared zesty Italian salad dressing**

In a large bowl, combine the peas, peanuts, celery, bacon and red onion. In a small bowl, combine the mayonnaise and Italian dressing. Pour over salad and toss to coat. Chill until serving. **Yield:** 5 servings.

Lively Leaves

Chopping celery for refreshing Pea 'n' Peanut Salad or another recipe leaves you with unused celery leaves. Instead of discarding them, save them to enhance your meal's presentation. Use the leaves to create an inexpensive garnish for your entree or another dish on the menu.

Crispy Crouton Salad

Prep/Total Time: 20 min.

LaNae Sanchez, Canyon Country, California

In our house, nothing says "summer" quite like a big bowl of this unique and colorful salad. I've brought it to many women's luncheons at church, too. You'll want to toss in your homegrown tomatoes and basil from the garden.

- 3 cups cubed Italian bread
- 3 medium tomatoes, chopped
- 6 ounces cubed part-skim mozzarella cheese
- 1 medium sweet yellow pepper, cut into 1-inch pieces
- 1/3 cup minced fresh basil
- 6 tablespoons olive oil
- 3 tablespoons white *or* brown balsamic vinegar
- 1-1/2 teaspoons minced garlic
- 1/8 teaspoon salt
- 1/8 teaspoon pepper

1. Place bread cubes in a single layer in an ungreased 15-in. x 10-in. x 1-in. baking pan. Bake at 450° for 6-8 minutes or until golden brown, stirring twice. Cool.

2. In a large bowl, combine the tomatoes, mozzarella, yellow pepper and basil. In a small bowl, whisk the oil, vinegar, garlic, salt and pepper. Pour over salad and toss to coat. Sprinkle with croutons. **Yield:** 8 servings.

Grandma's Spinach Salad

Prep/Total Time: 20 min.

Shelley Riebel, Armada, Michigan

My grandmother often fixed this favorite for get-togethers... and the rest of the family was happy to make it disappear! Pretty to present in a glass bowl, the layered medley combines spinach, mushrooms, hard-cooked eggs, bacon and red onion with a sweet-sour homemade dressing.

- 1/2 cup sugar
- 1/2 cup canola oil
- 1/4 cup white vinegar
- 1/2 teaspoon celery seed
- 1 package (10 ounces) fresh baby spinach
- 1 small red onion, thinly sliced
- 1/2 pound sliced fresh mushrooms
- 5 hard-cooked eggs, sliced
- 8 bacon strips, cooked and crumbled

1. In a small bowl, whisk the sugar, oil, vinegar and celery seed.

2. In a large salad bowl, layer half of the spinach, onion, mushrooms and eggs. Repeat layers. Top with bacon. Drizzle with dressing. **Yield:** 8 servings.

Microwave Potato Salad

Prep: 20 min. + chilling

Bonnie Carelli, Charlton Heights, West Virginia

Microwaving potatoes for this salad is a nice time-saver—especially in warm weather. I discovered the original recipe in an old cookbook and added roasted peppers and olives for color and zip. Chop your ingredients while the potatoes cook, and everything's ready to chill in just 20 minutes.

- 7 cups cubed red potatoes (about 2 pounds)
- 1 cup water
- 1-1/2 cups (6 ounces) shredded sharp cheddar cheese
- 1 cup mayonnaise
- 4 hard-cooked eggs, chopped
- 3/4 cup pimiento-stuffed olives, halved
- 3/4 cup chopped roasted sweet red peppers
- 1/2 cup sliced green onions
- 1/2 teaspoon pepper

1. Place potatoes in a shallow 2-qt. microwave-safe dish; add water. Cover and microwave on high for 9-11 minutes or until tender, stirring once. Drain and rinse in cold water.

2. In a large bowl, combine the remaining ingredients. Add the potatoes and gently toss to coat. Cover and

refrigerate salad for at least 1 hour before serving. **Yield:** 10 servings.

Editor's Note: This recipe was tested in a 1,100-watt microwave.

Asian Veggie Gelatin

Prep: 15 min. + chilling

Janice Scott, Spokane Valley, Washington

While trying the different offerings at a potluck, I just had to sample this unusual gelatin. It's a delicious change of pace from sweeter molds. The secret ingredient is soy sauce.

 This recipe includes Nutrition Facts & Diabetic Exchange.

- 1 package (.3 ounce) sugar-free orange gelatin
- 3/4 cup boiling water
- 1 cup cold water
- 4-1/2 teaspoons reduced-sodium soy sauce
- 1 tablespoon lemon juice
- 1/2 cup canned bean sprouts
- 1/2 cup sliced celery
- 1/2 cup shredded carrots
- 1/4 cup sliced water chestnuts, halved
- 1 tablespoon chopped green onion

1. In a large bowl, dissolve gelatin in boiling water. Stir in the cold water, soy sauce and lemon juice. Add the bean sprouts, celery, carrots, water chestnuts and onion; mix well.

2. Spoon into four 6-oz. bowls coated with cooking spray. Refrigerate for 1 hour or until set. Invert onto salad plates. **Yield:** 4 servings.

Nutrition Facts: 1 serving equals 30 calories, trace fat (trace saturated fat), 0 cholesterol, 307 mg sodium, 5 g carbohydrate, 1 g fiber, 2 g protein. **Diabetic Exchange:** 1 Free Food.

Colorful Corn 'n' Bean Salad

Prep/Total Time: 15 min.

TerryAnn Moore, Vineland, New Jersey

This quick recipe couldn't be much easier to fix—the liquid from the corn relish creates the fuss-free dressing! And with no mayo, this a great choice for outings on hot days.

 This recipe includes Nutrition Facts & Diabetic Exchange.

> 1 can (15 ounces) black beans, rinsed and drained
> 1 jar (13 ounces) corn relish
> 1/2 cup canned kidney beans, rinsed and drained
> 1/2 cup quartered cherry tomatoes
> 1/2 cup chopped celery
> 1/4 cup chopped sweet orange pepper
> 1/4 cup sliced pimiento-stuffed olives
> 2 teaspoons minced fresh parsley

In a large bowl, combine all ingredients. Cover and refrigerate until serving. **Yield:** 12 servings.

Nutrition Facts: 1/2 cup equals 80 calories, 1 g fat (trace saturated fat), 0 cholesterol, 217 mg sodium, 16 g carbohydrate, 2 g fiber, 2 g protein. **Diabetic Exchange:** 1 starch.

Confetti Broccoli Slaw

Prep: 15 min. + chilling

Kathy Murphy, Fort Thomas, Arizona

Want a super side for a variety of summertime meals? This pretty coleslaw is loaded with terrific flavor. If you like, use broccoli stalks instead of purchasing the packaged broccoli coleslaw mix—simply peel the stalks and shred them in your food processor. You'll want about 3 cups for this recipe.

> 1 package (12 ounces) broccoli coleslaw mix
> 1 medium green pepper, chopped
> 1 medium tomato, seeded and chopped
> 1 small onion, finely chopped
> 1/2 teaspoon salt
> 1/4 teaspoon pepper
> DRESSING:
> 1/2 cup mayonnaise
> 1/3 cup sugar
> 2 tablespoons cider vinegar
> 2 tablespoons ketchup
> 1 tablespoon vegetable oil
> 1-1/2 teaspoons prepared mustard
> 1 teaspoon lemon juice
> 1/8 teaspoon paprika
> 1/8 teaspoon pepper
> 1/8 teaspoon salt
> Dash garlic powder
> Dash hot pepper sauce

In a large bowl, combine the broccoli coleslaw mix, green pepper, tomato, onion, salt and pepper. In a blender or food processor, combine the dressing ingredients; cover and process until blended. Pour over coleslaw and toss to coat. Cover and refrigerate for at least 2 hours before serving. **Yield:** 6 servings.

Lemon-Linguine Shrimp Salad

Prep/Total Time: 30 min.

Laureen Pittman, Riverside, California

Bring a touch of elegance to any outdoor gathering or luncheon with this summery medley of fresh asparagus, spicy marinated shrimp and pasta. Splashed with lemon, it goes perfectly with cold glasses of iced tea. If you're making the recipe ahead of time, add the fresh basil just before serving.

- 1/4 cup olive oil
- 2 tablespoons white wine vinegar
- 2 tablespoons minced fresh parsley
- 1/2 to 1 teaspoon cayenne pepper
- 1/2 teaspoon dried oregano
- 1/4 teaspoon salt
- 1 pound cooked small shrimp, peeled and deveined
- 1 package (16 ounces) linguine
- 1/2 pound fresh asparagus, trimmed and cut into 1-inch pieces

LEMON DRESSING:
- 2/3 cup olive oil
- 2/3 cup shredded Parmesan cheese
- 1/2 cup lemon juice
- 1 tablespoon grated lemon peel
- 1/3 cup minced fresh basil

1. In a large resealable plastic bag, combine the oil, vinegar, parsley, cayenne pepper, oregano and salt; add shrimp. Seal bag and turn to coat; set aside.

2. Cook linguine according to package directions, adding asparagus during the last 3 minutes; drain and rinse in cold water. In a large bowl, combine the oil, Parmesan cheese, lemon juice and peel; add linguine mixture and toss to coat.

3. Drain and discard the marinade. Add shrimp to linguine; gently toss to coat. Cover and refrigerate until serving. Sprinkle with basil. **Yield:** 6 servings.

Asparagus Advice

It's best to use asparagus within a few days of purchase. Look for firm, straight, uniform-size spears. The tips should be closed with crisp stalks. To clean asparagus, soak it in cold water. Cut or snap off the tough white portion.

Smoked Turkey Pasta Salad

Prep: 30 min. + chilling

- 1 cup uncooked tricolor spiral pasta
- 1/4 pound cubed deli smoked turkey
- 1 cup (4 ounces) cubed Monterey Jack cheese
- 1/2 small cucumber, thinly sliced and halved
- 1/3 cup chopped sweet red pepper
- 1 green onion, thinly sliced
- 3 tablespoons sour cream
- 2 tablespoons mayonnaise
- 1-1/2 teaspoons 2% milk
- 1 teaspoon honey
- 1 teaspoon Dijon mustard
- Dash pepper

1. Cook the tricolor spiral pasta according to the package directions; drain and rinse in cold water. In a serving bowl, combine the pasta, deli turkey, Monterey Jack cheese, cucumber, red pepper and green onion.

2. In a small bowl, whisk sour cream, mayonnaise, milk, honey, mustard and pepper. Pour over salad and toss to coat. Cover and refrigerate for at least 2 hours before serving. **Yield:** 4 cups.

ANA COLON WISCONSIN RAPIDS, WISCONSIN

I fixed a big batch of this hearty, colorful salad for a football party, and my guests couldn't get enough of it. They wanted to know the "secret ingredient" that made it taste so good.

GRAND PRIZE WINNER

Summer Avocado Salad

Prep/Total Time: 30 min.

Deb Williams, Peoria, Arizona

Garden-fresh veggies, creamy avocado and a sprinkling of feta cheese make this chunky salad a summer standout.

- 1/2 **cup chopped seeded peeled cucumber**
- 1/3 **cup chopped sweet yellow pepper**
- 6 **cherry tomatoes, seeded and quartered**
- 2 **tablespoons finely chopped sweet onion**
- 1 **tablespoon minced fresh basil** *or* 1 **teaspoon dried basil**
- 1-1/2 **teaspoons lemon juice**
- 1-1/2 **teaspoons olive oil**

Dash garlic powder

- 1 **medium ripe avocado, peeled and chopped**
- 2 **tablespoons crumbled feta cheese**

Bibb lettuce leaves, optional

In a small bowl, combine the first eight ingredients; cover and refrigerate for 15-20 minutes. Add the avocado; toss gently. Sprinkle with the feta cheese. Serve the salad immediately on lettuce-lined plates if desired. **Yield:** 2 servings.

Cheddar-Almond Lettuce Salad

Prep/Total Time: 30 min.

Julia Musser, Lebanon, Pennsylvania

With lots of sugared almonds and a homemade honey-mustard dressing, this salad always impresses guests. In fact, I keep slivered almonds in my freezer just so I can toss this together for spur-of-the-moment special occasions. For added nutrition, color and variety, I sometimes toss in broccoli and tomatoes.

- 1/2 **cup slivered almonds**
- 3 **tablespoons sugar**
- 9 **cups torn romaine**
- 2 **hard-cooked eggs, sliced**
- 1 **cup (4 ounces) shredded cheddar cheese**

HONEY-MUSTARD DRESSING:

- 1/4 **cup sugar**
- 2 **tablespoons white vinegar**
- 2 **tablespoons honey**
- 1 **tablespoon lemon juice**
- 1/2 **teaspoon onion powder**
- 1/2 **teaspoon celery seed**
- 1/2 **teaspoon ground mustard**
- 1/2 **teaspoon paprika**
- 1/4 **teaspoon salt**
- 1/2 **cup canola oil**

1. In a small heavy skillet, combine the almonds and sugar. Cook and stir over medium heat for 5-6 minutes or until nuts are coated and golden. Spread onto foil to cool. Divide romaine among salad plates; top with eggs and cheese.

2. In a blender, combine the sugar, vinegar, honey, lemon juice, onion powder, celery seed, mustard, paprika and salt. While processing, gradually add oil in a steady stream. Drizzle over salads; sprinkle with almonds. **Yield:** 9 servings.

Cashew-Chicken Rotini Salad

Prep: 30 min. + chilling

Kara Cook, Elk Ridge, Utah

I've tried many different recipes for chicken salad over the years, and this version is my all-time favorite. It gets refreshing fruit flavor from pineapple, grapes and cranberries, and the cashews add a fun crunch. Every time I bring it to a potluck or picnic, I come home with an empty bowl.

- 1 package (16 ounces) spiral or rotini pasta
- 4 cups cubed cooked chicken
- 1 can (20 ounces) pineapple tidbits, drained
- 1-1/2 cups sliced celery
- 3/4 cup thinly sliced green onions
- 1 cup seedless red grapes
- 1 cup seedless green grapes
- 1 package (6 ounces) dried cranberries
- 1 cup ranch salad dressing
- 3/4 cup mayonnaise
- 2 cups salted cashews

1. Cook the pasta according to package directions. Meanwhile, in a large bowl, combine the chicken, pineapple, celery, onions, grapes and cranberries.

Drain the pasta and rinse in cold water; stir into the chicken mixture.

2. In a small bowl, whisk the ranch dressing and mayonnaise. Pour over salad and toss to coat. Cover and refrigerate for at least 1 hour. Just before serving, stir in cashews. **Yield:** 12 servings.

Mixed Greens with French Dressing

Prep: 10 min. + chilling

Thelma Harrison, Califon, New Jersey

You won't miss the oil in this salad's wonderful homemade French dressing. People have told me it's so good, they wonder why I haven't bottled and marketed it! Plus, preparation time is a mere 10 minutes, so it's convenient.

- 2/3 cup cider vinegar
- 2/3 cup ketchup
- 1/2 cup sugar
- 1/4 cup chopped onion
- 1-1/2 teaspoons celery salt
- 1-1/2 teaspoons paprika
- 1 teaspoon salt
- 1/2 teaspoon celery seed
- 3 cups torn curly endive
- 3 cups chopped escarole *or* torn romaine

1. For dressing, place the first eight ingredients in a blender or food processor; cover and process until blended. Transfer to a jar with a tight-fitting lid; cover and refrigerate for at least 1 hour.

2. Just before serving, combine endive and escarole. Shake prepared dressing and drizzle over greens. Refrigerate leftover dressing. **Yield:** 4-6 servings (about 1-1/2 cups dressing).

Heirloom Tomato Salad

Prep: 20 min. + chilling

Jessie Apfel, Berkeley, California

Here's a simple yet elegant dish that always pleases my guests with its fresh flavor. Not only is it tasty, but it's also wholesome and healthy. The more varied the colors of the tomatoes you choose, the prettier the salad will be.

 This recipe includes Nutrition Facts & Diabetic Exchanges.

- **2 cups torn fresh spinach**
- **2 cups sliced multicolored heirloom tomatoes**
- **1 cup red and yellow cherry tomatoes, halved**
- **1 cup sliced red onion**

DRESSING:
- **3 tablespoons olive oil**
- **2 tablespoons white balsamic vinegar**
- **1 garlic clove, minced**
- **1/2 teaspoon salt**
- **1/4 teaspoon *each* dried basil, oregano, thyme and sage**
- **1/4 teaspoon dried rosemary, crushed**
- **1/4 teaspoon pepper**
- **1/8 teaspoon dried parsley flakes**

In a large bowl, combine the spinach, tomatoes and red onion. In a small bowl, whisk dressing ingredients. Pour over the salad and toss to coat. Cover and refrigerate salad for at least 2 hours. Serve with a slotted spoon. **Yield:** 6 servings.

Nutrition Facts: 2/3 cup equals 79 calories, 5 g fat (1 g saturated fat), 0 cholesterol, 165 mg sodium, 8 g carbohydrate, 2 g fiber, 1 g protein. **Diabetic Exchanges:** 1 vegetable, 1 fat.

Mincing Method

Minced garlic brings zip to the homemade dressing for Heirloom Tomato Salad. To mince fresh garlic, crush a garlic clove with the blade of a chef's knife. Peel away the skin and cut the garlic into pieces no larger than 1/8 inch.

Calico Black Bean Salad

Prep: 15 min. + chilling

Linda Holland, Lantana, Florida

This unique recipe reflects the Caribbean culture in South Florida. The combination of black beans, tomatoes and onions with a made-from-scratch vinaigrette is great alongside a main course of pork or chicken. I also love the convenience—I can make it ahead and just keep it in the fridge.

- **2 cans (15 ounces *each*) black beans, rinsed and drained**
- **4 green onions, thinly sliced**
- **2 plum tomatoes, chopped**
- **1 medium onion, chopped**
- **1 large sweet red pepper, chopped**
DRESSING:
- **2 tablespoons olive oil**
- **2 tablespoons red wine vinegar**
- **1 tablespoon lemon juice**
- **1/2 teaspoon salt**
- **1/4 teaspoon pepper**
- **3/4 teaspoon minced fresh basil *or* 1/4 teaspoon dried basil**

In a salad bowl, combine the beans, green onions, tomatoes, onion and red pepper. In a small bowl, whisk the dressing ingredients. Drizzle over vegetables and toss to coat. Cover and refrigerate for at least 1 hour before serving. **Yield:** 6 servings.

Antipasto Picnic Salad

Prep: 30 min. **Cook:** 15 min.

Michele Larson, Baden, Pennsylvania

Everybody likes this tempting blend of meats, vegetables and pasta. It tastes as good at room temperature as it does cold.

- 1 **package (16 ounces) medium pasta shells**
- 2 **jars (16 ounces *each*) giardiniera**
- 1 **pound fresh broccoli florets**
- 1/2 **pound cubed part-skim mozzarella cheese**
- 1/2 **pound hard salami, cubed**
- 1/2 **pound deli ham, cubed**
- 2 **packages (3-1/2 ounces *each*) sliced pepperoni, halved**
- 1 **large green pepper, cut into chunks**
- 1 **can (6 ounces) pitted ripe olives, drained**

DRESSING:
- 1/2 **cup olive oil**
- 1/4 **cup red wine vinegar**
- 2 **tablespoons lemon juice**
- 1 **teaspoon Italian seasoning**
- 1 **teaspoon coarsely ground pepper**
- 1/2 **teaspoon salt**

1. Cook the pasta according to package directions. Meanwhile, drain giardiniera, reserving 3/4 cup liquid. In a large bowl, combine the giardiniera, broccoli, mozzarella, salami, ham, pepperoni, green pepper and olives. Drain pasta and rinse in cold water; stir into meat mixture.

2. For dressing, in a small bowl, whisk the oil, vinegar, lemon juice, Italian seasoning, pepper, salt and reserved giardiniera liquid. Pour over salad and toss to coat. Refrigerate until serving. **Yield:** 25 servings.

Editor's Note: Giardiniera, a pickled vegetable mixture, is available in mild and hot varieties and can be found in the Italian or pickle section of your grocery store.

Strawberry Chicken Salad

Prep/Total Time: 15 min.

Michelle Hallock, Warwick, Rhode Island

This dish is similar to one I loved at a local restaurant. When we moved away, I created my own version so I could still enjoy it. The recipe goes together in just 15 minutes and makes a wonderful picnic contribution or light main course.

 This recipe includes Nutrition Facts & Diabetic Exchanges.

- 1 package (5 ounces) spring mix salad greens
- 1 small red onion, thinly sliced and separated into rings
- 1/2 cup cubed fresh pineapple
- 2 packages (6 ounces *each*) ready-to-use grilled chicken breast strips
- 2 medium tomatoes, seeded and chopped
- 1 medium cucumber, chopped
- 1 pint fresh strawberries, sliced
- 3/4 cup crumbled blue cheese
- 3/4 cup raspberry vinaigrette

Place the salad greens in a large shallow bowl. In rows, arrange the onion, pineapple, chicken, tomatoes, cucumber and strawberries. Sprinkle with blue cheese. Drizzle with vinaigrette. **Yield:** 10 servings.

Nutrition Facts: 1-1/2 cups (prepared with fat-free raspberry vinaigrette) equals 130 calories, 4 g fat

(2 g saturated fat), 30 mg cholesterol, 538 mg sodium, 13 g carbohydrate, 2 g fiber, 11 g protein. **Diabetic Exchanges:** 1 lean meat, 1 vegetable, 1/2 starch.

Chunky Cranberry Salad

Prep: 25 min. + chilling

Joyce Butterfield, Nancy, Kentucky

I discovered this recipe while taking a cooking class. Full of mixed fruit, celery and pecans, the salad is a nice alternative to jellied cranberry sauce. When cranberries are in season, I buy extra and freeze them so I can make this year-round.

- 4 cups fresh *or* frozen cranberries
- 3-1/2 cups unsweetened pineapple juice
- 2 envelopes unflavored gelatin
- 1/2 cup cold water
- 2 cups sugar
- 1 can (20 ounces) unsweetened pineapple tidbits, drained
- 1 cup chopped pecans
- 1 cup green grapes, chopped
- 1/2 cup finely chopped celery
- 2 teaspoons grated orange peel

1. In a large saucepan, combine the cranberries and pineapple juice. Cook over medium heat until berries pop, about 15 minutes.

2. Meanwhile, in a small bowl, sprinkle gelatin over cold water; let stand for 5 minutes. In a large bowl, combine the berry mixture, sugar and softened gelatin. Chill until partially set.

3. Fold in the pineapple, pecans, grapes, celery and orange peel. Pour into individual serving dishes. Chill until firm. **Yield:** 12 servings.

Gorgonzola Pear Salad

Prep: 15 min. **Bake:** 25 min.

Melinda Singer, Tarzana, California

Need an extra-special first course for a holiday feast or dinner party? Consider this simple but impressive medley of pears, greens, plum tomatoes, Gorgonzola cheese and toasted pecans. Balsamic vinaigrette tops everything off deliciously.

- 3 medium pears, halved and cored
- 3 tablespoons olive oil
- 1/2 teaspoon salt
- 6 cups spring mix salad greens
- 2 plum tomatoes, seeded and chopped
- 1 cup crumbled Gorgonzola cheese
- 1/2 cup pecan halves, toasted
- 3/4 cup balsamic vinaigrette

1. Place the pears in an ungreased 13-in. x 9-in. baking dish. Drizzle with oil and sprinkle with salt. Bake, uncovered, at 400° for 25-30 minutes, basting occasionally with cooking juices.

2. In a large salad bowl, combine the greens, tomatoes, cheese and pecans. Drizzle with dressing and toss to coat. Divide among six serving plates; top each with a pear half. **Yield:** 6 servings.

Pina Colada Molded Salad

Prep: 25 min. + chilling

Carol Gillespie, Chambersburg, Pennsylvania

I like experimenting in the kitchen in my spare time, and this is one of my favorite creations. The pretty molded gelatin gets a tropical twist from coconut, pineapple and macadamia nuts. I fill the center with more fruit and coconut.

- 1 can (20 ounces) unsweetened crushed pineapple
- 2 envelopes unflavored gelatin
- 1/2 cup cold water
- 1 cup cream of coconut
- 1 cup (8 ounces) sour cream
- 3/4 cup lemon-lime soda
- 3/4 cup flaked coconut
- 1/2 cup chopped macadamia nuts

Pineapple chunks and freshly shredded coconut, optional

1. Drain the pineapple, reserving the juice; set the pineapple aside. In a large saucepan, sprinkle gelatin over cold water; let stand for 1 minute. Cook and stir over low heat until gelatin is completely dissolved, about 2 minutes.

2. Remove from the heat; stir in the cream of coconut, sour cream, soda and reserved pineapple juice. Transfer to a large bowl. Cover and refrigerate for 30 minutes or until thickened, stirring occasionally.

3. Fold in the coconut, macadamia nuts and reserved pineapple. Pour into a 6-cup ring mold coated with cooking spray. Cover and refrigerate for 3 hours or until firm.

4. To serve, unmold salad onto a platter. Fill the center with pineapple chunks and shredded coconut if desired. **Yield:** 8 servings.

Editor's Note: This recipe was tested with Coco Lopez cream of coconut.

Special Salads **51**

PG. 65

PG. 71

PG. 55

SOUPS & SANDWICHES

Whether your family is in the mood for chunky chili, big grilled burgers loaded with the works, fun veggie wraps or a hot and hearty stew, casual comfort foods just don't get better than the recipes here!

PG. 66

Italian Sausage Calzone

Prep: 20 min. **Bake:** 30 min. + standing

Terri Gallagher, King George, Virginia

My teenage daughter and I have been experimenting in the kitchen to re-create some old-time family dishes. This calzone featuring spinach, Italian sausage, mushrooms and mozzarella is definitely a favorite. Using refrigerated pizza crust, we can easily prepare one for us or several for a crowd.

- 1 tube (13.8 ounces) refrigerated pizza crust
- 1 can (8 ounces) pizza sauce
- 1 package (10 ounces) frozen chopped spinach, thawed and squeezed dry
- 1 pound bulk Italian sausage, cooked and drained
- 1 jar (4-1/2 ounces) sliced mushrooms, drained
- 2 cups (8 ounces) shredded part-skim mozzarella cheese

1. Unroll the pizza dough onto an ungreased baking sheet; pat into a 14-in. x 11-in. rectangle. Spread the pizza sauce over one long side of the pizza dough to within 1/2 in. of the edges.

2. Layer the spinach, sausage, mushrooms and cheese over the sauce. Fold the dough over the filling; pinch the seams to seal.

3. Bake at 400° for 30-35 minutes or until golden brown. Let calzone stand for 10-15 minutes before slicing. **Yield:** 6 servings.

Kielbasa Split Pea Soup

Prep: 15 min. **Cook:** 55 min.

Sandra Bonde, Brainerd, Minnesota

Slices of turkey kielbasa bring wonderful flavor to this simple yet heartwarming split pea soup. It's been a hit with my entire family—even our picky toddler eats it up.

 This recipe includes Nutrition Facts & Diabetic Exchanges.

- 2 celery ribs, thinly sliced
- 1 medium onion, chopped
- 1 package (16 ounces) dried green split peas
- 9 cups water, *divided*
- 1 package (14 ounces) smoked turkey kielbasa, halved and sliced
- 4 medium carrots, halved and thinly sliced
- 2 medium potatoes, peeled and cubed
- 1 tablespoon minced fresh parsley
- 1 teaspoon dried basil
- 1-1/2 teaspoons salt
- 1/2 teaspoon pepper

1. In a Dutch oven coated with cooking spray, cook the celery and onion until tender. Stir in split peas and 6 cups water. Bring to a boil. Reduce heat; cover and simmer for 25 minutes.

2. Stir in the kielbasa, carrots, potatoes, parsley, basil, salt, pepper and remaining water. Return to a boil. Reduce heat; cover and simmer for 20-25 minutes or until peas and vegetables are tender. **Yield:** 12 servings (3 quarts).

Nutrition Facts: 1 cup equals 208 calories, 2 g fat (trace saturated fat), 13 mg cholesterol, 635 mg sodium, 34 g carbohydrate, 11 g fiber, 15 g protein. **Diabetic Exchanges:** 2 starch, 2 very lean meat.

Speedy Weeknight Chili

Prep/Total Time: 30 min.

Cynthia Hudson, Greenville, South Carolina

Super-fast and great-tasting, this chili makes a big batch of crowd-pleasing party fare. I cut down on prep time by using my food processor to chop up the vegetables.

- 1-1/2 pounds ground beef
- 2 small onions, chopped
- 1/2 cup chopped green pepper
- 1 teaspoon minced garlic
- 2 cans (16 ounces *each*) kidney beans, rinsed and drained
- 2 cans (14-1/2 ounces *each*) stewed tomatoes
- 1 can (28 ounces) crushed tomatoes
- 1 bottle (12 ounces) beer *or* nonalcoholic beer
- 1 can (6 ounces) tomato paste
- 1/4 cup chili powder
- 3/4 teaspoon dried oregano
- 1/2 teaspoon hot pepper sauce
- 1/4 teaspoon sugar
- 1/4 teaspoon salt
- 1/4 teaspoon pepper

In a large saucepan or Dutch oven, cook the beef, onions and green pepper over medium heat until meat

is no longer pink. Add garlic; cook 1 minute longer. Drain. Add the remaining ingredients; bring to a boil. Reduce heat; simmer, uncovered, for 10 minutes. **Yield:** 15 servings.

Hearty Veggie Sandwiches

Prep/Total Time: 20 min.

Micki Sannar, Highland, Utah

This meatless delight stacked with avocado, tomato, onion, olives and cheese is a lighter choice that tastes terrific. Pack it in your lunch bag with some pretzels or potato chips.

 This recipe includes Nutrition Facts.

- 2 teaspoons mayonnaise
- 2 teaspoons prepared mustard
- 4 slices whole wheat bread
- 4 slices cheddar cheese (3/4 ounce *each*)
- 2 slices red onion
- 1/4 cup sliced ripe olives, drained
- 1 small tomato, sliced
- 1 medium ripe avocado, peeled and sliced
- 1/8 teaspoon pepper
- 4 tablespoons Italian salad dressing
- 2 lettuce leaves

1. Spread mayonnaise and mustard over two slices of bread; layer with the cheese, onion, olives, tomato and avocado. Sprinkle with pepper.

2. Drizzle each sandwich with 1 tablespoon of Italian salad dressing. Top with lettuce. Drizzle the remaining salad dressing over remaining bread; place over the sandwiches. **Yield:** 2 servings.

Nutrition Facts: 1 sandwich (prepared with reduced-fat mayonnaise, reduced-fat cheddar cheese and fat-free Italian salad dressing) equals 479 calories, 29 g fat (8 g saturated fat), 27 mg cholesterol, 1,259 mg sodium, 42 g carbohydrate, 10 g fiber, 22 g protein.

Meat Loaf Gyros

Prep: 30 min. **Bake:** 1 hour + chilling

Sharon Rawlings, Tampa, Florida

I always wanted to learn how to make Greek gyros, but they sounded intimidating. Then I tried this recipe, and the results were great. Now I slice my leftover dinner meat into individual portions and freeze it so I can satisfy a craving anytime.

- 1 **egg, lightly beaten**
- 6 **garlic cloves, minced**
- 3 **tablespoons dried oregano**
- 1-1/2 **teaspoons kosher salt**
- 1 **teaspoon pepper**
- 1 **pound ground lamb**
- 1 **pound ground beef**

TZATZIKI SAUCE:
- 1 **cup (8 ounces) plain yogurt**
- 1 **medium cucumber, peeled, seeded and chopped**
- 2 **tablespoons lemon juice**
- 2 **garlic cloves, minced**
- 1/2 **teaspoon salt**
- 1/4 **teaspoon pepper**
- 8 **whole pita breads**
- 3 **tablespoons olive oil,** *divided*
- 16 **slices tomato**
- 8 **slices sweet onion, halved**

1. In a large bowl, combine the egg, garlic, oregano, kosher salt and pepper. Crumble lamb and beef over mixture; mix well.

2. Pat into an ungreased 9-in. x 5-in. loaf pan. Bake, uncovered, at 350° for 60-70 minutes or until no pink remains and a meat thermometer reads 160°. Cool completely on a wire rack. Refrigerate for 1-2 hours.

3. For sauce, in a small bowl, combine the yogurt, cucumber, lemon juice, garlic, salt and pepper. Cover and refrigerate until serving.

4. Brush the pita breads with 1 tablespoon oil; heat on a lightly greased griddle for 1 minute on each side. Keep warm. Cut the meat loaf into very thin slices. In a large skillet, fry meat loaf in the remaining oil in batches until crisp.

5. On each pita bread, layer tomato, onion and meat loaf slices; top with some tzatziki sauce. Carefully fold the pitas in half. Serve with the remaining sauce. **Yield:** 8 servings.

Onion Advice

Sweet onions are high in sugar and water content and low in tear-inducing sulfur compounds. Because of these properties, they are not suited for long-term storage and should be used within several weeks of purchase.

Chicken Salad Panini

Prep/Total Time: 25 min.

- 1/4 **cup mayonnaise**
- 1-1/2 **teaspoons honey**
- 3/4 **teaspoon snipped fresh dill**
- 3/4 **teaspoon Dijon mustard**
- **Dash salt**
- **Dash pepper**
- 1 **cup cubed cooked chicken breast**
- 3/4 **cup shredded cheddar cheese**
- 1/2 **cup chopped peeled apple**
- 1/4 **cup chopped pecans, toasted**
- 6 **slices white bread**
- 4 **teaspoons butter, softened**

1. In a small bowl, combine the first six ingredients. In another bowl, combine chicken, cheese, apple and nuts; add prepared dressing and toss to coat.

2. Spread half of the prepared chicken salad on two slices of bread. Top each with another slice of bread, remaining chicken salad and remaining bread. Spread butter on both sides of sandwiches. Cook on a panini maker or indoor grill until bread is toasted and cheese is melted. **Yield:** 2 servings.

LISA HUFF CLIVE, IOWA

Grilled indoors, this scrumptious sandwich can be enjoyed year-round. The honey-mustard dressing gives the chicken plenty of pizzazz, and the apple and pecans lend a lively crunch.

GRAND PRIZE WINNER

Greek Turkey Pitas

Prep: 25 min. + chilling

Jean Graf-Joyce, Albany, Oregon

We like to fix these stuffed pita sandwiches whenever we have extra turkey from a meal. They're easy to assemble and make a perfect dinner for two on the deck or patio.

- 1/4 cup plain yogurt
- 1/4 cup chopped seeded peeled cucumber
- 1/4 teaspoon lemon-pepper seasoning
- 1/4 teaspoon dried oregano
- 1/8 teaspoon garlic powder
- 1/4 pound cooked turkey breast, cubed
- 2 whole pita breads, warmed
- 1 small tomato, sliced
- 2 slices red onion, halved
- 2 pitted Greek olives, sliced
- 2 pepperoncinis, sliced
- 1/2 cup shredded lettuce
- 2 tablespoons crumbled feta cheese

1. In a small bowl, combine the first five ingredients. Stir in the turkey. Cover mixture and refrigerate for at least 1 hour.

2. Spoon the turkey mixture onto each pita; top with tomato, onion, olives, pepperoncinis, lettuce and feta cheese. Fold in half. **Yield:** 2 servings.

Pizza Meatball Subs

Prep: 30 min. **Bake:** 25 min.

Heather Begin, Athens, Maine

I served these hot sandwiches one evening for supper, and they were a huge hit with everyone in the family—including the picky eaters! The baked meatballs are surrounded with mayo, two kinds of cheese and plenty of pizza sauce.

- 1 egg, lightly beaten
- 1/3 cup steak sauce
- 1 cup crushed saltines
- 1 teaspoon onion powder
- 1/4 teaspoon seasoned salt
- 1/8 teaspoon pepper
- 1-1/2 pounds ground beef
- 6 to 7 tablespoons mayonnaise
- 6 to 7 submarine buns, split
- 9 to 11 slices process American cheese, cut into strips
- 1 jar (14 ounces) pizza sauce
- 2 cups (8 ounces) shredded part-skim mozzarella cheese

1. In a large bowl, combine the egg, steak sauce, saltines, onion powder, salt and pepper. Crumble the ground beef over the mixture and mix well. Shape into 1-1/2-in. meatballs.

2. Place meatballs on a greased rack in a shallow baking pan. Bake at 375° for 20-25 minutes or until no longer pink. Drain on paper towels.

3. Spread the mayonnaise over the bottoms of buns; top each with American cheese, 1 tablespoon pizza sauce, meatballs and remaining pizza sauce. Sprinkle with mozzarella cheese. Place on a baking sheet.

4. Bake for 5-10 minutes or until cheese is melted. **Yield:** 6-7 servings.

Texas-Sized Beef Sandwiches

Prep/Total Time: 25 min.

Utha Bonham, Blairsville, Georgia

One day, I surprised my ceramics class with these as a special lunch. The hearty open-faced sandwiches went over so well, the students wanted them every week!

    1/2 medium green pepper, thinly sliced
    1/3 cup thinly sliced onion
    1/4 cup sliced fresh mushrooms
    1/4 teaspoon ground cumin
      1 teaspoon butter
      2 teaspoons mayonnaise
      1 teaspoon Dijon mustard
    1/4 teaspoon prepared horseradish
      2 slices Texas toast, toasted
      6 slices deli roast beef *or* ham (1/2 ounce *each*)
    1/2 medium tomato, sliced
    1/2 cup shredded cheddar cheese

1. In a nonstick skillet, saute the green pepper, onion, mushrooms and cumin in butter until the vegetables are tender.

2. In a small bowl, combine the mayonnaise, mustard and horseradish; spread over the toast. Top with the pepper mixture, beef, tomato and cheese.

3. Broil 4-6 in. from the heat for 2-3 minutes or until cheese is melted. **Yield:** 2 servings.

Anytime Turkey Chili

Prep: 15 min. Cook: 1-1/4 hours

Brad Bailey, Cary, North Carolina

I created this hoping to grab the attention of voters at a chili contest we held in our backyard. Calling for canned pumpkin, brown sugar and cooked turkey, this recipe is also a great way to use up leftovers from a Thanksgiving feast.

 This recipe includes Nutrition Facts & Diabetic Exchanges.

    2/3 cup chopped sweet onion
    1/2 cup chopped green pepper

  1-1/2 teaspoons dried oregano
      1 teaspoon ground cumin
      1 teaspoon olive oil
      2 garlic cloves, minced
      1 can (16 ounces) kidney beans, rinsed and drained
      1 can (15-1/2 ounces) great northern beans, rinsed and drained
      1 can (15 ounces) solid-pack pumpkin
      1 can (15 ounces) crushed tomatoes
      1 can (14-1/2 ounces) reduced-sodium chicken broth
    1/2 cup water
      2 tablespoons brown sugar
      2 tablespoons chili powder
    1/2 teaspoon pepper
      3 cups cubed cooked turkey breast

1. In a large saucepan, saute the onion, green pepper, oregano and cumin in oil until vegetables are tender. Add garlic; cook 1 minute longer.

2. Stir in the beans, pumpkin, tomatoes, broth, water, brown sugar, chili powder and pepper; bring to a boil. Reduce heat; cover and simmer for 1 hour. Add turkey; heat through. **Yield:** 8 servings (2 quarts).

Nutrition Facts: 1 cup chili equals 241 calories, 2 g fat (trace saturated fat), 45 mg cholesterol, 478 mg sodium, 32 g carbohydrate, 10 g fiber, 25 g protein. **Diabetic Exchanges:** 3 very lean meat, 1-1/2 starch, 1 vegetable.

Greek Turkey Burgers

Prep/Total Time: 30 min.

Marianne Shira, Osceola, Wisconsin

A dear friend gave me this recipe, which I pared down a bit. Cumin and cayenne pepper give the turkey great flavor.

 This recipe includes Nutrition Facts & Diabetic Exchanges.

1/3 cup fat-free plain yogurt
1/3 cup reduced-fat mayonnaise
1/4 cup chopped seeded peeled cucumber
1/4 teaspoon Worcestershire sauce
1/4 teaspoon garlic powder
1/8 teaspoon salt
1/8 teaspoon pepper
Dash dried thyme

BURGERS:
1/2 cup finely chopped sweet onion
1/2 cup finely chopped green pepper
1 teaspoon ground cumin
1/4 teaspoon salt
1/4 teaspoon pepper
1/4 teaspoon cayenne pepper
1-1/2 pounds extra-lean ground turkey
1/2 cup thinly sliced cucumber
6 slices tomato
6 hamburger buns, split

1. For the cucumber sauce, in a small bowl, combine the first eight ingredients. Cover and refrigerate sauce until serving.

2. In a large bowl, combine the onion, green pepper, cumin, salt, pepper and cayenne. Crumble turkey over mixture and mix well. Shape into six patties.

3. Using long-handled tongs, moisten a paper towel with cooking oil and lightly coat the grill rack. Grill patties, covered, over medium heat or broil 4 in. from the heat for 5-7 minutes on each side or until a meat thermometer reads 165° and juices run clear.

4. Place the cucumber and tomato slices on the buns; top each bun with a burger and about 2 tablespoons cucumber sauce. **Yield:** 6 servings.

Nutrition Facts: 1 burger equals 316 calories, 9 g fat (1 g saturated fat), 51 mg cholesterol, 586 mg sodium, 28 g carbohydrate, 2 g fiber, 33 g protein. **Diabetic Exchanges:** 4 very lean meat, 1-1/2 starch, 1 vegetable, 1 fat.

Apple 'n' Prosciutto Sandwiches

Prep/Total Time: 20 min.

Elizabeth Bennett, Mill Creek, Washington

Prepared on an indoor grill, these Italian-style sandwiches are spread with a simple-to-make rosemary pesto. I think they taste especially good on a cold fall or winter afternoon.

1/4 cup olive oil
1/2 cup chopped walnuts
2 tablespoons grated Parmesan cheese
2 tablespoons minced fresh rosemary
1 loaf (12 ounces) focaccia bread
8 thin slices prosciutto
1 medium apple, sliced
6 ounces Brie cheese, rind removed and sliced

1. In a blender, combine the oil, walnuts, cheese and rosemary; cover and process until blended and nuts are finely chopped. With a bread knife, split focaccia into two horizontal layers. Spread rosemary mixture over cut sides of bread.

2. On bottom of bread, layer the prosciutto, apple and Brie; replace bread top. Cut into quarters.

3. Cook on an indoor grill for 2-3 minutes or until bread is browned and cheese is melted. To serve, cut each wedge in half. **Yield:** 8 servings.

Stuffed Pepper Soup

Prep/Total Time: 30 min.

Tracy Thompson, Cranesville, Pennsylvania

Ready in 30 minutes when I get home from work, this soup makes a satisfying meal paired with a salad, rolls or fruit. For variety, try chicken or turkey instead of ground beef.

- 1 package (8.8 ounces) ready-to-serve long grain and wild rice
- 1 pound ground beef
- 2 cups frozen chopped green peppers, thawed
- 1 cup chopped onion
- 1 jar (26 ounces) chunky tomato pasta sauce
- 1 can (14-1/2 ounces) Italian diced tomatoes, undrained
- 1 can (14 ounces) beef broth

Prepare the rice according to the package directions. Meanwhile, in a large saucepan, cook beef, peppers and onion until meat is no longer pink; drain. Stir in the pasta sauce, tomatoes, broth and prepared rice; heat through. **Yield:** 6-8 servings (about 2 quarts).

Italian Wedding Soup

Prep: 30 min. Cook: 45 min.

Noelle Myers, Grand Forks, North Dakota

I just love the combination of meatballs, vegetables and pasta in this recipe. I enjoyed something similar for lunch at work one day and decided to re-create it at home.

- 2 eggs, lightly beaten
- 1/2 cup seasoned bread crumbs
- 1 pound ground beef
- 1 pound bulk Italian sausage
- 3 medium carrots, sliced
- 3 celery ribs, diced
- 1 large onion, chopped
- 4-1/2 teaspoons olive oil
- 3 garlic cloves, minced
- 4 cans (14-1/2 ounces *each*) reduced-sodium chicken broth
- 2 cans (14-1/2 ounces *each*) beef broth
- 1 package (10 ounces) frozen chopped spinach, thawed and squeezed dry
- 1/4 cup minced fresh basil
- 1 envelope onion soup mix
- 4-1/2 teaspoons ketchup
- 1/2 teaspoon dried thyme
- 3 bay leaves
- 1-1/2 cups uncooked penne pasta

1. In a large bowl, combine eggs and bread crumbs. Crumble beef and sausage over mixture and mix well. Shape into 3/4-in. balls.

2. Place meatballs on a greased rack in a foil-lined 15-in. x 10-in. x 1-in. baking pan. Bake at 350° for 15-18 minutes or until no longer pink.

3. Meanwhile, in a Dutch oven, saute the carrots, celery and onion in oil until tender. Add garlic; cook 1 minute longer. Stir in the broth, spinach, basil, soup mix, ketchup, thyme and bay leaves.

4. Drain meatballs on paper towels. Bring soup to a boil; add meatballs. Reduce heat; simmer, uncovered, for 30 minutes. Add pasta; cook 13-15 minutes longer or until pasta is tender, stirring occasionally. Discard bay leaves. **Yield:** 10 servings (2-1/2 quarts).

Grilled Veggie Wraps

Prep: 15 min. + marinating **Grill:** 15 min.

Britani Sepanski, Indianapolis, Indiana

I love the veggie marinade in this recipe, but the real secret to its success is the spread made with feta, Parmesan and cream cheeses. My father is a real meat-and-potatoes man, but these meatless wraps passed his taste test with flying colors!

 This recipe includes Nutrition Facts & Diabetic Exchanges.

     2 tablespoons balsamic vinegar
 1-1/2 teaspoons minced fresh basil
 1-1/2 teaspoons olive oil
 1-1/2 teaspoons molasses
   3/4 teaspoon minced fresh thyme
   1/8 teaspoon salt
   1/8 teaspoon pepper
     1 medium zucchini, cut lengthwise into 1/4-inch slices
     1 medium sweet red pepper, cut into 1-inch pieces
     1 medium red onion, cut into 1/2-inch slices
     4 ounces whole fresh mushrooms, cut into 1/2-inch pieces
     4 ounces fresh sugar snap peas
   1/2 cup crumbled feta cheese
     3 tablespoons reduced-fat cream cheese
     2 tablespoons grated Parmesan cheese
     1 tablespoon reduced-fat mayonnaise
     4 flour tortillas (8 inches)
     4 romaine leaves

1. In a large resealable plastic bag, combine the first seven ingredients; add vegetables. Seal bag and turn to coat; refrigerate for 2 hours, turning once.

2. Drain and reserve marinade. Transfer vegetables to a grill wok or basket. Grill, uncovered, over medium-high heat for 5 minutes, stirring frequently.

3. Set aside 1 teaspoon marinade. Turn vegetables; baste with remaining marinade. Grill 5-8 minutes longer or until tender, stirring frequently. Meanwhile, in a small bowl, combine cheeses and mayonnaise; set aside.

4. Brush one side of each tortilla with the reserved marinade. Place tortillas, marinade side down, on grill for 1-3 minutes or until lightly toasted.

5. Spread 3 tablespoons of the cheese mixture over ungrilled side of each tortilla. Top with romaine and 1 cup grilled vegetables; roll up. **Yield:** 4 servings.

Editor's Note: If you do not have a grill wok or basket, use a disposable foil pan. Poke holes in the bottom of the pan with a meat fork to allow liquid to drain.

Nutrition Facts: 1 wrap equals 332 calories, 14 g fat (6 g saturated fat), 26 mg cholesterol, 632 mg sodium, 39 g carbohydrate, 4 g fiber, 13 g protein. **Diabetic Exchanges:** 2 starch, 2 vegetable, 2 fat.

Tex-Mex Turkey Burgers

Prep/Total Time: 25 min.

Nancy Bourget, Round Rock, Texas

Flavored with taco seasoning and cilantro, these Southwestern turkey patties are so good—and even better topped with salsa, sour cream and cheese. I round out the menu with corn on the cob and deep-fried pita pieces sprinkled with cinnamon.

1-1/4 pounds ground turkey
   1 envelope reduced-sodium taco seasoning
   1 tablespoon dried cilantro flakes
   1 cup (4 ounces) shredded Mexican cheese blend
1/2 cup sour cream
1/2 cup salsa
   4 hamburger buns, split
   4 lettuce leaves

1. In a large bowl, combine the turkey, taco seasoning and cilantro; shape into four patties. Grill, covered, over medium heat or broil 4-6 in. from the heat for 5 minutes on each side.

2. Sprinkle cheese over the burgers; grill 2-3 minutes longer or until a meat thermometer reads 165° and the

juices run clear. Combine the sour cream and salsa. Serve the burgers on buns with the sour cream mixture and lettuce. **Yield:** 4 servings.

Rich Broccoli Cream Soup

Prep: 10 min. **Cook:** 65 min.

Carol Macagno, Fresno, California

Want to warm up a chilly winter's day? Indulge in a steaming bowl of this creamy homemade soup. It's wonderfully thick, flavorful and loaded with wholesome ingredients.

   4 celery ribs, chopped
   1 large onion, chopped

   3 tablespoons butter
   2 bunches broccoli, trimmed and coarsely
     chopped (about 8 cups)
1-1/2 cups chicken broth
   2 teaspoons garlic salt
1/2 teaspoon pepper
   2 tablespoons cornstarch
1/4 cup cold water
   1 pint heavy whipping cream

1. In a large saucepan, saute celery and onion in butter until tender. Add the broccoli, broth, garlic salt and pepper; bring to a boil. Reduce heat; cover and simmer for 45 minutes or until broccoli is tender.

2. In a small bowl, combine cornstarch and water until smooth. Stir into soup. Bring to a boil; cook and stir for 2 minutes or until thickened. Reduce heat to low. Stir in cream; cook 10 minutes longer or until heated through. **Yield:** 6-8 servings.

Best Broccoli

When buying broccoli, look for bunches that have a deep green color, tightly closed buds and crisp leaves. Store broccoli in a resealable plastic bag in the refrigerator for up to 4 days. Wash it just before using.

Brats with Sauerkraut

Prep: 10 min. **Cook:** 6 hours

Darlene Dixon, Hanover, Minnesota

I've made many variations of this versatile slow cooker recipe. The bratwurst can be plain, smoked or cheese-flavored. Plus, you can serve it whole or sliced...and with a bun or without. Try it for your next football party or potluck.

- 8 uncooked bratwurst links
- 1 can (14 ounces) sauerkraut, rinsed and well drained
- 2 medium apples, peeled and finely chopped
- 3 bacon strips, cooked and crumbled
- 1/4 cup packed brown sugar
- 1/4 cup finely chopped onion
- 1 teaspoon ground mustard
- 8 brat buns, split

1. Place bratwurst in a 5-qt. slow cooker. In a large bowl, combine the sauerkraut, apples, bacon, brown sugar, onion and mustard; spoon over bratwurst. Cover and cook on low for 6-7 hours or until the sausage is no longer pink.

2. Place brats in buns; using a slotted spoon, top with sauerkraut mixture. **Yield:** 8 servings.

Colorful Beef Wraps

Prep/Total Time: 30 min.

Robyn Cavallaro, Easton, Pennsylvania

I stir-fry a combination of sirloin steak, onions and peppers to make these hearty roll-ups. Spreading a little fat-free ranch salad dressing on the tortillas really jazzes them up.

✔ This recipe includes Nutrition Facts & Diabetic Exchanges.

- 1 beef top sirloin steak (1 pound), cut into thin strips
- 1/4 teaspoon pepper
- 3 tablespoons reduced-sodium soy sauce, *divided*
- 3 teaspoons olive oil, *divided*
- 1 medium red onion, cut into wedges
- 3 garlic cloves, minced
- 1 jar (7 ounces) roasted sweet red peppers, drained and cut into strips
- 1/4 cup dry red wine *or* reduced-sodium beef broth
- 6 tablespoons fat-free ranch salad dressing
- 6 flour tortillas (8 inches)
- 1-1/2 cups torn iceberg lettuce
- 1 medium tomato, chopped
- 1/4 cup chopped green onions

1. In a large nonstick skillet coated with cooking spray, saute the beef, pepper and 2 tablespoons soy sauce in 2 teaspoons oil until meat is no longer pink. Remove and keep warm.

2. Saute the red onion and garlic in the remaining oil for 1 minute. Stir in the roasted sweet red peppers, red wine and remaining soy sauce; bring to a boil. Return the beef to the pan; simmer for 5 minutes or until heated through.

3. Spread ranch dressing over one side of each tortilla; sprinkle with lettuce, tomato and green onions. Spoon about 3/4 cup beef mixture down the center of each tortilla; roll up. **Yield:** 6 servings.

Nutrition Facts: 1 wrap equals 325 calories, 9 g fat (2 g saturated fat), 43 mg cholesterol, 830 mg sodium, 39 g carbohydrate, 1 g fiber, 20 g protein. **Diabetic Exchanges:** 2 starch, 2 lean meat, 1 vegetable, 1 fat.

Italian Sausage Subs

Prep/Total Time: 30 min.

Sue Hoyt, Portland, Oregon

This traditional favorite smothers Italian sausage with sauteed onion, sweet red pepper, garlic, provolone cheese and plenty of pizza sauce. Plus, it's on the table in just 30 minutes.

> 2 Italian sausage links (4 ounces *each*)
> 1/4 cup reduced-sodium chicken broth
> 1/3 cup thinly sliced onion
> 2 teaspoons olive oil
> 1/3 cup julienned sweet red pepper
> Dash pepper
> 1 garlic clove, minced
> 2 teaspoons balsamic vinegar
> 2 Italian rolls *or* submarine buns, split
> 1/4 cup pizza sauce
> 1 slice provolone cheese, halved (3/4 ounce)

1. In a small nonstick skillet, brown sausages on all sides over medium heat. Add chicken broth; cover and simmer for 10 minutes. Remove sausages and keep warm; discard broth.

2. In the same pan, saute onion in oil until crisp-tender. Add the red pepper and pepper; cook until red pepper is crisp-tender. Add garlic; cook 1 minute longer. Stir in vinegar and sausages; heat through.

3. Spread the rolls with pizza sauce; top with sausage, cheese and onion mixture. Broil 4-6 in. from the heat for 2-3 minutes or until cheese is melted. **Yield:** 2 servings.

Turkey Burgers With Herb Sauce

Prep/Total Time: 30 min.

Lily Julow, Gainesville, Florida

Cooking for just two people can be a challenge, but this recipe is a breeze to prepare…and can easily be doubled for drop-in dinner guests. The moist ground-turkey burgers stuffed with feta cheese are topped off with a tangy cream sauce.

> 1/4 cup finely chopped red onion
> 2 tablespoons minced fresh parsley
> 1 tablespoon plus 1/3 cup sour cream, *divided*
> 1/2 pound lean ground turkey
> 1 tablespoon crumbled feta cheese
> 1-1/2 teaspoons minced chives
> 1-1/2 teaspoons minced fresh basil *or* 1/2 teaspoon dried basil
> 1-1/2 teaspoons lemon juice
> 3/4 teaspoon minced fresh tarragon *or* 1/4 teaspoon dried tarragon
> 1/8 teaspoon salt
> 1/8 teaspoon pepper
> 2 lettuce leaves
> 2 sesame seed hamburger buns, split

1. In a small bowl, combine the onion, parsley and 1 tablespoon sour cream. Crumble turkey over mixture and mix well. Shape into four thin patties. Top two patties with feta cheese; top with remaining patties and press edges firmly to seal.

2. Using long-handled tongs, moisten a paper towel with cooking oil and lightly coat the grill rack. Grill burgers, covered, over medium heat or broil 4 in. from the heat for 5-6 minutes on each side or until a meat thermometer reads 165°.

3. In a small bowl, combine the chives, basil, lemon juice, tarragon, salt, pepper and remaining sour cream. Serve burgers on lettuce-lined buns with prepared herb sauce. **Yield:** 2 servings.

Ham and Bean Soup

Prep: 30 min. + soaking **Cook:** 1-1/2 hours

Amanda Reed, Milford, Delaware

I learned to prepare this soup when we lived in Pennsylvania, near several Amish families. It's a wonderful way to use up leftover ham and mashed potatoes.

- 1 **pound dried navy beans**
- 2 **medium onions, chopped**
- 2 **teaspoons canola oil**
- 2 **celery ribs, chopped**
- 10 **cups water**
- 4 **cups cubed fully cooked ham**
- 1 **cup mashed potatoes (without added milk and butter)**
- 1/2 **cup shredded carrot**
- 2 **tablespoons Worcestershire sauce**
- 1 **teaspoon salt**
- 1/2 **teaspoon dried thyme**
- 1/2 **teaspoon pepper**
- 2 **bay leaves**
- 1 **meaty ham bone or 2 smoked ham hocks**
- 1/4 **cup minced fresh parsley**

1. Place the beans in a Dutch oven; add water to cover beans by 2 in. Bring to a boil; boil for 2 minutes. Remove from the heat; cover and let stand for 1 to 4 hours or until beans are softened. Drain and rinse beans, discarding liquid.

2. In the same pan, saute onions in oil for 2 minutes. Add the celery; cook until tender. Stir in the beans, water, ham, potatoes, carrot, Worcestershire sauce, salt, thyme, pepper and bay leaves. Add ham bone. Bring to a boil. Reduce heat; cover and simmer for 1-1/4 to 1-1/2 hours or until beans are tender.

3. Discard the bay leaves. Remove ham bone and set aside until cool enough to handle. Remove ham from bone and cut into cubes. Discard bone. Return ham to soup; heat through. Garnish soup with parsley. **Yield:** 15 servings (3-3/4 quarts).

Special Turkey Sandwiches

Prep/Total Time: 25 min.

Maria Bertram, Waltham, Massachusetts

Every Saturday, my family has "lunch" for supper. The rich cream cheese spread makes these sandwiches a favorite.

 This recipe includes Nutrition Facts & Diabetic Exchanges.

- 4 **ounces reduced-fat cream cheese**
- 1/2 **cup finely chopped fresh spinach**
- 1/2 **cup minced fresh basil**
- 1/3 **cup shredded Parmesan cheese**
- 1 **garlic clove, minced**
- 1/2 **large red onion, sliced**
- 2 **tablespoons dry red wine or reduced-sodium beef broth**
- 8 **slices whole wheat bread, toasted**
- 3/4 **pound sliced deli turkey**
- 8 **slices tomato**
- 8 **lettuce leaves**

1. In a small bowl, beat the cream cheese, spinach, basil, Parmesan cheese and garlic until blended; set aside. In a small skillet, cook onion in wine until tender; set aside.

2. Place four slices of toast on a broiler pan; top with turkey. Place remaining toast on broiler pan; spread with cream cheese mixture.

3. Broil 3-4 in. from the heat for 2-3 minutes or until heated through. Layer the onion, tomato and lettuce over turkey. Top with remaining toast. **Yield:** 4 servings.

Nutrition Facts: 1 sandwich equals 348 calories, 11 g fat (6 g saturated fat), 63 mg cholesterol, 1,426 mg sodium, 36 g carbohydrate, 5 g fiber, 29 g protein. **Diabetic Exchanges:** 3 lean meat, 2 starch, 1-1/2 fat.

Vegetable Soup With Dumplings

Prep: 25 min. Cook: 40 min.

Karen Mau, Jacksboro, Tennessee

This satisfying meatless soup is jam-packed with wholesome and flavorful vegetables—carrots, celery, onions, potatoes, tomatoes, cabbage and peas. Plus, the simmering pot is topped off with fluffy homemade dumplings garnished with shredded cheddar cheese. It all adds up to a hot, hearty meal-in-one and a great change of pace at dinnertime.

 This recipe includes Nutrition Facts & Diabetic Exchanges.

1-1/2 **cups chopped onions**
    4 **medium carrots, sliced**
    3 **celery ribs, sliced**
    2 **tablespoons canola oil**
    3 **cups vegetable broth**
    4 **medium potatoes, peeled and sliced**
    4 **medium tomatoes, chopped**
    2 **garlic cloves, minced**
1/2 **teaspoon salt**
1/2 **teaspoon pepper**
1/4 **cup all-purpose flour**
1/2 **cup water**
    1 **cup chopped cabbage**
    1 **cup frozen peas**

CARROT DUMPLINGS:
2-1/4 **cups reduced-fat biscuit/baking mix**
    1 **cup shredded carrots**
    1 **tablespoon minced fresh parsley**
    1 **cup cold water**
  10 **tablespoons shredded reduced-fat cheddar cheese**

1. In a Dutch oven, cook the onions, carrots and celery in oil for 6-8 minutes or until crisp-tender. Stir in the vegetable broth, potatoes, tomatoes, garlic, salt and pepper. Bring to a boil. Reduce the heat; cover and simmer for 15-20 minutes or until the vegetables are tender.

2. In a small bowl, combine the flour and water until smooth; stir into vegetable mixture. Bring to a boil; cook and stir for 2 minutes or until thickened. Stir in cabbage and peas.

3. For dumplings, in a small bowl, combine baking mix, carrots and parsley. Stir in water until moistened. Drop in 10 mounds onto simmering soup. Cover and simmer for 15 minutes or until a toothpick inserted in a dumpling comes out clean (do not lift cover while simmering). Garnish with cheese. **Yield:** 10 servings.

Nutrition Facts: 1-1/4 cups soup with 1 dumpling equals 258 calories, 7 g fat (2 g saturated fat), 5 mg cholesterol, 826 mg sodium, 44 g carbohydrate, 5 g fiber, 8 g protein. **Diabetic Exchanges:** 2 starch, 2 vegetable, 1 fat.

Meatball Stew

Prep: 1 hour Cook: 30 min.

Joan Chasse, Berlin, Connecticut

Hearty and homey, this saucy stew is chock-full of meatballs made with beef, pork and veal. It's guaranteed to please your family when there's an autumn chill in the air.

- 3 eggs, lightly beaten
- 2/3 cup seasoned bread crumbs
- 1/3 cup grated Parmesan cheese
- Dash pepper
- 1/2 pound *each* ground beef, pork and veal
- 4 medium potatoes, peeled and cut into small chunks
- 3 medium carrots, sliced
- 1-1/2 cups chopped celery
- 1 medium onion, cut into wedges
- 1 garlic clove, minced
- 1 envelope onion soup mix
- 2-1/4 cups water
- 1 cup frozen peas, thawed
- 4-1/2 teaspoons minced fresh parsley

1. In a large bowl, combine the eggs, bread crumbs, cheese and pepper. Crumble beef, pork and veal over mixture and mix well. Shape into 1-1/2-in. balls.

2. Place meatballs on a greased rack in a shallow baking pan. Bake at 350° for 20-25 minutes or until no longer pink. Drain on paper towels.

3. Place the meatballs, potatoes, carrots, celery, onion and garlic in a Dutch oven. In a small bowl, combine the soup mix and water; pour over meatball mixture. Bring to a boil. Reduce heat; cover and simmer for 25-30 minutes or until the vegetables are tender. Stir in the peas and parsley; heat through. **Yield:** 10 servings (2-1/2 quarts).

Sensational Sloppy Joes

Prep/Total Time: 30 min.

Jessica Mergen, Cuba City, Wisconsin

I've always enjoyed sloppy joes but was feeling that my own recipe lacked pizzazz. Then a coworker gave me hers—and I knew I'd never go back! This flavorful mixture gets a hint of sweetness from grape jelly, but I often use more than called for because my husband likes his extra sweet.

- 1 pound ground beef
- 1/2 cup chopped onion
- 1/2 cup condensed tomato soup, undiluted
- 1/2 cup ketchup
- 3 tablespoons grape jelly
- 1 tablespoon brown sugar
- 1 tablespoon cider vinegar
- 1 tablespoon prepared mustard
- 1/2 teaspoon salt
- 1/2 teaspoon celery seed
- 5 hamburger buns, split

In a large skillet, cook beef and onion over medium heat until meat is no longer pink; drain. Stir in the soup, ketchup, jelly, brown sugar, vinegar, mustard, salt and celery seed. Bring to a boil. Reduce heat; simmer, uncovered, for 10 minutes or until heated through. Serve on buns. **Yield:** 5 servings.

Curry Chicken Salad Wraps

Prep/Total Time: 25 min.

Robyn Cavallaro, Easton, Pennsylvania

Featuring curry powder and mango chutney, these scrumptious sandwiches give traditional chicken salad a twist.

- 1/2 cup mayonnaise
- 1/2 cup sour cream
- 1/4 cup finely chopped green onions
- 2 tablespoons curry powder
- 1 tablespoon mango chutney
- 1/2 teaspoon salt
- 1/2 teaspoon pepper
- 1 package (9 ounces) ready-to-serve roasted chicken breast strips
- 1 cup seedless red grapes, halved
- 1/2 cup julienned carrot
- 6 tablespoons chopped pecans, toasted
- 1/4 cup thinly sliced onion
- 6 lettuce leaves
- 6 flour tortillas (10 inches), room temperature
- 3/4 cup fresh mint (about 24 leaves)

1. For dressing, in a small bowl, combine the first seven ingredients. Set aside 1-1/2 cups for serving. In a large bowl, combine the chicken, grapes, carrot, pecans and onion. Stir in the remaining dressing.

2. Place a lettuce leaf on each flour tortilla; top with 2/3 cup chicken salad and mint leaves. Roll up. Serve with reserved dressing. **Yield:** 6 servings.

Spicy Two-Bean Chili

Prep: 20 min. Cook: 8 hours

Lesley Pew, Lynn, Massachusetts

Chili lovers are sure to get a kick out of this nontraditional recipe. It gets its distinctive taste from lime juice and tomatoes with green chilies, as well as both kidney and black beans. Try ladling it over rice and sprinkling on some cheddar cheese.

- **2 pounds ground beef**
- **3 large onions, chopped**
- 6 garlic cloves, minced
- 2 cans (16 ounces *each*) kidney beans, rinsed and drained
- 2 cans (15 ounces *each*) black beans, rinsed and drained
- 2 cans (10 ounces *each*) diced tomatoes and green chilies, undrained
- 1 can (14-1/2 ounces) chicken broth
- 1/2 cup lime juice
- 6 tablespoons cornmeal
- 1/4 cup chili powder
- 4 teaspoons dried oregano
- 3 teaspoons ground cumin
- 2 teaspoons salt
- 2 teaspoons rubbed sage
- 1/2 teaspoon white pepper
- 1/2 teaspoon paprika
- 1/2 teaspoon pepper

Hot cooked rice
Shredded cheddar cheese

1. In a Dutch oven, cook ground beef and onions over medium heat until meat is no longer pink. Add garlic; cook 1 minute longer. Drain.

2. Transfer to a 5-qt. slow cooker. Stir in the beans, tomatoes, chicken broth, lime juice, cornmeal and seasonings.

3. Cover and cook on low for 8 hours or until heated through. Serve with rice; sprinkle with cheese. **Yield:** 11 servings.

Lime Chicken Chili

Prep: 25 min. **Cook:** 40 min.

Diane Randazzo, Sinking Spring, Pennsylvania

A burst of lime juice gives this chicken chili refreshing flavor while canned tomatoes and beans make preparation a breeze. Top off each serving with toasted tortilla strips.

 This recipe includes Nutrition Facts & Diabetic Exchanges.

1 medium onion, chopped
1 *each* medium sweet yellow, red and green pepper, chopped
2 tablespoons olive oil
3 garlic cloves, minced
1 pound ground chicken
1 tablespoon all-purpose flour
1 tablespoon baking cocoa
1 tablespoon ground cumin
1 tablespoon chili powder
2 teaspoons ground coriander
1/2 teaspoon salt
1/2 teaspoon garlic pepper blend
1/4 teaspoon pepper
2 cans (14-1/2 ounces *each*) diced tomatoes, undrained
1/4 cup lime juice
1 teaspoon grated lime peel
1 can (15 ounces) white kidney *or* cannellini beans, rinsed and drained
2 flour tortillas (8 inches), cut into 1/4-inch strips
6 tablespoons reduced-fat sour cream

1. In a large saucepan, saute the onion and peppers in oil for 7-8 minutes or until crisp-tender. Add the garlic; cook 1 minute longer. Add the chicken; cook and stir over medium heat for 8-9 minutes or until no longer pink.

2. Stir in the flour, cocoa and seasonings. Add the tomatoes, lime juice and lime peel. Bring to a boil. Reduce heat; simmer, uncovered, for 20-25 minutes or until thickened, stirring frequently. Stir in the kidney beans; heat through.

3. Meanwhile, place tortilla strips on a baking sheet coated with cooking spray. Bake at 400° for 8-10 minutes or until crisp. Serve chili with sour cream and tortilla strips. **Yield:** 6 servings.

Nutrition Facts: 1 cup with 5 baked tortilla strips and 1 tablespoon sour cream equals 357 calories, 14 g fat (4 g saturated fat), 55 mg cholesterol, 643 mg sodium, 40 g carbohydrate, 8 g fiber, 21 g protein. **Diabetic Exchanges:** 3 vegetable, 2 lean meat, 1-1/2 starch, 1 fat.

Crunchy Ham and Cheese

Prep/Total Time: 25 min.

Karen Wolf, Niles, Illinois

Crushed potato chips put the delightful crunch in this winning spin on traditional ham-and-cheese sandwiches. Round out the meal with a bowl of your favorite soup—you'll have one of the best comfort-food meals ever!

    1 tablespoon butter, softened
    4 slices white bread
    1 tablespoon Dijon mustard
    4 slices process American cheese
    2 slices deli ham (1 ounce *each*)
  1/2 medium tomato, thinly sliced
    2 eggs, lightly beaten
    2 tablespoons 2% milk
  1/8 teaspoon onion powder
    1 cup crushed ridged potato chips

1. Butter one side of each slice of bread. Spread Dijon mustard over the unbuttered side of two slices; layer each with one slice of cheese, ham, tomato, remaining cheese and remaining bread, buttered side up.

2. In a shallow bowl, beat the eggs, milk and onion powder. Place the potato chips in another bowl. Dip each sandwich into the egg mixture, then coat with potato chips.

3. In a large nonstick skillet or griddle coated with cooking spray, toast sandwiches for 4 minutes on each side or until golden brown. **Yield:** 2 servings.

Cheese-Topped Vegetable Soup

Prep: 15 min. **Cook:** 25 min.

Anna Minegar, Zolfo Springs, Florida

Garden-fresh taste makes this mozzarella-topped veggie soup a summertime staple, but you're sure to love it year-round.

    1 can (28 ounces) Italian stewed tomatoes
1-1/2 cups water
    1 can (8-3/4 ounces) whole kernel corn, drained
  3/4 cup chopped sweet red pepper
  2/3 cup chopped red onion
  2/3 cup chopped green pepper
  1/4 cup minced fresh basil
    1 garlic clove, minced
  1/2 teaspoon salt
  1/4 teaspoon pepper
  1/2 cup salad croutons
  1/4 cup shredded part-skim mozzarella cheese

1. In a large saucepan, combine the first 10 ingredients. Bring to a boil. Reduce heat; simmer, uncovered, for 20-25 minutes or until heated through and vegetables are tender.

2. Ladle the soup into ovenproof bowls. Top each with croutons and cheese. Broil 6 in. from the heat until cheese is melted. **Yield:** 4 cups.

Great Garnishes

Cheese-Topped Vegetable Soup is finished off with mozzarella cheese and croutons. Other flavorful garnishes for soups include finely chopped green onions or chives, minced fresh parsley and dollops of sour cream.

PG. 85

PG. 76

PG. 74

BREAKFAST & BRUNCH

Whether you want grab-and-go muffins for your family or a hearty egg bake for holiday guests, the sunrise specialties here will open your eyes to just how scrumptious mornings can be!

PG. 87

Raspberry Key Lime Crepes

Prep: 20 min. + chilling

Wolfgang Hanau, West Palm Beach, Florida

Key lime juice turns cream cheese into the refreshing filling for these lightened-up berry crepes. Sometimes I even pipe it into phyllo-dough cones that I bake separately.

 This recipe includes Nutrition Facts & Diabetic Exchanges.

> 3 tablespoons key lime juice
> 1 package (12.3 ounces) silken firm tofu, crumbled
> 6 ounces reduced-fat cream cheese, cubed
> 2/3 cup confectioners' sugar, *divided*
> 2-1/2 teaspoons grated lime peel
> Dash salt
> Dash ground nutmeg
> 6 prepared crepes (9 inches)
> 1-1/2 cups fresh raspberries

1. In a blender, combine the lime juice, tofu and cream cheese; cover and process until smooth. Set aside 1 teaspoon confectioners' sugar. Add the lime peel, salt, nutmeg and remaining confectioners' sugar; cover and process until blended. Cover and refrigerate for at least 1 hour.

2. Spread cream cheese mixture over crepes. Sprinkle with berries; roll up. Dust with reserved confectioners' sugar. **Yield:** 6 servings.

Nutrition Facts: 1 filled crepe equals 222 calories, 9 g fat (5 g saturated fat), 26 mg cholesterol, 247 mg sodium, 28 g carbohydrate, 3 g fiber, 8 g protein. **Diabetic Exchanges:** 1-1/2 starch, 1 lean meat, 1 fat, 1/2 fruit.

Pecan Apple Pancakes

Prep: 15 min. **Cook:** 10 min./batch

Sharon Richardson, Dallas, Texas

Weekend breakfasts are a big deal here in Texas, and these yummy pancakes make any morning special.

> 2 cups all-purpose flour
> 1 cup sugar
> 2 teaspoons baking powder
> 1 teaspoon baking soda
> 1 teaspoon ground cinnamon
> 1/2 teaspoon salt
> 1/2 teaspoon ground ginger
> 1/2 teaspoon ground mace
> 1/2 teaspoon ground cloves
> 2 eggs
> 1-3/4 cups buttermilk
> 3 tablespoons canola oil
> 1-3/4 cups shredded peeled apples
> 1/2 cup chopped pecans

1. In a large bowl, combine the first nine ingredients. In another bowl, combine the eggs, buttermilk and oil; stir into dry ingredients just until blended. Stir in apples and pecans.

2. Pour pancake batter by 1/4 cupfuls onto a greased griddle over medium-low heat. Turn when bubbles form on top; cook until the second side is golden brown. **Yield:** 1-1/2 dozen.

Buttermilk Blend

Keeping powdered buttermilk blend (found near the dry and canned milk in stores) in your pantry is a convenient way to always have buttermilk on hand. You can reconstitute the amount needed for a recipe in just seconds.

Tomato Quiche

Prep: 20 min. **Bake:** 50 min.

Heidi Anne Quinn, West Kingston, Rhode Island

I first sampled this recipe at a family gathering, and I absolutely loved it. The cheesy quiche is fairly simple to fix and makes a great meatless brunch dish, whether served hot or cold. It's become my most-requested contribution to parties.

 1 cup chopped onion
 2 tablespoons butter
 4 large tomatoes, peeled, seeded, chopped and
  drained
 1 teaspoon salt
1/4 teaspoon pepper
1/4 teaspoon dried thyme
 2 cups (8 ounces) Monterey Jack cheese, *divided*
 1 unbaked pastry shell (10 inches)
 4 eggs
1-1/2 cups half-and-half cream

1. In a large skillet, saute onion in butter until tender. Add tomatoes, salt, pepper and thyme. Cook over medium-high heat until liquid is almost evaporated, about 10 to 15 minutes. Remove from heat.

2. Sprinkle 1 cup cheese into the bottom of the pie shell. Cover with the tomato mixture; sprinkle with remaining cheese.

3. In a small bowl, beat the eggs until foamy. Stir in cream; mix well. Pour into pie shell.

4. Bake at 425° for 10 minutes. Reduce the heat to 325°; bake 40 minutes longer or until the top begins to brown and a knife inserted near the center comes out clean. Let the quiche stand 10 minutes before cutting. **Yield:** 6-8 servings.

Jumbo Caramel Banana Muffins

Prep: 20 min. **Bake:** 25 min. + cooling

Katherine McClelland, Deep Brook, Nova Scotia

Love banana bread? These flavorful jumbo muffins, drizzled with a luscious caramel icing, are sure to satisfy your craving.

1/4 cup shortening
 1 cup sugar
 1 egg
1-1/2 cups mashed ripe bananas (about 3 large)
 1 teaspoon vanilla extract
1-1/2 cups all-purpose flour
 1 teaspoon baking soda
1/4 teaspoon salt
CARAMEL ICING:
 2 tablespoons butter
1/4 cup packed brown sugar
 1 tablespoon 2% milk
1/2 cup confectioners' sugar

1. In a large bowl, cream shortening and sugar until light and fluffy. Beat in egg. Beat in bananas and vanilla. Combine the flour, baking soda and salt; add to creamed mixture just until moistened.

2. Fill paper-lined jumbo muffin cups three-fourths full. Bake at 350° for 23-28 minutes or until a toothpick inserted near the center comes out clean. Cool for 5 minutes before removing from pan to a wire rack to cool completely.

3. For icing, in a small saucepan, melt butter over medium heat. Stir in brown sugar and milk; bring to a boil. Cool slightly. Beat in confectioners' sugar until smooth. Transfer to a small resealable plastic bag; cut a small hole in a corner of the bag and drizzle over muffins. **Yield:** 6 muffins.

White Chocolate Macadamia Muffins

Prep: 20 min. **Bake:** 15 min.

Lorie Roach, Buckatunna, Mississippi

I love making muffins because they're versatile and everyone likes them. These chocolaty, nutty bites remind me of one of my favorite cookies and are real kid-pleasers, too.

1-3/4 cups all-purpose flour
3/4 cup sugar
2-1/2 teaspoons baking powder
1/2 teaspoon salt
1 egg
1/2 cup 2% milk
1/4 cup butter, melted
3/4 cup white baking chips
3/4 cup chopped macadamia nuts
GLAZE:
1/2 cup white baking chips
2 tablespoons heavy whipping cream

1. In a large bowl, combine the flour, sugar, baking powder and salt. In another bowl, combine the egg, milk and butter; stir into dry ingredients just until moistened. Fold in chips and nuts.

2. Fill paper-lined muffin cups two-thirds full. Bake at 400° for 15-18 minutes or until a toothpick inserted near the center comes out clean. Cool for 5 minutes before removing from pan to a wire rack.

3. For the glaze, in a microwave, melt the white chips; stir until smooth. Drizzle over warm muffins. Serve warm. **Yield:** 1 dozen.

Muffins in Moments

To save time in the morning, start muffins the night before. Combine the dry ingredients in a plastic bag and measure any other ingredients that will hold. The next day, you can quickly stir together the batter and bake.

Berry Cheesecake Muffins

Prep: 30 min. **Bake:** 25 min./batch

1/3 cup butter, softened
3/4 cup sugar
2 eggs
1/3 cup 2% milk
1-1/2 cups all-purpose flour
1-1/2 teaspoons baking powder
1 teaspoon ground cinnamon
CREAM CHEESE FILLING:
2 packages (3 ounces *each*) cream cheese, softened
1/3 cup sugar
1 egg
3/4 cup fresh raspberries
3/4 cup fresh blueberries
STREUSEL TOPPING:
1/4 cup all-purpose flour
2 tablespoons brown sugar
1/2 teaspoon ground cinnamon
1 tablespoon cold butter

1. In a large bowl, cream butter and sugar until light and fluffy. Add eggs, one at a time, beating well after each addition. Beat in milk. Combine the flour, baking powder and cinnamon; gradually add to creamed mixture just until moistened. Fill greased or paper-lined muffin cups one-third full.

2. For filling, in a small bowl, beat cream cheese, sugar and egg until smooth. Fold in berries. Drop a rounded tablespoonful into center of each muffin.

3. For topping, combine flour, brown sugar and cinnamon in a small bowl; cut in butter until crumbly. Sprinkle over the batter. (Muffin cups will be full.)

4. Bake at 375° for 25-30 minutes or until a toothpick inserted near the center comes out clean. Cool for 5 minutes before removing from pans to wire racks. Serve warm. Refrigerate leftovers. **Yield:** 21 muffins.

JEANNE BILHIMER MIDLAND, MICHIGAN

I adapted this recipe over the years for my family, and they think it's wonderful. Baked with a streusel topping, these goodies taste almost like miniature desserts.

GRAND
PRIZE
WINNER

Orange-Rhubarb Breakfast Bread

Prep: 20 min. **Bake:** 55 min. + cooling

Sonya Goergen, Moorhead, Minnesota

I love starting my day with this fabulous sweet loaf alongside eggs, sausage and a glass of orange juice.

     1/3 cup butter, softened
       1 cup sugar
       2 eggs
       1 teaspoon vanilla extract
       2 cups all-purpose flour
 1-1/2 teaspoons baking powder
     1/2 teaspoon baking soda
     1/2 teaspoon salt
     1/4 teaspoon ground ginger
     1/4 teaspoon ground nutmeg
     1/2 cup orange juice
       1 cup chopped fresh *or* frozen rhubarb
     1/2 cup slivered almonds
       2 teaspoons grated orange peel

1. In a large bowl, cream butter and sugar until light and fluffy. Add eggs, one at a time, beating well after each addition. Beat in vanilla.

2. Combine the flour, baking powder, baking soda, salt, ginger and nutmeg; add to creamed mixture alternately with orange juice. Fold in the rhubarb, almonds and orange peel.

3. Transfer to a greased 9-in. x 5-in. loaf pan. Bake at 350° for 55-65 minutes or until a toothpick inserted near the center comes out clean. Cool for 10 minutes before removing from pan to a wire rack. **Yield:** 1 loaf (16 slices).

Editor's Note: If using frozen rhubarb, measure rhubarb while still frozen, then thaw completely. Drain in a colander, but do not press liquid out.

Rhubarb Do's

Using fresh rhubarb? Select stalks that are crisp and brightly colored. Tightly wrap them in a plastic bag and store them in the refrigerator for up to 3 days. Wash the stalks and remove the poisonous leaves before fixing your recipe.

Walnut Raspberry Muffins

Prep: 25 min. **Bake:** 20 min./batch

Elisa Lochridge, Tigard, Oregon

Raspberries are my favorite berry, so I often turn to this recipe when I'm in the mood for some fresh-baked muffins.

     2/3 cup cream cheese, softened
     1/3 cup butter, softened
 1-1/2 cups sugar
       2 egg whites
       1 egg
     1/2 cup buttermilk
 1-1/2 teaspoons vanilla extract
       2 cups all-purpose flour
       1 teaspoon baking powder
     1/4 teaspoon baking soda
       2 cups fresh *or* frozen raspberries
     1/4 cup chopped walnuts

1. In a large bowl, beat the cream cheese, butter and sugar until light and fluffy. Add the egg whites, egg, buttermilk and vanilla; mix well. Combine the flour, baking powder and baking soda; add to creamed

mixture just until moistened. Fold in the raspberries and walnuts.

2. Fill paper-lined muffin cups three-fourths full. Bake at 350° for 20-24 minutes or until a toothpick inserted near the center comes out clean. Cool for 5 minutes before removing from pans to wire racks. Serve warm. **Yield:** 1-1/2 dozen.

Editor's Note: If using frozen raspberries, do not thaw before adding to batter.

Cranberry Almond Muffins

Prep: 20 min. Bake: 20 min.

Janice Pletscher, Basking Ridge, New Jersey

My youngest daughter baked a batch of these golden-brown goodies for breakfast when my husband and I were visiting her in Virginia, and now we enjoy them at our home.

1-1/2 cups all-purpose flour
1/2 cup sugar
1 teaspoon baking powder
1/4 teaspoon baking soda
1/4 teaspoon salt
2 eggs
1/2 cup sour cream
1/4 cup butter, melted
1/4 teaspoon almond extract
3/4 cup sliced almonds, *divided*
1/2 cup whole-berry cranberry sauce

1. In a large bowl, combine the flour, sugar, baking powder, baking soda and salt. In another bowl, combine the eggs, sour cream, butter and almond extract; stir into the dry ingredients just until moistened. Fold in 1/2 cup almonds.

2. Fill greased or paper-lined muffin cups half full; drop 1 tablespoon cranberry sauce into the center of each muffin. Cover with enough batter to fill cups three-fourths full; sprinkle with remaining almonds.

3. Bake at 375° for 20-25 minutes or until a toothpick inserted near the center comes out clean. Cool for 5 minutes before removing from pan to a wire rack. Serve warm. **Yield:** 8 muffins.

Fajita Frittata

Prep/Total Time: 25 min.

Mary Ann Gomez, Lombard, Illinois

It takes less than 30 minutes to put together this tasty egg dish packed with chicken, cheese, veggies and spices. The frittata is perfect for brunch, but it's a popular choice in our house for dinner, too. Serve salsa and sour cream on the side.

 This recipe includes Nutrition Facts & Diabetic Exchanges.

1/2 pound boneless skinless chicken breast, cut into strips
1 small onion, cut into thin strips
1/2 medium green pepper, cut into thin strips
1 teaspoon lime juice
1/2 teaspoon salt
1/2 teaspoon ground cumin
1/2 teaspoon chili powder
2 tablespoons canola oil
8 eggs, lightly beaten
1 cup (4 ounces) shredded Colby-Monterey Jack cheese
Salsa and sour cream, optional

1. In a large ovenproof skillet, saute the chicken, onion, green pepper, lime juice, salt, cumin and chili powder in oil until chicken is no longer pink.

2. Pour eggs over chicken mixture. Cover and cook over medium-low heat for 8-10 minutes or until eggs are nearly set. Uncover; broil 6 in. from the heat for 2-3 minutes or until eggs are set.

3. Sprinkle with the cheese. Cover and let stand for 1 minute or until cheese is melted. Serve with salsa and sour cream if desired. **Yield:** 8 servings.

Nutrition Facts: 1 serving (prepared with egg substitute and reduced-fat cheese; calculated without salsa and sour cream) equals 137 calories, 7 g fat (2 g saturated fat), 23 mg cholesterol, 393 mg sodium, 3 g carbohydrate, trace fiber, 15 g protein. **Diabetic Exchanges:** 2 lean meat, 1 fat.

Cornmeal Ham Cakes

Prep/Total Time: 30 min.

Priscilla Gilbert, Indian Harbour Beach, Florida

These savory breakfast cakes topped with pineapple-flavored maple syrup are wonderful in the morning, but my husband and I also like to have them for supper.

- 1/2 cup all-purpose flour
- 1/2 cup cornmeal
- 2 tablespoons sugar
- 1/2 teaspoon baking powder
- 1/4 teaspoon baking soda
- 1/8 teaspoon salt
- 2 eggs, lightly beaten
- 1 cup buttermilk
- 3 tablespoons butter, melted
- 1 teaspoon vanilla extract
- 1-1/2 cups diced fully cooked ham

PINEAPPLE MAPLE SYRUP:
- 1 cup diced fresh pineapple
- 1/4 teaspoon ground cinnamon
- 1 tablespoon butter
- 1 cup maple syrup

1. In a large bowl, combine the first six ingredients. Combine the eggs, buttermilk, butter and vanilla; stir into dry ingredients until well blended. Fold in ham. Pour batter by 1/4 cupfuls onto a greased hot griddle. Turn when bubbles form on top; cook until second side is golden brown.

2. For syrup, in a small saucepan, saute pineapple and cinnamon in butter for 4-6 minutes or until pineapple is browned. Stir in the maple syrup. Serve with the pancakes. **Yield:** 4 servings.

Miniature Orange Muffins

Prep: 30 min. Bake: 10 min./batch

Bonita Kinney, Firth, Nebraska

Orange peel and orange juice bring a burst of citrus to these fun, streusel-topped mini muffins. The accompanying orange marmalade butter makes them extra special.

- 1-1/2 cups plus 2 tablespoons all-purpose flour, *divided*
- 1/2 cup sugar
- 2 teaspoons baking powder
- 1/2 teaspoon salt
- 1 egg
- 1 cup 2% milk
- 9 tablespoons butter, melted, *divided*
- 3 tablespoons orange juice concentrate
- 2-1/2 teaspoons grated orange peel, *divided*
- 1/4 cup packed brown sugar
- 1/4 cup chopped pecans

ORANGE BUTTER:
- 1/2 cup butter, softened
- 1/4 cup sweet orange marmalade
- 1 teaspoon honey

1. In a large bowl, combine 1-1/2 cups flour, sugar, baking powder and salt. In another bowl, whisk egg, milk, 8 tablespoons butter, concentrate and 2 teaspoons peel; stir into dry ingredients just until moistened.

2. Fill greased miniature muffin cups half full. Combine the brown sugar, pecans and remaining flour, butter and orange peel; sprinkle over batter.

3. Bake at 400° for 10-12 minutes or until a toothpick inserted near the center comes out clean. Cool for 5 minutes before removing from pans to wire racks.

4. In a small bowl, beat orange butter ingredients until blended. Serve with warm muffins. **Yield:** 4-1/2 dozen.

Chicken Club Brunch Ring

Prep: 20 min. **Bake:** 20 min.

Rebecca Clark, Warrior, Alabama

A few tubes of refrigerated crescent rolls make this impressive recipe a snap. I fill the ring with chicken salad and serve warm slices with mustard-flavored mayonnaise.

 This recipe includes Nutrition Facts & Diabetic Exchanges.

- 1/2 cup mayonnaise
- 1 tablespoon minced fresh parsley
- 2 teaspoons Dijon mustard
- 1-1/2 teaspoons finely chopped onion
- 1-3/4 cups cubed cooked chicken breast (1/2-inch cubes)
- 2 bacon strips, cooked and crumbled
- 1 cup (4 ounces) shredded Swiss cheese, *divided*
- 2 tubes (8 ounces *each*) refrigerated crescent rolls
- 2 plum tomatoes
- 2 cups shredded lettuce

1. In a large bowl, combine the mayonnaise, parsley, Dijon mustard and onion. Stir in the chicken, bacon and 3/4 cup cheese.

2. Unroll crescent dough; separate into 16 triangles. Arrange on an ungreased 12-in. round pizza pan, forming a ring with pointed ends facing outer edge of pan and wide ends overlapping.

3. Spoon chicken mixture over the wide ends; fold the points over the filling and tuck under the wide ends (filling will be visible). Chop half of a tomato; set aside. Slice remaining tomatoes; place over filling and tuck into dough.

4. Bake at 375° for 20-25 minutes or until golden brown. Sprinkle with remaining cheese. Let stand for 5 minutes. Place lettuce in center of ring; sprinkle with chopped tomato. **Yield:** 16 servings.

Nutrition Facts: 1 piece equals 153 calories, 6 g fat (2 g saturated fat), 17 mg cholesterol, 368 mg sodium, 14 g carbohydrate, trace fiber, 9 g protein. **Diabetic Exchanges:** 1 starch, 1 very lean meat, 1 fat.

Golden Raisin Bran Muffins

Prep/Total Time: 30 min.

*Joanne Foote, Harbour Breton
Newfoundland and Labrador*

I tried many bran muffin recipes before coming up with this one. My family and friends say these moist goodies, flavored with applesauce and cinnamon, are the best they've tasted.

- 1 cup unsweetened applesauce
- 1/3 cup canola oil
- 1/4 cup milk
- 1 egg, lightly beaten
- 1 cup All-Bran
- 3/4 cup all-purpose flour
- 3/4 cup whole wheat flour
- 1/3 cup packed brown sugar
- 3 teaspoons baking powder
- 1 teaspoon ground cinnamon
- 1/2 teaspoon baking soda
- 1/4 teaspoon salt
- 1/2 cup golden raisins

1. In a large bowl, combine the applesauce, oil, milk and egg. Stir in bran; let stand for 5 minutes.

2. In another bowl, combine the flours, brown sugar, baking powder, cinnamon, baking soda and salt; stir in bran mixture just until moistened. Fold in raisins (batter will be thick).

3. Fill greased or paper-lined muffin cups two-thirds full. Bake at 375° for 15-20 minutes or until a toothpick inserted near the center comes out clean. Cool for 5 minutes before removing from pan to a wire rack. Serve warm. **Yield:** 1 dozen.

Chicken Broccoli Crepes

Prep: 40 min. + chilling **Bake:** 20 min.

Deanna Naivar, Temple, Texas

When I organized food and nutrition training for our county 4-H members, we had cooking demonstrations representing different countries. We chose crepes for France, and everyone really loved this version with a chicken-broccoli filling.

- 1 cup plus 2 tablespoons milk
- 2 eggs
- 2 tablespoons butter, melted
- 1 cup all-purpose flour
- 1/4 teaspoon salt

FILLING:
- 1/4 cup butter
- 1/4 cup all-purpose flour
- 2 cups chicken broth
- 2 teaspoons Worcestershire sauce
- 3 cups (12 ounces) shredded cheddar cheese, *divided*
- 2 cups (16 ounces) sour cream
- 2 packages (8 ounces *each*) frozen broccoli spears, cooked and drained
- 2-1/2 cups cubed cooked chicken

1. In a small bowl, beat the milk, eggs and butter. Combine flour and salt; add to egg mixture and beat until smooth. Cover and refrigerate for 1 hour.

2. Heat a lightly greased 8-in. nonstick skillet. Stir batter; pour 1/4 cup into the center of skillet. Lift and tilt pan to evenly coat bottom. Cook until top appears dry; turn and cook 15-20 seconds longer. Remove to a wire rack. Repeat with remaining batter, greasing skillet as needed. When cool, stack crepes with waxed paper or paper towels in between.

3. In a large saucepan, melt butter. Stir in flour until smooth. Gradually stir in broth and Worcestershire sauce. Bring to a boil; cook and stir for 2 minutes or until thickened. Reduce heat; stir in 2 cups of cheese. Cook and stir for 10 minutes or until cheese is melted. Remove from heat; stir in sour cream until smooth.

4. Place four broccoli spears and 1/3 cup of chicken down the center of each crepe; top with 1/3 cup cheese sauce. Roll up and place seam side down in a greased 13-in. x 9-in. baking dish. Pour remaining cheese sauce over crepes; sprinkle with remaining cheese.

5. Bake, uncovered, at 350° for 20 minutes or until heated through. **Yield:** 8 crepes.

Blueberry French Toast

Prep: 30 min. + chilling **Bake:** 55 min.

- 12 slices day-old white bread, crusts removed
- 2 packages (8 ounces *each*) cream cheese
- 1 cup fresh *or* frozen blueberries
- 12 eggs
- 2 cups milk
- 1/3 cup maple syrup *or* honey

SAUCE:
- 1 cup sugar
- 2 tablespoons cornstarch
- 1 cup water
- 1 cup fresh *or* frozen blueberries
- 1 tablespoon butter

1. Cut bread into 1-in. cubes; place half in a greased 13-in. x 9-in. baking dish. Cut cream cheese into 1-in. cubes; place over bread. Top with the blueberries and remaining bread. In a large bowl, beat the eggs. Add the milk and syrup; mix well. Pour over the bread mixture. Cover and refrigerate for 8 hours or overnight.

2. Remove from the refrigerator 30 minutes before baking. Cover and bake at 350° for 30 minutes. Uncover; bake 25-30 minutes longer or until golden brown and center is set.

3. In a small saucepan, combine sugar, cornstarch and water until smooth. Bring to a boil over medium heat; cook and stir for 3 minutes. Stir in blueberries; reduce heat. Simmer for 8-10 minutes or until berries have burst. Stir in butter until melted. Serve with French toast. **Yield:** 6-8 servings (1-3/4 cups sauce).

PATRICIA AXELSEN AURORA, MINNESOTA

This recipe was shared by a local blueberry grower and quickly became my all-time favorite breakfast dish. Juicy blueberries are tucked into the French toast and the sauce that goes on top. With the combination of berries and cream cheese, this treat reminds me of a dessert.

GRAND PRIZE WINNER

Lemon Pound Cake Muffins

Prep: 15 min. **Bake:** 20 min.

Lola Baxter, Winnebago, Minnesota

My family asks for these lemony goodies regularly, so I bake them for all kinds of occasions. The sweet-tart glaze on top is the perfect finishing touch and so easy to make.

- 1/2 cup butter, softened
- 1 cup sugar
- 2 eggs
- 1/2 cup sour cream
- 1 teaspoon vanilla extract
- 1/2 teaspoon lemon extract
- 1-3/4 cups all-purpose flour
- 1/2 teaspoon salt
- 1/4 teaspoon baking soda

GLAZE:
- 2 cups confectioners' sugar
- 3 tablespoons lemon juice

1. In a large bowl, cream the butter and sugar until light and fluffy. Add eggs, one at a time, beating well after each addition. Beat in the sour cream and extracts. Combine the flour, salt and baking soda; add to the creamed mixture just until moistened.

2. Fill greased or paper-lined muffin cups three-fourths full. Bake at 400° for 18-20 minutes or until a toothpick inserted near the center comes out clean. Cool for 5 minutes before removing from pan to a wire rack.

3. Combine the glaze ingredients; drizzle over muffins. Serve warm. **Yield:** 1 dozen.

Apple-Stuffed French Toast

Prep: 20 min. + chilling **Bake:** 35 min.

Kay Clark, Lawrenceburg, Kentucky

At my bed and breakfast and tearoom cafe, customers often request this luscious French toast. It's a great breakfast dish to prepare ahead for the holidays or a Sunday brunch.

- 1 cup packed brown sugar
- 1/2 cup butter, cubed
- 2 tablespoons light corn syrup
- 1 cup chopped pecans
- 12 slices Italian bread (1/2 inch thick)
- 2 large tart apples, peeled and thinly sliced
- 6 eggs
- 1-1/2 cups milk
- 1-1/2 teaspoons ground cinnamon
- 1 teaspoon vanilla extract
- 1/4 teaspoon salt
- 1/4 teaspoon ground nutmeg

CARAMEL SAUCE:
- 1/2 cup packed brown sugar
- 1/4 cup butter, cubed
- 1 tablespoon light corn syrup

1. In a small saucepan, combine the brown sugar, butter and corn syrup; cook and stir over medium heat until thickened. Pour into a greased 13-in. x 9-in. baking dish; top with half of the pecans, a single layer of bread and remaining pecans. Arrange apples and remaining bread over the top.

2. In a large bowl, whisk the eggs, milk, cinnamon, vanilla, salt and nutmeg. Pour over bread. Cover and refrigerate overnight.

3. Remove from the refrigerator 30 minutes before baking. Bake, uncovered, at 350° for 35-40 minutes or until lightly browned.

4. In a small saucepan, combine the sauce ingredients. Cook and stir over medium heat until thickened. Serve with French toast. **Yield:** 6 servings.

Savory Omelet Cups

Prep: 40 min. **Bake:** 10 min.

Joan Churchill, Dover, New Hampshire

I experimented a bit and replaced the pastry portion of this recipe with a crepe-like base. Baked in single-serving dishes, the cheesy cups are fun and yummy.

 This recipe includes Nutrition Facts & Diabetic Exchanges.

- 1/4 cup sun-dried tomatoes (not packed in oil)
- 1/2 cup water, *divided*
- 3 eggs
- 6 egg whites
- 2 tablespoons minced fresh cilantro
- 4 teaspoons butter, melted
- 1/2 teaspoon salt
- 1/4 teaspoon pepper
- 1/3 cup shredded provolone cheese
- 1 cup chopped leeks (white portion only)
- 2 green onions, chopped
- 1 tablespoon olive oil
- 2 tablespoons chopped Greek olives
- 2 teaspoons minced fresh oregano *or* 1/2 teaspoon dried oregano
- 1/4 cup grated Parmesan cheese
- 1 tablespoon honey

1. Place tomatoes in a small bowl. Cover with 1/4 cup water; let stand for 30 minutes. Meanwhile, in a large bowl, whisk the eggs, egg whites, cilantro, butter, salt, pepper and remaining water.

2. Heat an 8-in. nonstick skillet coated with cooking spray; pour about 1/2 cup egg mixture into center of skillet. Lift and tilt pan to evenly coat bottom. Cook for 1-1/2 to 2 minutes or until top appears dry; turn and cook 30-45 seconds longer or until set.

3. Remove from pan and press into a 1-cup baking dish or ramekin coated with cooking spray. Repeat with remaining egg mixture, making three more omelet cups (coat the skillet with cooking spray as needed). Sprinkle provolone cheese into cups.

4. Drain the tomatoes; chop and set aside. In a large nonstick skillet, saute leeks and onions in oil until tender. Stir in tomatoes, olives and oregano; cook over medium heat for 2-3 minutes. Spoon into omelet cups. Sprinkle with Parmesan cheese; drizzle with honey. Bake at 350° for 10-12 minutes or until heated through. **Yield:** 4 servings.

Nutrition Facts: 1 filled omelet cup equals 246 calories, 16 g fat (6 g saturated fat), 178 mg cholesterol, 764 mg sodium, 12 g carbohydrate, 1 g fiber, 15 g protein. **Diabetic Exchanges:** 2 lean meat, 2 fat, 1 vegetable.

Ham 'n' Egg Muffins

Prep/Total Time: 25 min.

Emily Chaney, Blue Hill, Maine

This quick but filling recipe makes not only a super breakfast, but also a satisfying main course for Saturday dinner.

- 1 English muffin, split
- 1/4 cup shredded Swiss cheese
- 1/4 cup sour cream
- 2 tablespoons mayonnaise
- 1 teaspoon lemon juice
- 2 slices deli ham (1 ounce *each*)
- 2 hard-cooked eggs, sliced

Paprika, optional

1. Place English muffin halves on a baking sheet. Sprinkle with cheese. Bake at 350° for 3-4 minutes or until cheese is melted.

2. Meanwhile, in a small bowl, combine the sour cream, mayonnaise and lemon juice. Place the deli ham and hard-cooked eggs on each English muffin half; top with the sour cream mixture. Sprinkle with paprika if desired.

3. Bake 15 minutes longer or until heated through. **Yield:** 2 servings.

10 slices day-old bread, crusts removed and cubed
1 medium onion, finely chopped
4 medium fresh mushrooms, finely chopped
1/4 cup butter, cubed
4 cups (16 ounces) shredded cheddar cheese
2 cups cubed fully cooked ham
2 tablespoons all-purpose flour
8 eggs
3 cups 2% milk
2 tablespoons prepared mustard
1 teaspoon garlic powder
1/2 teaspoon salt

Cheddar Ham Strata

Prep: 20 min. + chilling **Bake:** 1 hour + standing

Ann Pool, Jerome, Idaho

I put together this ham and egg dish on Christmas Eve and keep it in the refrigerator. Then, while we open our gifts on Christmas morning, I pop the pan in the oven.

1. Place the bread cubes in a greased 13-in. x 9-in. baking dish. In a small skillet, saute the onion and mushrooms in butter; spoon over bread. Sprinkle with cheese, ham and flour. In a large bowl, whisk the eggs, milk, mustard, garlic powder and salt. Pour over ham and cheese. Cover and refrigerate overnight.

2. Remove from refrigerator 30 minutes before baking. Bake, uncovered, at 350° for 60-70 minutes or until a knife inserted near center comes out clean. Let stand for 10 minutes before serving. **Yield:** 12 servings.

Gingerbread Muffins

Prep: 45 min. **Bake:** 15 min.

Kelly Trupkiewicz, Fort Collins, Colorado

This is my twist on my mother's gingerbread cake with lemon sauce. The spice-and-molasses-flavored muffins spread with homemade lemon curd are a new-generation favorite.

LEMON CURD:
2/3 cup sugar
3/4 teaspoon cornstarch
1/3 cup lemon juice
5 egg yolks, lightly beaten
1/4 cup butter, cubed
2 teaspoons grated lemon peel

MUFFINS:
2 cups all-purpose flour
1/4 cup sugar
2-1/2 teaspoons baking powder
2 teaspoons ground ginger
1 teaspoon ground cinnamon
1/4 teaspoon salt
1/4 teaspoon ground cloves
1 egg
3/4 cup milk
1/4 cup canola oil
1/4 cup molasses

1. In a large heavy saucepan, combine the sugar, cornstarch and lemon juice until smooth. Cook and stir over medium-high heat until thickened and bubbly. Reduce heat to low; cook and stir for 2 minutes longer. Remove from heat. Stir a small amount of hot filling into yolks; return all to pan, stirring constantly. Bring to a gentle boil; cook and stir for 2 minutes. Remove from the heat; gently stir in butter and peel until blended. Pour into a large bowl; cover surface with plastic wrap. Cover; refrigerate until serving.

2. In a large bowl, combine flour, sugar, baking powder, ginger, cinnamon, salt and cloves. In another bowl, combine the egg, milk, oil and molasses until smooth; stir into dry ingredients just until moistened.

3. Fill paper-lined muffin cups half full. Bake at 375° for 15-20 minutes or until a toothpick inserted near the center comes out clean. Cool for 5 minutes before removing from pan to a wire rack. Serve warm with lemon curd. **Yield:** 1 dozen (1 cup lemon curd).

Apple Streusel Muffins

Prep: 20 min. **Bake:** 15 min. + cooling

Dulcy Grace, Roaring Spring, Pennsylvania

My husband and children enjoy these tender, coffee cake-like bites not only as a quick breakfast, but also as a yummy snack on the run. The drizzle of glaze makes them pretty enough to serve company at weekend brunches.

2 cups all-purpose flour
1 cup sugar
1 teaspoon baking powder
1/2 teaspoon baking soda
1/2 teaspoon salt
2 eggs
1/2 cup butter, melted
1-1/4 teaspoons vanilla extract
1-1/2 cups chopped peeled tart apples
STREUSEL TOPPING:
1/3 cup packed brown sugar
1 tablespoon all-purpose flour
1/8 teaspoon ground cinnamon
1 tablespoon cold butter
GLAZE:
1-1/2 cups confectioners' sugar
1 to 2 tablespoons milk
1 teaspoon butter, melted
1/4 teaspoon vanilla extract
1/8 teaspoon salt

1. In a large bowl, combine the flour, sugar, baking powder, baking soda and salt. In another bowl, combine the eggs, butter and vanilla; stir into dry ingredients just until moistened (the batter will be stiff). Fold in the apples.

2. Fill greased or paper-lined muffin cups three-fourths full. In a small bowl, combine the brown sugar, flour and cinnamon; cut in butter until crumbly. Sprinkle over batter.

3. Bake at 375° for 15-20 minutes or until a toothpick inserted near the center comes out clean. Cool for 5 minutes before removing from pan to a wire rack to cool completely. Combine glaze ingredients; drizzle over muffins. Serve warm. **Yield:** 1 dozen.

Baked Peach Pancake

Prep: 10 min. **Bake:** 25 min.

Nancy Wilkinson, Princeton, New Jersey

Want something different from traditional pancakes? Try this impressive-looking baked treat. I usually take it right from the oven to the table, then fill it with the sliced peaches and sour cream. Round out your meal with bacon or ham.

2 cups fresh or frozen sliced peeled peaches
4 teaspoons sugar
1 teaspoon lemon juice
3 eggs
1/2 cup all-purpose flour
1/2 cup milk
1/2 teaspoon salt
2 tablespoons butter
Ground nutmeg
Sour cream, optional

1. In a small bowl, combine peaches with sugar and lemon juice; set aside. In a large bowl, beat eggs until fluffy. Add the flour, milk and salt; beat until smooth.

2. Place butter in a 10-in. skillet; bake at 400° for 3 to 5 minutes or until melted. Immediately pour batter into hot skillet. Bake for 20 to 25 minutes or until pancake has risen and puffed all over.

3. Fill pancake with peach slices and sprinkle with nutmeg. Serve immediately with sour cream if desired. **Yield:** 6 servings.

PG. 112

PG. 104

PG. 110

BEEF & POULTRY ENTREES

Whatever the occasion, your family and friends are sure to love hearty main courses such as Pepper Jack Chicken Pasta, German–Style Short Ribs, Pretzel–Crusted Drumsticks and Ginger Sirloin Strips.

Pepper Jack Chicken Pasta

Prep/Total Time: 25 min.

Mike Kirschbaum, Cary, North Carolina

My wife is the primary cook in our family but loved this result of my kitchen experimenting. If you can't find the soup called for in the recipe, just use cheese soup.

- 3 cups uncooked mostaccioli
- 1/4 cup chopped onion
- 1/4 cup chopped sweet red pepper
- 1 tablespoon canola oil
- 1/2 teaspoon minced garlic
- 1 can (10-3/4 ounces) condensed nacho cheese soup, undiluted
- 1 package (9 ounces) ready-to-use Southwestern chicken strips
- 3/4 cup water
- 1 can (15 ounces) black beans, rinsed and drained
- 1/4 cup shredded Monterey Jack cheese, optional

1. Cook mostaccioli according to package directions. Meanwhile, in a large skillet, saute the onion and red

pepper in oil until tender. Add garlic; cook 1 minute longer. Stir in the soup, chicken and water. Bring to a boil. Reduce heat; cover and simmer for 8 minutes.

2. Stir in the beans; heat through. Drain mostaccioli; transfer to a serving bowl; top with chicken mixture. Sprinkle with cheese if desired. **Yield:** 6 servings.

Chicken-Ricotta Stuffed Shells

Prep: 25 min. Bake: 30 min.

Amy Hixon, Ringgold, Georgia

My husband and I don't care for tomato-based sauces, so I came up with this variation of traditional stuffed shells. The taste reminds us of chicken Alfredo.

 This recipe includes Nutrition Facts.

- 6 uncooked jumbo pasta shells
- 2/3 cup ricotta cheese
- 2 ounces cream cheese, softened

- 1/8 teaspoon chicken bouillon granules
- 2/3 cup shredded cooked chicken breast
- 2 tablespoons shredded Parmesan cheese

SAUCE:
- 1/3 cup heavy whipping cream *or* half-and-half cream
- 1 tablespoon butter
- 5 tablespoons shredded Parmesan cheese, *divided*
- 1/2 teaspoon dried parsley flakes

1. Cook the pasta according to the package directions. Meanwhile, in a small bowl, beat the ricotta, cream cheese and bouillon until blended. Stir in chicken and Parmesan cheese. Drain the shells; stuff with chicken mixture. Place in a shallow 3-cup baking dish coated with cooking spray.

2. In a small saucepan, bring cream and butter to a boil. Whisk in 3 tablespoons cheese and parsley. Stir until cheese is melted. Pour over shells.

3. Cover and bake at 350° for 25 minutes. Uncover; sprinkle with remaining cheese. Bake 5-10 minutes longer or until cheese is melted and filling is heated through. **Yield:** 2 servings.

Nutrition Facts: 3 stuffed shells (prepared with reduced-fat ricotta, reduced-fat cream cheese, reduced-sodium bouillon and half-and-half) equals 499 calories, 26 g fat (16 g saturated fat), 124 mg cholesterol, 618 mg sodium, 28 g carbohydrate, 1 g fiber, 35 g protein.

Two-Cheese Turkey Enchiladas

Prep: 25 min. **Bake:** 20 min.

Shelly Platten, Amherst, Wisconsin

Sour cream and cream cheese create a rich, delicious filling for these enchiladas. I use reduced-fat and fat-free ingredients.

 This recipe includes Nutrition Facts & Diabetic Exchanges.

> 1 pound extra-lean ground turkey
> 1 large onion, chopped
> 1/2 cup chopped green pepper
> 1 teaspoon brown sugar
> 1 teaspoon garlic powder
> 1 teaspoon ground cumin
> 1 teaspoon chili powder
> 1 can (28 ounces) crushed tomatoes, *divided*
> 1 package (8 ounces) reduced-fat cream cheese
> 1/4 cup fat-free sour cream
> 1 can (4 ounces) chopped green chilies
> 1 cup salsa
> 8 fat-free flour tortillas (8 inches), warmed
> 1/2 cup shredded reduced-fat cheddar cheese

1. Crumble turkey into a large nonstick skillet; add onion, pepper, brown sugar and seasonings. Cook and stir over medium heat until turkey is no longer pink. Stir in 1 cup crushed tomatoes. Reduce heat; simmer, uncovered, for 10 minutes, stirring occasionally.

2. In a small bowl, beat the cream cheese, sour cream and chilies until blended; set aside. Combine salsa and remaining tomatoes; spread 1 cup into a 13-in. x 9-in. baking dish coated with cooking spray.

3. Spoon about 3 tablespoons cream cheese mixture and 1/3 cup turkey mixture down the center of each tortilla. Roll up and place seam side down in baking dish. Top with remaining salsa mixture; sprinkle with cheddar cheese. Bake, uncovered, at 350° for 20-25 minutes or until bubbly. **Yield:** 8 servings.

Nutrition Facts: 1 enchilada equals 329 calories, 9 g fat (5 g saturated fat), 49 mg cholesterol, 776 mg sodium, 39 g carbohydrate, 5 g fiber, 24 g protein. **Diabetic Exchanges:** 2 starch, 2 lean meat, 2 vegetable.

German-Style Short Ribs

Prep: 15 min. **Cook:** 8 hours

Bregitte Rugman, Shanty Bay, Ontario

Our whole family gets excited when I plug in the slow cooker to make these fall-off-the-bone-tender ribs. We like them best served over a bed of rice or egg noodles.

> 3/4 cup dry red wine *or* beef broth
> 1/2 cup mango chutney
> 3 tablespoons quick-cooking tapioca
> 1/4 cup water
> 3 tablespoons brown sugar
> 3 tablespoons cider vinegar
> 1 tablespoon Worcestershire sauce
> 1/2 teaspoon salt
> 1/2 teaspoon ground mustard
> 1/2 teaspoon chili powder
> 1/2 teaspoon pepper
> 4 pounds bone-in beef short ribs
> 2 medium onions, sliced
> Hot cooked egg noodles

1. In a 5-qt. slow cooker, combine the first 11 ingredients. Add the ribs and turn to coat. Top with the onions.

2. Cover and cook on low for 8-10 hours or until the meat is tender.

3. Remove the ribs from slow cooker. Skim fat from the cooking juices; serve with ribs and egg noodles. **Yield:** 8 servings.

Ginger Sirloin Strips

Prep/Total Time: 20 min.

Jill Cox, Lincoln, Nebraska

A wonderful blend of fruit flavors with just the right touch of fresh ginger makes this meaty stir-fry a dinnertime winner in our house. I came up with the idea one night while trying to do something new with beef strips.

- 1 can (14 ounces) pineapple tidbits
- 1 can (11 ounces) mandarin oranges
- 2 tablespoons cornstarch
- 1-1/2 pounds beef top sirloin steak, cut into strips
- 4-1/2 teaspoons minced fresh gingerroot
- 1 tablespoon olive oil
- 1 can (14 ounces) whole-berry cranberry sauce
- 1 cup thinly sliced green onions
- Hot cooked rice

1. Drain pineapple and oranges, reserving juice; set fruit aside. In a small bowl, combine cornstarch and juices until smooth; set aside.

2. In a large skillet or wok, stir-fry beef and ginger in oil until meat is no longer pink. Add the cranberry sauce, onions and pineapple. Stir cornstarch mixture and gradually add to skillet; cook and stir until slightly thickened. Gently stir in the oranges. Serve with the rice. **Yield:** 7 servings.

Fresh Facts

Wrapped in a paper towel and placed in a plastic bag, unpeeled fresh gingerroot may be refrigerated for up to 3 weeks. For longer storage, tightly wrap fresh gingerroot and keep it in the freezer for up to 2 months.

Peppery Grilled Turkey Breast

Prep: 15 min. Grill: 1–1/2 hours + standing

 This recipe includes Nutrition Facts & Diabetic Exchanges.

- 2 tablespoons light brown sugar
- 1 tablespoon salt
- 2 teaspoons ground cinnamon
- 1 teaspoon cayenne pepper
- 1/2 teaspoon ground mustard
- 1 bone-in turkey breast (5 pounds)
- 1 cup reduced-sodium chicken broth
- 1/4 cup white vinegar
- 1/4 cup jalapeno pepper jelly
- 2 tablespoons olive oil

1. In a small bowl, combine the brown sugar, salt, cinnamon, cayenne pepper and ground mustard. With fingers, carefully loosen the skin from both sides of the turkey breast. Spread half of the spice mixture under the turkey skin; secure the skin to the underside of the breast with wooden toothpicks. Spread the remaining spice mixture over the skin.

2. Using long-handled tongs, moisten a paper towel with cooking oil and lightly coat the grill rack. Prepare the grill for indirect heat, using a drip pan. Place turkey over drip pan; grill, covered, over indirect medium heat for 30 minutes.

3. In a small saucepan, combine the broth, vinegar, jelly and oil. Cook and stir over medium heat for 2 minutes or until jelly is melted. Set aside 1/2 cup. Baste the turkey with some of the remaining jelly mixture. Grill 1 to 1-1/2 hours longer or until a meat thermometer reads 170°, basting every 15 minutes.

4. Cover and let stand for 10 minutes. Remove and discard turkey skin if desired. Brush with reserved jelly mixture before slicing. **Yield:** 15 servings.

Nutrition Facts: 4 ounces cooked turkey (with skin removed) equals 167 calories, 3 g fat (trace saturated fat), 78 mg cholesterol, 565 mg sodium, 6 g carbohydrate, trace fiber, 29 g protein. **Diabetic Exchanges:** 4 lean meat, 1/2 starch, 1/2 fat.

MARY RELYEA CANASTOTA, NEW YORK

This is a combination of several of our family's favorite recipes. People who sample it for the first time are amazed to learn that it's not only flavorful, but also light.

GRAND PRIZE WINNER

Saucy Chicken Thighs

Prep: 20 min. **Cook:** 4 hours

Kim Puckett, Reagan, Tennessee

Everyone raves about the honey-sweetened sauce that flavors these slow-cooked chicken thighs. They're a breeze to prepare because they simmer in the slow cooker, giving me the chance to do other things. Round out the meal with a side of corn... or even serve these as a hearty appetizer.

>   9 bone-in chicken thighs (about 3-1/4 pounds)
>   1/2 teaspoon salt
>   1/4 teaspoon pepper
> 1-1/2 cups barbecue sauce
>   1/2 cup honey
>   2 teaspoons prepared mustard
>   2 teaspoons Worcestershire sauce
>   1/8 to 1/2 teaspoon hot pepper sauce

1. Sprinkle the chicken with salt and pepper. Place on a broiler pan. Broil 4-5 in. from the heat for 3-4 minutes on each side or until lightly browned. Transfer to a 5-qt. slow cooker.

2. In a small bowl, combine the barbecue sauce, honey, mustard, Worcestershire sauce and pepper sauce. Pour over the chicken; stir to coat. Cover and cook on low for 4-5 hours or until the meat is tender. **Yield:** 9 servings.

Stuffed Cornish Hens

Prep: 20 min. **Bake:** 65 min.

Jenny Holliday, Roanoke, Alabama

I first made these hens for Thanksgiving one year when only a few of us gathered to celebrate the holiday.

> 1 package (6.2 ounces) fast-cooking long grain and wild rice mix
> 2 celery ribs, chopped
> 1 small onion, chopped
> 2 tablespoons butter, *divided*
> 1 can (10-3/4 ounces) condensed cream of mushroom soup, undiluted
> 1 can (4 ounces) mushroom stems and pieces, drained
> 4 Cornish game hens (20 to 24 ounces *each*)
> 1/4 teaspoon salt
> 1/4 teaspoon pepper

1. Cook rice according to the package directions. In a small skillet, saute celery and onion in 1 tablespoon butter until tender. Stir in the soup, mushrooms and prepared rice.

2. Sprinkle inside and outside of hens with salt and pepper. Stuff with rice mixture. Place on a rack in a greased shallow roasting pan; cover with foil.

3. Bake at 350° for 40 minutes. Remove the foil. Melt the remaining butter; brush over the hens. Bake 25-35 minutes longer or until the juices run clear and a meat thermometer reads 180° for the hens and 165° for the stuffing. **Yield:** 4 servings.

Sun-Dried Tomato Chicken

Prep: 30 min. Bake: 40 min.

Anna Rhyne, Kershaw, South Carolina

My husband often orders a particular chicken entree at a local restaurant, so I created a similar version he can enjoy at home. The sun-dried tomatoes are terrific with the goat cheese. We complete the menu with a green salad and Italian bread.

 This recipe includes Nutrition Facts & Diabetic Exchanges.

3/4 cup finely chopped onion
  1 garlic clove, minced
  1 tablespoon butter
1/2 cup sun-dried tomatoes (not packed in oil), chopped
1/2 cup white wine *or* reduced-sodium chicken broth
1/4 cup lemon juice
1/4 cup minced fresh basil *or* 4 teaspoons dried basil
  4 boneless skinless chicken breast halves (6 ounces *each*)
1/4 cup crumbled goat cheese
1/2 teaspoon salt
1/4 teaspoon pepper

1. In a large skillet, saute onion and garlic in butter for 3-4 minutes or until tender. Stir in the tomatoes, wine or broth and lemon juice; bring to a boil. Reduce heat; simmer, uncovered, for 10-15 minutes or until liquid is absorbed, stirring occasionally. Remove from the heat; stir in basil.

2. Flatten chicken to 1/4-in. thickness. Spread each with 1/4 cup tomato mixture to within 1/2 in. of edges. Crumble goat cheese over tomato mixture. Roll up jelly-roll style, starting with a short side; secure with a toothpick or small metal skewer. Sprinkle with salt and pepper.

3. Place the chicken in an 11-in. x 7-in. baking dish coated with cooking spray. Bake, uncovered, at 350° for 40-45 minutes or until juices run clear. Spoon pan juices over the chicken and remove toothpicks before serving. **Yield:** 4 servings.

Nutrition Facts: 1 serving equals 299 calories, 11 g fat (6 g saturated fat), 113 mg cholesterol, 622 mg sodium, 9 g carbohydrate, 2 g fiber, 39 g protein. **Diabetic Exchanges:** 5 very lean meat, 1-1/2 fat, 1 vegetable.

Meat Sauce for Spaghetti

Prep: 30 min. Cook: 8 hours

Mary Tallman, Arbor Vitae, Wisconsin

With both beef and sausage, this thick and hearty sauce turns ordinary spaghetti and garlic bread into a filling feast.

  1 pound ground beef
  1 pound bulk Italian sausage
  1 can (28 ounces) crushed tomatoes, undrained
  1 medium green pepper, chopped
  1 medium onion, chopped
  1 cup finely chopped carrots
  1 cup water
  1 can (8 ounces) tomato sauce
  1 can (6 ounces) tomato paste
  1 tablespoon brown sugar
  1 tablespoon Italian seasoning
  2 garlic cloves, minced
1/2 teaspoon salt
1/4 teaspoon pepper
Hot cooked spaghetti

1. In a large skillet, cook the beef and sausage over medium heat until no longer pink; drain.

2. Transfer to a 5-qt. slow cooker. Stir in the tomatoes, green pepper, onion, carrots, water, tomato sauce, tomato paste, brown sugar, Italian seasoning, garlic, salt and pepper. Cover and cook on low for 8-10 hours or until bubbly. Serve the sauce with spaghetti. **Yield:** 9 servings.

Meat Loaf Wellington

Prep: 20 min. Bake: 1-1/4 hours

Janine Talbot, Santaquin, Utah

I borrowed from a few different recipes and put it all together to create this cheese-stuffed loaf covered in refrigerated dough. It looks complicated but is actually easy to prepare.

    1 egg, lightly beaten
    1 cup meatless spaghetti sauce, *divided*
1/4 cup dry bread crumbs
1/2 teaspoon salt
1/4 teaspoon pepper
1-1/2 pounds ground beef
    2 cups (8 ounces) shredded part-skim
      mozzarella cheese, *divided*
    1 tablespoon minced fresh parsley
    1 tube (8 ounces) refrigerated crescent rolls

1. In a large bowl, combine the egg, 1/3 cup spaghetti sauce, bread crumbs, salt and pepper. Crumble beef over mixture and mix well.

2. On a piece of heavy-duty foil, pat beef mixture into a 12-in. x 8-in. rectangle. Sprinkle 1 cup cheese and parsley to within 1 in. of edges. Roll up jelly-roll style, starting with a long side and peeling foil away while rolling. Seal seam and ends. Place seam side down in a greased 13-in. x 9-in. baking dish.

3. Bake, uncovered, at 350° for 1 hour; drain. Unroll crescent dough; seal seams and perforations. Drape dough over meat loaf to cover the top, sides and ends; seal ends. Bake 15-20 minutes longer or until a meat thermometer reads 160° and crust is golden brown. Let stand for 5 minutes.

4. Using two large spatulas, carefully transfer meat loaf to a serving platter. Sprinkle with the remaining cheese. Serve with the remaining spaghetti sauce. **Yield:** 8 servings.

Corsican Chicken

Prep: 20 min. Cook: 4-1/2 hours

    3 tablespoons butter, softened
    2 tablespoons herbes de Provence
    1 teaspoon salt
    2 garlic cloves, minced
1/2 teaspoon coarsely ground pepper
    2 pounds boneless skinless chicken
      thighs
    1 large onion, chopped
1/2 cup oil-packed sun-dried tomatoes,
      julienned
    1 can (10-1/2 ounces) condensed beef
      consomme, undiluted
1/2 cup dry vermouth or orange juice
1/2 cup pitted Greek olives, quartered
    1 teaspoon grated orange peel
    2 teaspoons cornstarch
    1 tablespoon cold water
    2 tablespoons minced fresh basil
    2 tablespoons diced pimientos
    2 tablespoons minced fresh parsley

1. In a small bowl, combine the butter, herbes de Provence, salt, garlic and pepper; rub over the chicken thighs.

2. Place in a 5-qt. slow cooker. Add the onion, sun-dried tomatoes, beef consomme and vermouth. Cover and cook on low for 4-5 hours or until the chicken thighs are no longer pink. Add the Greek olives and orange peel. Cover and cook on high for 30 minutes.

3. Remove the chicken and vegetables to a serving platter; keep warm. Skim fat from cooking juices; transfer to a small saucepan. Bring liquid to a boil. Combine the cornstarch and water until smooth. Gradually stir into the pan. Bring to a boil; cook and stir for 2 minutes or until thickened. Pour over the chicken. Sprinkle with basil, pimientos and parsley. **Yield:** 6-8 servings.

Editor's Note: Look for herbes de Provence in the spice aisle.

MARY BERGFELD EUGENE, OREGON

On chilly days, these tender chicken thighs make a delicious hot dinner served alongside a tossed green salad and lemon dessert. I like to set the table with warm, sunny Mediterranean shades and patterns that look gorgeous with this colorful meal.

Chicken Artichoke Pasta

Prep/Total Time: 25 min.

Beth Washington, Ayer, Massachusetts

Here's a main course my whole family likes—including the kids. Similar to one of our favorite menu items at a restaurant, it calls for canned artichokes, ripe olives and a jar of sun-dried tomatoes. It's so fuss-free to make, I often leave the ingredients on the counter for my husband to do the prep work.

    8 ounces uncooked bow tie pasta
1-1/2 pounds boneless skinless chicken breasts,
        cubed
  1/2 teaspoon dried oregano
  1/4 teaspoon salt
  1/4 teaspoon pepper
    3 tablespoons olive oil
    1 to 2 tablespoons minced garlic
    2 cans (14 ounces *each*) water-packed artichoke
        hearts, rinsed, drained and quartered
    1 jar (8-1/2 ounces) oil-packed sun-dried
        tomatoes, quartered
    1 can (2-1/4 ounces) sliced ripe olives, drained
Shredded Parmesan cheese

1. Cook pasta according to the package directions. Meanwhile, sprinkle chicken with the oregano, salt and pepper. In a large skillet, saute chicken in oil until no longer pink. Add garlic; cook 1 minute longer.

2. Stir in artichokes, tomatoes and ripe olives; heat through. Drain the pasta; toss with chicken mixture. Sprinkle with cheese. **Yield:** 6 servings.

Cheese-Topped Meat Loaves

Prep/Total Time: 20 min.

Lois Kinneberg, Phoenix, Arizona

This is always a terrific choice when you're cooking for two. I found the tender meat loaf recipe in a supermarket's cookbook more than 20 years ago and have been enjoying it ever since. Sometimes I substitute ground turkey or chicken for the ground beef...or make extra loaves to freeze for later meals.

    1 egg
    2 tablespoons plus 1/3 cup picante sauce,
        divided
  1/4 cup old-fashioned oats
    1 teaspoon dried minced onion
  1/4 teaspoon chili powder
  1/8 teaspoon salt
  1/2 pound ground beef
  1/4 cup shredded cheddar cheese

1. In a small bowl, combine the egg, 2 tablespoons picante sauce, oats, onion, chili powder and salt. Crumble beef over mixture and mix well. Shape into two 4-in. x 2-in. loaves.

2. Place loaves in a microwave-safe dish. Cover and microwave on high for 5-6 minutes or until no longer pink and a meat thermometer reads 160°.

3. Place the remaining picante sauce in a small microwave-safe bowl; cover and microwave on high for 30 seconds. Pour over meat loaves. Sprinkle with cheese. Cover and microwave on high for 45 seconds or until cheese is melted. **Yield:** 2 servings.

Editor's Note: This recipe was tested in a 1,100-watt microwave.

Taco Casserole

Prep: 15 min. **Bake:** 30 min.

Kathy Wilson, Romeoville, Illinois

When my preschooler never wanted to eat ground beef unless it was taco-flavored, I came up with this casserole we all like. To make assembly easy, I prepare the meat and freeze several bags at a time. I also cook the noodles over the weekend for a streamlined supper later in the week.

      3 **cups uncooked bow tie pasta**
      1 **pound ground beef**
  1/4 **cup chopped onion**
      2 **cups (8 ounces) shredded cheddar cheese**
      1 **jar (16 ounces) salsa**
      1 **can (14-1/2 ounces) diced tomatoes, undrained**
      1 **envelope taco seasoning**
      2 **cups nacho tortilla chips, crushed**

1. Cook pasta according to the package directions. Meanwhile, in a large skillet, cook beef and onion over medium heat until meat is no longer pink; drain. Add the cheese, salsa, tomatoes and taco seasoning. Drain pasta; stir into beef mixture.

2. Transfer to a greased 11-in. x 7-in. baking dish. Cover and bake at 350° for 20 minutes. Uncover; sprinkle with tortilla chips. Bake 10 minutes longer or until heated through. **Yield:** 7 servings.

Pretzel-Crusted Drumsticks

Prep: 10 min. **Bake:** 50 min.

Joann Frazier Hensley, McGaheysville, Virginia

The first time I served this simple chicken to guests, I received many requests for the recipe. You'll need just pretzels, pecans, cayenne and three other pantry staples to cover the oven-baked drumsticks with a crunchy, yummy coating.

  1/2 **cup butter, melted**
      1 **teaspoon cayenne pepper**
  1/8 **teaspoon garlic powder**
      1 **cup finely crushed pretzels**
  1/4 **cup chopped pecans**
  1/2 **teaspoon pepper**
1-1/2 **to 2 pounds chicken drumsticks**

1. In a shallow bowl, combine the butter, cayenne and garlic powder. In another shallow bowl, combine the pretzels, pecans and pepper. Dip chicken in butter mixture, then roll in pretzel mixture.

2. Place in a greased 13-in. x 9-in. baking dish. Bake, uncovered, at 350° for 50-55 minutes or until a meat thermometer reads 180°, turning once. **Yield:** 5 servings.

Measuring Method

When melted butter is called for in a recipe, the butter is measured first and then melted. The convenient markings on the wrappers of sticks of butter make it easy to slice off the amount you need and melt it.

Italian-Style Cabbage Rolls

Prep: 45 min. **Bake:** 50 min.

Erika Niehoff, Eveleth, Minnesota

Here's a terrific way to get your family to eat their vegetables. Not only is this lightened-up recipe one of my gang's favorite main dishes, but children also like to help prepare it by rolling the turkey filling into the cabbage leaves.

 This recipe includes Nutrition Facts & Diabetic Exchanges.

1/3 cup uncooked brown rice
  1 medium head cabbage
1/2 cup shredded carrot

1/4 cup finely chopped onion
1/4 cup egg substitute
  1 can (10-3/4 ounces) reduced-sodium condensed tomato soup, undiluted, *divided*
  1 can (10-3/4 ounces) reduced-fat reduced-sodium condensed vegetable beef soup, undiluted, *divided*
  2 tablespoons Italian seasoning, *divided*
1/4 teaspoon cayenne pepper
1/4 teaspoon pepper
  1 pound lean ground turkey

1. Cook the rice according to the package directions. Meanwhile, cook cabbage in boiling water just until leaves fall off head. Set aside 10 large leaves for rolls (Refrigerate remaining cabbage for another use.) Cut out the thick vein from the bottom of each reserved leaf, making a V-shaped cut.

2. In a large bowl, combine the carrot, onion, egg substitute, 2 tablespoons tomato soup, 2 tablespoons vegetable soup, 1 tablespoon Italian seasoning, cayenne, pepper and rice. Crumble turkey over the mixture and mix well. Place about 1/3 cupful on each cabbage leaf. Overlap cut ends of leaf; fold in sides, beginning from the cut end. Roll up completely to enclose filling.

3. Place the rolls seam side down in an 11-in. x 7-in. baking dish coated with cooking spray. Combine the remaining soups; pour over cabbage rolls. Sprinkle with remaining Italian seasoning. Cover and bake at 350° for 50-60 minutes or until cabbage is tender and a meat thermometer reads 165°. **Yield:** 5 servings.

Nutrition Facts: 2 cabbage rolls equals 293 calories, 10 g fat (3 g saturated fat), 74 mg cholesterol, 582 mg sodium, 29 g carbohydrate, 4 g fiber, 22 g protein. **Diabetic Exchanges:** 3 lean meat, 1-1/2 starch, 1 vegetable.

Apricot Chicken

Prep/Total Time: 15 min.

1/2 cup apricot preserves
  2 tablespoons soy sauce
  1 tablespoon chicken broth *or* sherry
  1 tablespoon canola oil
  1 tablespoon cornstarch
  1 teaspoon minced garlic
1/4 teaspoon ground ginger
  1 pound boneless skinless chicken breasts, cut into strips
  1 medium green pepper, chopped
1/2 cup salted cashews
Hot cooked rice

1. In a large resealable bag, combine the first seven ingredients; add the chicken. Seal the bag and turn to coat. Transfer to a shallow microwave-safe dish. Cover and microwave on high for 3 minutes, stirring once.

2. Add the green pepper and cashews. Cover and microwave on high for 2-4 minutes or until chicken is no longer pink, stirring once. Let chicken stand for 3 minutes. Serve with rice. **Yield:** 4 servings.

Editor's Note: This recipe was tested in a 1,100-watt microwave.

VICKI RUIZ TWIN FALLS, IDAHO

This is my go-to option when I want chicken in a hurry. Everybody loves it, and any leftovers are just as good the next day. For variation, I've used pork instead of chicken and added other ingredients such as pineapple, mandarin oranges, snow peas and broccoli.

GRAND PRIZE WINNER

Soft Chicken Tacos

Prep: 30 min. **Cook:** 5 hours

Cheryl Newendorp, Pella, Iowa

The chicken filling for these tacos goes in the slow cooker, so I throw it together before I leave for work. At the end of the day, all I have to do is roll up the meat in a tortilla with some lettuce, cheese, salsa, tomato and sour cream.

- 1 broiler/fryer chicken (3-1/2 pounds), cut up and skin removed
- 1 can (8 ounces) tomato sauce
- 1 can (4 ounces) chopped green chilies
- 1/3 cup chopped onion
- 2 tablespoons chili powder
- 2 tablespoons Worcestershire sauce
- 1/4 teaspoon garlic powder
- 10 flour tortillas (8 inches), warmed
- 1-1/4 cups shredded cheddar cheese
- 1-1/4 cups salsa
- 1-1/4 cups shredded lettuce
- 1 large tomato, chopped
- 3/4 cup sour cream, optional

1. Place the chicken in a 3-qt. slow cooker. In a small bowl, combine the tomato sauce, chilies, onion, chili powder, Worcestershire sauce and garlic powder; pour

over chicken. Cover and cook on low for 5-6 hours or until chicken is tender and juices run clear.

2. Remove the chicken. Shred meat with two forks and return to the slow cooker; heat through. Spoon 1/2 cup chicken mixture down the center of each tortilla. Top with cheese, salsa, lettuce, tomato and sour cream if desired; roll up. **Yield:** 5 servings.

Hearty Chicken Casserole

Prep: 25 min. **Bake:** 10 min.

Janet Applin, Gladstone, Michigan

I discovered this in a cookbook we received as a wedding gift, and I altered the recipe to suit our tastes. Now, I always cook extra chicken so we can have this casserole the next day.

- 2-1/2 cups frozen mixed vegetables
- 1/2 cup chopped onion
- 1/2 cup butter, *divided*
- 1/3 cup all-purpose flour
- 1/2 teaspoon dried sage leaves
- 1/2 teaspoon pepper
- 1/4 teaspoon salt
- 2 cups chicken broth
- 3/4 cup 2% milk
- 3 cups cubed cooked chicken
- 1 can (14-1/2 ounces) sliced potatoes, drained and quartered
- 2 cups seasoned stuffing cubes

1. Cook mixed vegetables according to the package directions; drain.

2. Meanwhile, in a large saucepan, saute the onion in 1/4 cup butter for 2-3 minutes or until tender. Stir in the flour, sage, pepper and salt until blended. Gradually add chicken broth and milk. Bring to a boil; cook and stir until thickened. Stir in the chicken, potatoes and mixed vegetables; heat through.

3. Transfer to a greased 13-in. x 9-in. baking dish. Melt the remaining butter; toss with stuffing cubes. Sprinkle over chicken mixture.

4. Bake, uncovered, at 450° for 10-12 minutes or until heated through. **Yield:** 6 servings.

Honey-Ginger Chicken Stir-Fry

Prep/Total Time: 25 min.

April Walcher, Hutchinson, Kansas

When I was first married, we didn't have a working oven or grill, so I had to use the stovetop for everything. After a few months of preparing the same things, I needed some new ideas and put together this easy stir-fry. I fix half of it when we're home alone and can easily double it for company.

- 1/4 cup honey
- 3 to 4 teaspoons soy sauce
- 1-1/2 teaspoons lemon juice
- 1 teaspoon ground ginger
- 1-1/4 pounds boneless skinless chicken breasts, cut into 1/4-inch slices
- 1/2 teaspoon salt
- 1/4 teaspoon pepper
- 1 tablespoon canola oil
- 1 package (16 ounces) frozen stir-fry vegetable blend
- 1 can (8 ounces) sliced water chestnuts, drained
- 4 to 6 cups hot cooked rice

1. In a small bowl, combine the honey, soy sauce, lemon juice and ginger; set aside.

2. Sprinkle chicken with salt and pepper. In a large skillet or wok, stir-fry chicken in oil for 3-4 minutes or until lightly browned. Add vegetables and water chestnuts; stir-fry 3-4 minutes longer or until vegetables are crisp-tender.

3. Stir the honey mixture and stir into the chicken mixture. Cook for 3-5 minutes or until heated through and the chicken is no longer pink. Serve with rice. **Yield:** 4 servings.

Dad's Swedish Meatballs

Prep: 30 min. **Cook:** 35 min.

Michelle Lizotte, Cumberland, Rhode Island

My father used to make these tender meatballs every year at Christmastime when I was a kid. I've carried on the tradition, and everyone loves them just as much today.

- 1 egg, lightly beaten
- 1/2 cup milk
- 1 cup soft bread crumbs
- 1/2 cup finely chopped onion
- 1 teaspoon salt
- 1/4 teaspoon ground nutmeg
- 1/4 teaspoon pepper
- 1 pound ground beef
- 1/2 pound ground pork
- 1/4 cup butter, cubed

DILL CREAM SAUCE:
- 2 tablespoons all-purpose flour
- 1 cup heavy whipping cream
- 1 cup beef broth
- 1 teaspoon salt
- 1/2 teaspoon dill seed

1. In a large bowl, combine the first seven ingredients. Crumble the beef and pork over the mixture and mix well. Shape into 1-1/2-in. balls. In a large skillet, cook meatballs in butter in batches until no longer pink. Remove and keep warm.

2. In a small bowl, combine the sauce ingredients until blended. Stir into skillet. Bring to a boil; cook and stir for 2 minutes or until thickened. Serve with meatballs. **Yield:** 6 servings.

Skewered Chicken 'n' Sweet Potatoes

Prep: 20 min. + marinating **Grill:** 15 min.

Janice Elder, Charlotte, North Carolina

Want a different combination for your kabobs? Consider this out-of-the-ordinary option. The flavored butter really enhances the chicken, sweet potatoes and sweet onion.

4 medium sweet potatoes, peeled and cut into
    1-inch cubes
2 tablespoons water
1/4 cup olive oil
2 tablespoons lemon juice
2 tablespoons Worcestershire sauce
2 garlic cloves, minced
1/2 teaspoon pepper
1/4 teaspoon salt
1-1/2 pounds boneless skinless chicken breasts,
    cut into 1-inch cubes
2 large sweet onions, cut into chunks
CHIPOTLE MOLASSES BUTTER:
1/2 cup butter, softened
2 tablespoons molasses
2 teaspoons minced chipotle pepper in adobo
    sauce
1 teaspoon grated lemon peel

1. Place the sweet potatoes and water in a large microwave-safe dish. Cover and microwave on high for 8 minutes or until tender; drain and set aside.

2. In a small bowl, combine the oil, lemon juice, Worcestershire sauce, garlic, pepper and salt. Place chicken in a large resealable plastic bag; add half of marinade. Place onions and sweet potatoes in another large resealable plastic bag; add remaining marinade. Seal bags and turn to coat; refrigerate for 30 minutes.

3. In a small bowl, combine the butter, molasses, chipotle peppers and lemon peel. Cover and refrigerate until serving.

4. Drain and discard marinade. On 12 metal or soaked wooden skewers, alternately thread the chicken, sweet potatoes and onions. Grill, covered, over medium-hot heat for 6-8 minutes on each side or until the chicken is no longer pink. Serve with the chipotle molasses butter. **Yield:** 6 servings.

Editor's Note: This recipe was tested in a 1,100-watt microwave.

Chicken and Asparagus Kabobs

Prep: 25 min. + marinating **Grill:** 10 min.

DIPPING SAUCE:
2 cups mayonnaise
1/4 cup sugar
1/4 cup soy sauce
2 tablespoons sesame seeds, toasted
1 tablespoon sesame oil
1/2 teaspoon white pepper
KABOBS:
1/4 cup soy sauce
2 tablespoons brown sugar
2 tablespoons water
1 tablespoon sesame oil
1 teaspoon crushed red pepper flakes
1 teaspoon minced fresh gingerroot
1-1/2 pounds boneless skinless chicken breasts,
    cut into 1-1/2-inch pieces
1 pound fresh asparagus, trimmed and cut
    into 2-inch pieces
2 tablespoons olive oil
1/2 teaspoon salt

1. In a small bowl, combine the sauce ingredients. Cover and refrigerate for 2-4 hours.

2. In a large resealable plastic bag, combine the soy sauce, brown sugar, water, sesame oil, pepper flakes and ginger. Add the chicken; seal bag and turn to coat. Refrigerate for 2 hours, turning occasionally.

3. Drain and discard the marinade. In a large bowl, toss the asparagus with olive oil and salt. On six metal or soaked wooden skewers, alternately thread one chicken piece and two asparagus pieces.

4. Grill, covered, over medium heat for 4-5 minutes on each side or until chicken is no longer pink and asparagus is crisp-tender. Serve with the dipping sauce. **Yield:** 6 servings.

KELLY TOWNSEND SYRACUSE, NEBRASKA

Served with a tasty dipping sauce, these Asian-inspired skewers are special enough to make for guests at your next backyard get-together. Sometimes I substitute salmon for the chicken.

GRAND
PRIZE
WINNER

Feta-Stuffed Chicken

Prep: 10 min. Bake: 40 min.

Lisa Herbert, Wadsworth, Ohio

When I was a newlywed, I knew how to prepare only a few meals that we'd rotate throughout the week. After I did some experimenting in the kitchen, I came up with this cheese-stuffed chicken that's still a favorite today.

- 4 boneless skinless chicken breast halves (6 ounces *each*)
- 1 package (4 ounces) crumbled tomato and basil feta cheese, *divided*
- 1 cup seasoned bread crumbs
- 4 tablespoons balsamic vinegar
- 4 tablespoons olive oil
- 4 plum tomatoes, sliced
- 8 fresh basil leaves

1. Flatten the chicken to 1/4-in. thickness. Place a tablespoon of feta cheese on each chicken breast half; roll up and secure with toothpicks. Coat with bread

crumbs. Place seam side down in a greased 13-in. x 9-in. baking pan. Sprinkle with remaining cheese.

2. Bake, uncovered, at 350° for 40-45 minutes or until the chicken is no longer pink. Immediately drizzle the vinegar and oil over the chicken. Discard toothpicks. Garnish with tomatoes and basil. **Yield:** 4 servings.

Chicken in a Hurry

Prep: 20 min. Cook: 10 min.

Barbara Frasier, Fyffe, Alabama

I cook meat and vegetables in my microwave all the time, but these stuffed chicken breasts filled with chilies and cheese are especially easy and take just 30 minutes from start to finish. I serve sweet-and-sour or duck sauce on top.

- 4 boneless skinless chicken breast halves (6 ounces *each*)
- 3 tablespoons butter, softened

- 3 tablespoons sharp American cheese spread
- 2 tablespoons chopped green chilies
- 2 teaspoons dried minced onion
- 1/4 teaspoon salt
- 1/4 cup butter, melted
- 1 cup seasoned bread crumbs

1. Flatten the chicken to 1/4-in. thickness. In a small bowl, combine butter, cheese spread, chilies, onion and salt. Spread 2 tablespoons on each chicken breast half; roll up and secure with toothpicks.

2. Place melted butter and bread crumbs in separate shallow bowls. Dip the chicken rolls in butter, then coat with crumbs.

3. Place in a greased 8-in. square microwave-safe dish. Cover and microwave on high for 10 minutes or until the chicken is no longer pink. Discard the toothpicks. **Yield:** 4 servings.

Editor's Note: This recipe was tested in a 1,100-watt microwave.

Flat-Out Easy

To flatten chicken, put it inside a heavy-duty resealable plastic bag or between two sheets of heavy plastic wrap to prevent splatters. Use the smooth side of a meat mallet to gently pound the chicken to the desired thickness.

Beef Fillets with Grilled Vegetables

Prep/Total Time: 30 min.

Cindie Haras, Boca Raton, Florida

Why bother with pots and pans when you can have this? The colorful grilled entree will have mouths watering and looks as good as it tastes. Basting with butter seals in the meat's juices and adds extra flavor. Make sure to use romaine lettuce leaves because they stand up well to grilling.

- 4 beef tenderloin fillets (1-1/2 inches thick and 4 ounces *each*)
- 3 teaspoons pepper, *divided*
- 1/2 cup creamy Caesar salad dressing
- 8 to 12 romaine leaves
- 2 medium tomatoes, cut into 1-inch slices
- 1 medium onion, sliced
- 3 tablespoons olive oil
- 2 tablespoons butter, melted
- 1/2 teaspoon salt

1. Rub fillets with 2 teaspoons pepper; place in a large resealable plastic bag. Add salad dressing; seal bag and turn to coat. Refrigerate for 10 minutes.

2. Meanwhile, brush romaine, tomatoes and onion with oil. Grill tomatoes and onion, uncovered, over medium heat for 4-5 minutes on each side or until onion is crisp-tender. Grill romaine for 30 seconds on each side or until heated through. Wrap vegetables in foil and set aside.

3. Drain and discard marinade. Grill fillets, covered, over medium heat for 7-8 minutes on each side or until meat reaches desired doneness (for medium-rare, a meat thermometer should read 145°; medium, 160°; well-done, 170°), basting occasionally with butter.

4. Serve with grilled vegetables. Sprinkle with salt and remaining pepper. **Yield:** 4 servings.

Tangy Meat Sauce

Prep/Total Time: 25 min.

Adalia Schweitzer, Hamilton, Ontario

This is the best meat sauce I've ever tried. It's quick to make, economical and absolutely delicious! I like to prepare batches for new moms because it can be frozen for future dinners. If you prefer, substitute ground chicken for the beef.

- 1/2 pound lean ground beef (90% lean)
- 1/2 cup chopped onion
- 1/2 cup chopped green pepper
- 1/2 teaspoon minced garlic
- 1 can (15 ounces) tomato sauce
- 1 can (6 ounces) tomato paste
- 1 tablespoon sugar
- 1 tablespoon red wine vinegar
- 1/2 teaspoon salt
- 1/2 teaspoon dried basil
- 1/4 teaspoon dried oregano

Hot cooked spaghetti

1. Crumble beef into a 2-qt. microwave-safe dish. Add the onion, green pepper and garlic. Cover and microwave on high for 5-6 minutes or until the meat is no longer pink and the vegetables are tender, stirring frequently; drain.

2. Stir in tomato sauce, tomato paste, sugar, vinegar, salt, basil and oregano. Cover and microwave at 70% power for 6-8 minutes or until heated through, stirring once. Serve with spaghetti. **Yield:** 3 cups.

Editor's Note: This recipe was tested in a 1,100-watt microwave.

Prosciutto-Stuffed Meat Loaf

Prep: 45 min. **Bake:** 1-1/4 hours

Carole Hermenau, Oviedo, Florida

With an amazing blend of ingredients including two cheeses, prosciutto, fresh basil and sun-dried tomatoes, this rolled meat loaf is a standout. Try it—you'll be glad you did!

- 1 cup finely chopped red onion
- 1 tablespoon olive oil
- 1 tablespoon butter
- 2 garlic cloves, minced
- 1/2 pound whole fresh mushrooms, coarsely chopped
- 3/4 teaspoon salt
- 1/2 teaspoon pepper
- 2 eggs, lightly beaten
- 1-3/4 cups soft sourdough bread crumbs
- 3/4 cup grated Parmesan cheese
- 1/3 cup minced fresh parsley
- 1 teaspoon minced fresh thyme
- 1-1/2 pounds lean ground beef
- 3/4 pound bulk Italian sausage

FILLING:
- 3 ounces thinly sliced prosciutto
- 5 ounces thinly sliced Havarti cheese
- 1-1/4 cups loosely packed basil leaves, cut into thin strips
- 1/3 cup oil-packed sun-dried tomatoes, drained and cut into strips

1. In a large skillet, saute the onion in oil and butter for 2 minutes. Add the garlic; cook 1 minute longer. Add the mushrooms; cook 6-8 minutes longer or until mushrooms are tender and no liquid remains. Stir in salt and pepper.

2. In a large bowl, combine the eggs, bread crumbs, Parmesan cheese, parsley, thyme and mushroom mixture. Crumble beef and sausage over the mixture; mix well.

3. On a large piece of heavy-duty foil, pat beef mixture into a 15-in. x 10-in. rectangle. Layer the prosciutto, Havarti, basil and tomatoes to within 1 in. of edges. Roll up jelly-roll style, starting with a short side and peeling foil away while rolling. Seal seams and ends.

4. Place the meat loaf seam side down in a greased 13-in. x 9-in. baking dish. Bake, uncovered, at 350° for 75-85 minutes or until no pink remains and a meat thermometer reads 160°. Let stand for 5 minutes. Using two large spatulas, carefully transfer meat loaf to a serving platter. **Yield:** 6-8 servings.

Chicken in Lime Butter

Prep/Total Time: 20 min.

- 4 boneless skinless chicken breast halves (4 ounces *each*)
- 1/8 teaspoon salt
- 1/8 teaspoon pepper
- 2 tablespoons canola oil
- 1/4 cup butter
- 1 tablespoon lime juice
- 1/2 teaspoon dill weed
- 1/4 teaspoon minced chives

1. Sprinkle the chicken with salt and pepper. In a large skillet, cook the chicken in oil over medium heat for 5-7 minutes on each side or until a meat thermometer reaches 170°; drain. Remove chicken and keep warm.

2. Add butter and lime juice to the skillet; cook and stir until the butter is melted. Stir in dill and chives. Drizzle over chicken. **Yield:** 4 servings.

DENISE SEGURA DRAPER, UTAH

Combining a few ordinary ingredients on the stovetop makes this moist, tender chicken truly extraordinary. The rich, buttery sauce with a splash of lime juice is delectable and adds so much flavor. It's been a hands-down winner at our house for many years.

GRAND PRIZE WINNER

Zippy Peanut Steak Kabobs

Prep: 40 min. + marinating **Grill:** 10 min.

Sheri Nutter, Oneida, Kentucky

If you like your kabobs with a kick, you're sure to enjoy these tongue-tingling skewers seasoned with habanero pepper sauce. The zippy steak chunks are balanced with refreshing pineapple and red pepper. Sometimes I substitute chicken for the beef.

    3/4 cup packed brown sugar
    3/4 cup water
      1 cup chunky peanut butter
      1 cup reduced-sodium soy sauce
    3/4 cup honey barbecue sauce
    1/3 cup canola oil
      1 to 2 tablespoons habanero pepper sauce
      3 garlic cloves, minced
      2 pounds beef top sirloin steak, cut into thin
         strips
      2 teaspoons ground ginger
      1 fresh pineapple, cut into 1-inch cubes
      2 large sweet red peppers, cut into 1-inch pieces
    Hot cooked jasmine rice

1. In a small saucepan, combine brown sugar and water. Cook and stir over low heat until the sugar is completely dissolved. Remove from the heat. Whisk in peanut butter until blended. Stir in the soy sauce, barbecue sauce, oil, pepper sauce and garlic.

2. Pour 3 cups of the marinade into a large resealable plastic bag; add the beef. Seal bag and turn to coat; refrigerate for 4 hours. Cover and refrigerate remaining marinade until serving.

3. Drain and discard marinade. Sprinkle ginger over the pineapple. On 16 metal or soaked wooden skewers, alternately thread beef, pineapple and red peppers.

4. Grill, covered, over medium heat for 5-7 minutes on each side or until meat reaches desired doneness. Serve with rice and reserved marinade for dipping. **Yield:** 8 servings.

Favorite Barbecued Chicken

Prep: 15 min. **Grill:** 35 min.

Bobbie Morgan, Woodstock, Georgia

What better place is there to find a sensational barbecue sauce than Texas? That's where this barbecued chicken recipe comes from—it's my father-in-law's own creation. We've served it at many family reunions and think it's the best.

      1 broiler/fryer chicken (3 pounds), cut up
    Salt and pepper to taste
    BARBECUE SAUCE:
      1 small onion, finely chopped
      1 tablespoon canola oil
      1 cup ketchup
      2 tablespoons lemon juice
      1 tablespoon brown sugar
      1 tablespoon water
    1/2 teaspoon ground mustard
    1/4 teaspoon garlic powder
    1/8 teaspoon pepper
    Dash salt
    Dash hot pepper sauce

1. Sprinkle the chicken with salt and pepper. Grill the chicken, skin side down, uncovered, over medium heat for 20 minutes.

2. Meanwhile, in a small saucepan, saute the onion in oil until tender. Stir in remaining sauce ingredients. Bring to a boil. Reduce heat; simmer, uncovered, for 10 minutes.

3. Turn the chicken; grill 15-25 minutes longer or until juices run clear, brushing often with barbecue sauce. **Yield:** 6 servings.

Mozzarella-Stuffed Meatballs

Prep: 20 min. **Cook:** 15 min.

Michaela Rosenthal, Woodland Hills, California

It's fun to watch people eat these for the first time—everyone is surprised to find the melted cheese in the middle. These meatballs are also great in a hot sub sandwich.

- 1 egg, lightly beaten
- 1/4 cup prepared Italian salad dressing
- 1-1/2 cups cubed bread
- 2 tablespoons minced fresh parsley
- 2 garlic cloves, minced
- 1/2 teaspoon dried oregano
- 1/2 teaspoon pepper
- 1/4 teaspoon salt
- 1/2 pound ground pork
- 1/2 pound ground sirloin
- 3 ounces fresh mozzarella cheese
- 2 tablespoons canola oil
- 1 jar (26 ounces) marinara sauce

Hot cooked pasta

1. In a large bowl, combine the first eight ingredients. Crumble the pork and beef over the mixture; mix well. Cut the mozzarella into eighteen 1/2-in. cubes.

Divide the meat mixture into 18 portions; shape each around a cheese cube.

2. In a large skillet, cook meatballs in oil in batches until no pink remains; drain. In a large saucepan, heat marinara sauce; add meatballs and heat through. Serve over pasta. **Yield:** 6 servings.

Blue Cheese Stroganoff

Prep/Total Time: 30 min.

Doris Heath, Franklin, North Carolina

Looking to break out of the dinnertime doldrums? Try this! The out-of-the-ordinary Stroganoff goes together with bacon, sugar snap peas and a mild blue cheese sauce. Cook some egg noodles or use any leftover pasta you have in the fridge.

- 1 bacon strip, diced
- 1/2 pound boneless beef sirloin steak, cut into thin strips
- 1/4 teaspoon beef bouillon granules
- 1/4 cup hot water
- 3/4 cup frozen sugar snap peas
- 4 ounces cream cheese, softened
- 1/3 cup crumbled blue cheese
- 1 tablespoon all-purpose flour
- 1/8 teaspoon salt
- 1/8 teaspoon pepper
- 1/3 cup 2% milk

Hot cooked egg noodles

1. In a small skillet, cook bacon over medium heat until crisp. Using a slotted spoon, remove to paper towel. In the same skillet, cook the beef over medium heat until no longer pink. Combine beef bouillon and water; stir into the skillet. Add peas. Bring to a boil. Reduce heat; cover and simmer for 10 minutes or until peas are tender.

2. Meanwhile, in a small bowl, beat the cream cheese, blue cheese, flour, salt and pepper until smooth. Stir in milk. Gradually stir into beef mixture. Cook and stir for 2-3 minutes or until heated through. Serve over noodles; sprinkle with bacon. **Yield:** 2 servings.

Southwestern Stuffed Turkey Breast

Prep: 40 min. **Bake:** 1-1/4 hours + standing

Bernice Janowski, Stevens Point, Wisconsin

This special-looking turkey breast is a guaranteed hit during the holiday season. The moist stuffing with tomatoes, spices, corn and lime adds south-of-the-border flair.

 This recipe includes Nutrition Facts & Diabetic Exchanges.

1/3 cup sun-dried tomatoes (not packed in oil)
2/3 cup boiling water
1-1/2 teaspoons dried oregano
1 teaspoon salt
3/4 teaspoon ground cumin
1/2 teaspoon ground coriander
1/4 teaspoon crushed red pepper flakes

1 small onion, chopped
1 small green pepper, diced
1 garlic clove, minced
1 tablespoon olive oil
1 cup frozen corn, thawed
1/2 cup dry bread crumbs
1-1/2 teaspoons grated lime peel
1 boneless skinless turkey breast half
   (2 pounds)

1. Place the tomatoes in a small bowl; cover with boiling water. Cover; let stand for 5 minutes. Drain, reserving 3 tablespoons liquid; set aside. Meanwhile, combine seasonings in a small bowl.

2. In a large skillet, saute the tomatoes, onion, green pepper and garlic in oil until tender. Stir in corn and 2 teaspoons seasonings; remove from the heat. Stir in bread crumbs and reserved tomato liquid. Add lime peel to remaining seasonings; set side.

3. Cover the turkey breast with plastic wrap. Flatten to 1/2-in. thickness; remove plastic. Sprinkle turkey with half of the lime-seasoning mixture; spread the vegetable mixture to within 1 in. of the edges. Roll up jelly-roll style, starting with a short side; tie with kitchen string. Sprinkle with remaining lime-seasoning mixture. Place on a rack in a shallow roasting pan; cover loosely with foil.

4. Bake at 350° for 1 hour. Uncover; bake 15-30 minutes longer or until a meat thermometer reads 170°, basting occasionally with pan drippings. Let stand for 15 minutes before slicing. **Yield:** 8 servings.

Nutrition Facts: 1 slice equals 200 calories, 3 g fat (1 g saturated fat), 70 mg cholesterol, 458 mg sodium, 12 g carbohydrate, 2 g fiber, 30 g protein. **Diabetic Exchanges:** 4 very lean meat, 1 starch.

Smothered Chicken Breasts

Prep/Total Time: 30 min.

4 boneless skinless chicken breast halves
   (6 ounces *each*)
1/4 teaspoon salt
1/4 teaspoon lemon-pepper seasoning
1 tablespoon canola oil
8 bacon strips
1 medium onion, sliced
1/4 cup packed brown sugar
1/2 cup shredded Colby-Monterey Jack cheese

1. Sprinkle chicken with salt and lemon-pepper. In a large skillet, cook chicken in oil for 6-7 minutes

on each side or until a meat thermometer reads 170°; remove and keep warm.

2. In the same skillet, cook the bacon over medium heat until crisp. Using a slotted spoon, remove the bacon to paper towels; drain, reserving 2 tablespoons drippings.

3. In the drippings, saute the onion and brown sugar until the onion is tender and golden brown. Place two bacon strips on each chicken breast half; top with the caramelized onions and cheese. **Yield:** 4 servings.

BRENDA CARPENTER WARRENSBURG, MISSOURI

After sampling a wonderful entree in a restaurant, I decided to try re-creating it in my own kitchen. Topped with bacon strips, caramelized onions and shredded cheese, this chicken comes together in no time with ingredients I usually have on hand.

GRAND
PRIZE
WINNER

Beef & Poultry Entrees **113**

Pecan-Crusted Chicken

Prep: 10 min. **Bake:** 25 min.

Ramona Parris, Marietta, Georgia

After trying something similar while dining out, I cooked up these baked chicken breasts covered with a pecan coating. For a special-occasion dinner, I'll serve them with mashed sweet potatoes and a side of cooked canned cherries.

> 3 **egg whites**
> 1 **package (4.2 ounces) seasoned coating mix**
> 1/2 **cup chopped pecans**
> 1/8 **teaspoon Chinese five-spice powder**
> 6 **boneless skinless chicken breast halves**
>   **(4 ounces *each*)**

1. In a shallow bowl, lightly beat the egg whites. In another shallow bowl, combine coating mix, pecans and five-spice powder. Dip chicken into egg whites, then roll into coating mixture.

2. Place in a greased 15-in. x 10-in. x 1-in. baking pan. Bake, uncovered, at 400° for 25 minutes or until a meat thermometer reads 170°. **Yield:** 6 servings.

Chicken 'n' Dressing Casserole

Prep: 1 hour **Bake:** 35 min.

Billie Blanton, Kingsport, Tennessee

A family favorite, this casserole is true comfort food. It's also a great solution for leftover chicken or turkey…and so easy to make that even beginner cooks will have success.

> 4 **cups cubed cooked chicken**
> 2 **tablespoons all-purpose flour**
> 1/2 **cup chicken broth**
> 1/2 **cup milk**
> **Salt and pepper to taste**
> **DRESSING:**
> 2 **celery ribs, chopped**
> 1 **small onion, finely chopped**
> 1 **tablespoon butter**
> 1 **teaspoon rubbed sage**
> 1/2 **teaspoon poultry seasoning**
> 1/4 **teaspoon salt**
> 1/8 **teaspoon pepper**
> 2 **cups unseasoned stuffing cubes, crushed**
> 2 **cups coarsely crumbled corn bread**
> 1/2 **cup chicken broth**
> 1 **egg, beaten**
> **GRAVY:**
> 1/4 **cup butter**
> 6 **tablespoons all-purpose flour**
> 2 **cups chicken broth**
> 1/2 **cup milk**

1. Place chicken in a greased 2-qt. baking dish; set aside. In a small saucepan, combine the flour, broth and milk until smooth. Bring to a boil; cook and stir for 2 minutes. Season with salt and pepper. Spoon over chicken.

2. In a large skillet, saute celery and onion in butter until tender. Stir in seasonings. Remove from the heat; add the stuffing cubes, corn bread, broth and egg. Mix well. Spoon over chicken mixture. Cover and bake at 350° for 35-40 minutes or until a thermometer inserted near the center reads 160°.

3. For gravy, melt butter in a small saucepan. Stir in flour until smooth; gradually add broth and milk. Bring to a boil; cook and stir for 2 minutes or until thickened. Serve with chicken and dressing. **Yield:** 8 servings.

Honey Orange Chicken

Prep: 20 min. **Cook:** 15 min.

Marie Hannah, Hemet, California

This chicken-and-pasta entree is elegant enough for company and tastes like you spent all day in the kitchen.

- 1 pound boneless skinless chicken breasts, cut into 1/2-inch strips
- 3 tablespoons butter, *divided*
- 1 teaspoon salt
- 1/2 teaspoon paprika
- 1/4 teaspoon pepper
- 1 medium onion, sliced
- 1 tablespoon cornstarch
- 1/2 teaspoon ground ginger
- 1/4 teaspoon ground nutmeg
- 1 cup orange juice
- 1/4 cup honey
- 1/2 cup pitted ripe olives, halved
- Hot cooked linguine

1. In a large skillet, saute the chicken in 2 tablespoons butter until chicken is no longer pink. Sprinkle with the salt, paprika and pepper. Remove and keep warm.

In the same pan, saute the onion in remaining butter until tender.

2. In a small bowl, combine the cornstarch, ginger, nutmeg, orange juice and honey; gradually pour over onion. Bring to a boil; cook and stir for 2 minutes or until thickened. Add the olives and chicken. Simmer, uncovered, for 5 minutes or until the chicken is heated through. Serve with linguine. **Yield:** 4 servings.

Greek Pasta Bake

Prep: 20 min. **Bake:** 25 min.

Anne Taglienti, Kennett Square, Pennsylvania

Whenever I bring this hot dish to potlucks or other gatherings, there's never a crumb left. Best of all, it's a simple, wholesome and hearty supper made with easy-to-find ingredients.

 This recipe includes Nutrition Facts & Diabetic Exchanges.

- 1 package (13-1/4 ounces) whole wheat penne pasta
- 4 cups cubed cooked chicken breast
- 1 can (29 ounces) tomato sauce
- 1 can (14-1/2 ounces) diced tomatoes, drained
- 1 package (10 ounces) frozen chopped spinach, thawed and squeezed dry
- 2 cans (2-1/4 ounces *each*) sliced ripe olives, drained
- 1/4 cup chopped red onion
- 2 tablespoons chopped green pepper
- 1 teaspoon dried basil
- 1 teaspoon dried oregano
- 1/2 cup shredded part-skim mozzarella cheese
- 1/2 cup crumbled feta cheese

1. Cook pasta according to package directions; drain. In a large bowl, combine the pasta, chicken, tomato sauce, tomatoes, spinach, olives, onion, green pepper, basil and oregano.

2. Transfer to a 13-in. x 9-in. baking dish coated with cooking spray. Sprinkle with cheeses. Bake, uncovered, at 400° for 25-30 minutes or until heated through and cheese is melted. **Yield:** 8 servings.

Nutrition Facts: 1-1/2 cups equals 366 calories, 7 g fat (2 g saturated fat), 62 mg cholesterol, 847 mg sodium, 43 g carbohydrate, 6 g fiber, 32 g protein. **Diabetic Exchanges:** 3 very lean meat, 2-1/2 starch, 1 vegetable, 1/2 fat.

Meatballs with Spaghetti Sauce

Prep: 30 min. **Bake:** 25 min.

Denise Linnett, Picton, Ontario

A friend gave me the recipe for this traditional main dish. It's her Italian mother-in-law's recipe from the old country—and it tastes like it! Sauce from a jar just can't compare.

    1/2 cup soft bread crumbs
    1/4 cup grated Parmesan cheese
      1 tablespoon 2% milk
      1 egg, lightly beaten
  1-1/2 teaspoons minced fresh parsley
    1/4 teaspoon garlic powder
    1/8 teaspoon salt
    1/8 teaspoon pepper
      6 ounces lean ground beef
      2 ounces ground pork
  SAUCE:
    1/2 cup chopped onion
      1 garlic clove, minced
      1 tablespoon olive oil
      1 can (14-1/2 ounces) whole tomatoes,
        quartered
      1 can (8 ounces) tomato sauce
      1 can (6 ounces) tomato paste
    1/2 cup water
      3 tablespoons minced fresh parsley
      1 teaspoon sugar
      1 teaspoon dried basil
    1/4 teaspoon pepper
  Hot cooked spaghetti

1. In a large bowl, combine the first eight ingredients. Crumble beef and pork over mixture and mix well. Shape into 1-3/4-in. balls.

2. Place the meatballs on a greased rack in a shallow baking pan. Bake at 350° for 25-30 minutes or until meatballs are no longer pink; drain.

3. Meanwhile, in a large saucepan, saute onion and garlic in oil until tender. Stir in the tomatoes, tomato sauce and paste, water, parsley, sugar, basil and pepper. Bring to a boil. Reduce heat; simmer, uncovered, for 15 minutes, stirring occasionally.

4. Add the meatballs to the sauce; simmer 5 minutes longer or until heated through. Serve with spaghetti. **Yield:** 2 servings.

Taco Meat Loaves

Prep: 25 min. **Bake:** 1 hour + standing

      3 eggs, lightly beaten
      2 cups picante sauce, *divided*
      1 can (16 ounces) kidney beans, rinsed and
        drained
      1 can (11 ounces) Mexicorn, drained
      1 medium onion, chopped
      2 cans (2-1/4 ounces *each*) sliced ripe olives,
        drained
    3/4 cup dry bread crumbs
      1 envelope taco seasoning
      1 teaspoon ground cumin
      1 teaspoon chili powder
      2 pounds ground beef
      2 cups (8 ounces) shredded cheddar cheese
  Additional picante sauce, optional

1. In a large bowl, combine eggs, 1/2 cup picante sauce, beans, corn, onion, olives, bread crumbs, taco seasoning, cumin and chili powder. Crumble beef over mixture and mix well.

2. Pat mixture into two ungreased 9-in. x 5-in. loaf pans. Bake, uncovered, at 350° for 50-55 minutes or until no pink remains and a meat thermometer reads 160°.

3. Spoon the remaining picante sauce over each meat loaf; sprinkle with cheese. Bake 10-15 minutes longer or until the cheese is melted. Let meat loaves stand for 10 minutes before slicing. Serve with additional picante sauce if desired. **Yield:** 2 meat loaves (6 servings each).

SUSAN GAROUTTE GEORGETOWN, TEXAS

Here in Texas, we love the Southwest style of cooking. This zesty meat loaf gets spiced up with picante sauce, chili powder, taco seasoning and more.

GRAND PRIZE WINNER

Tortilla-Salsa Meat Loaf

Prep: 15 min. Bake: 1-1/4 hours

Steven Espinosa, Salt Lake City, Utah

I'm asked to fix this recipe at least once a month during the winter, especially for birthdays. Guests always enjoy it with braised asparagus and garlic mashed potatoes.

- 2 slices day-old white bread
- 2 eggs, lightly beaten
- 1 cup salsa
- 1/2 cup crushed tortilla chips
- 1/2 cup *each* chopped green pepper, onion and celery
- 1 jalapeno pepper, seeded and chopped
- 6 garlic cloves, minced
- 1 teaspoon pepper
- 1/2 teaspoon Italian seasoning
- 1/4 teaspoon seasoned salt
- 1 pound ground beef
- 1 pound ground pork

1. Place bread in an ungreased 9-in. x 5-in. loaf pan; set aside. In a large bowl, combine the eggs, salsa, tortilla chips, green pepper, onion, celery, jalapeno,

garlic, pepper, Italian seasoning and seasoned salt. Crumble beef and pork over mixture and mix well. Pat into prepared pan.

2. Bake, uncovered, at 375° for 1-1/4 to 1-1/2 hours or until no pink remains and a meat thermometer reads 160°. Invert the meat loaf onto a serving platter; discard the bread. Let stand for 5 minutes before slicing. **Yield:** 8 servings.

Editor's Note: When cutting hot peppers, disposable gloves are recommended. Avoid touching your face.

Cherry-Topped Chicken

Prep/Total Time: 15 min.

Tabetha Moore, New Braunfels, Texas

Looking for a main course that's simple enough to make on busy weeknights but special enough to serve company? This scrumptious option really fills the bill. It goes together in just minutes and uses only four ingredients.

 This recipe includes Nutrition Facts & Diabetic Exchanges.

- 4 boneless skinless chicken breast halves (4 ounces *each*)
- 1 tablespoon canola oil
- 1/2 cup cherry preserves
- 1/4 teaspoon ground allspice

1. Flatten the chicken to 1/4-in. thickness. In a large skillet, cook the chicken in oil over medium heat for 5 minutes on each side or until meat is no longer pink.

2. Meanwhile, in a small microwave-safe bowl, combine preserves and allspice until blended. Heat in the microwave until warmed. Serve with chicken. **Yield:** 4 servings.

Nutrition Facts: 1 chicken breast half with 2 tablespoons preserves equals 252 calories, 6 g fat (1 g saturated fat), 63 mg cholesterol, 55 mg sodium, 26 g carbohydrate, trace fiber, 23 g protein. **Diabetic Exchanges:** 3 very lean meat, 2 fruit, 1/2 fat

Boning Chicken Breasts

Didn't buy boneless chicken? Simply insert a small boning or paring knife between the ribs and breast meat. Pressing the knife along the bones, cut to remove the meat. Remove the skin by pulling it from the breast meat.

Honey-Ginger Turkey Kabobs

Prep: 30 min. + marinating **Grill:** 10 min.

Pam Thomas, Marion, Iowa

Lime juice and fresh pineapple chunks lend tropical taste to these grilled skewers. You won't want to skip the accompanying rice flavored with more fruit and cilantro.

- 2 tablespoons chopped green onion
- 2 tablespoons soy sauce
- 1 tablespoon honey
- 1 tablespoon minced fresh gingerroot
- 1 teaspoon lime juice
- 2 garlic cloves, minced
- 1 pound turkey breast tenderloins, cut into 1-inch cubes
- 2 cups cubed fresh pineapple
- 1 medium sweet red pepper, cut into 1-inch pieces
- 1 medium red onion, cut into chunks
- 1 medium lime, cut into wedges

PINEAPPLE RICE:
- 2-1/2 cups water
- 1 cup uncooked long grain rice
- 1/2 cup chopped dried pineapple
- 2 teaspoons butter
- 1/2 teaspoon grated lime peel
- 1/4 teaspoon salt
- 1/4 cup minced fresh cilantro
- 1/4 cup chopped green onions
- 2 tablespoons lime juice

1. In a large resealable plastic bag, combine the first six ingredients; add turkey. Seal bag and turn to coat; refrigerate for at least 2 hours.

2. Drain and discard the marinade. On eight metal or soaked wooden skewers, alternately thread the turkey, pineapple, sweet red pepper, red onion and lime wedges; set aside.

3. In a large saucepan, bring water to a boil. Stir in the rice, dried pineapple, butter, lime peel and salt. Reduce heat; cover and simmer for 15-20 minutes or until tender.

4. Meanwhile, grill kabobs, covered, over medium heat or broil 4-6 in. from the heat for 4-6 minutes on each side or until the turkey is no longer pink and the vegetables are tender. Stir cilantro, onions and lime juice into rice. Serve with kabobs. **Yield:** 4 servings.

Tuxedo Pasta

Prep/Total Time: 20 min.

Jackie Hannahs, Fountain, Michigan

This colorful pasta medley in a lemon and wine sauce makes a complete meal. I like to keep leftover chicken or turkey on hand so I can prepare this dish whenever I want.

- 2 cups uncooked bow tie pasta
- 2 cups cubed cooked chicken
- 1 medium zucchini, sliced
- 1-1/2 cups sliced fresh mushrooms
- 1/2 cup chopped sweet red pepper
- 3 tablespoons butter, *divided*
- 1/4 cup lemon juice
- 2 tablespoons white wine *or chicken broth*
- 3/4 cup shredded Parmesan cheese
- 3 tablespoons minced fresh basil *or* 1 tablespoon dried basil

1. Cook the bow tie pasta according to the package directions. Meanwhile, in a large skillet, saute the chicken, zucchini, mushrooms and sweet red pepper in 2 tablespoons butter for 4-5 minutes or until the vegetables are tender. Add the lemon juice and white wine. Bring to a boil. Reduce the heat; cook and stir for 2 minutes or until heated through.

2. Drain the bow tie pasta; add to the skillet. Stir in the Parmesan cheese, basil and remaining butter. **Yield:** 6 servings.

Southern Barbecued Brisket

Prep: 10 min. **Bake:** 3 hours + standing

Lorraine Hodge, McLean, Virginia

Ever since a former neighbor shared this recipe with me, it's been one of my mainstays. It's perfect when you're expecting a crowd for a dinner buffet or other get-together. The brisket gets nice and tender from baking slowly for several hours.

 This recipe includes Nutrition Facts & Diabetic Exchanges.

1 fresh beef brisket (5 pounds)
1 large onion, chopped
1 cup ketchup
1/4 cup water
3 tablespoons brown sugar
1 tablespoon Liquid Smoke, optional
2 teaspoons celery seed
1 teaspoon salt
1 teaspoon ground mustard
1/8 teaspoon cayenne pepper

1. Place the brisket on a large sheet of heavy-duty foil; seal tightly. Place in a greased shallow roasting pan. Bake at 325° for 2 to 2-1/2 hours or until the meat is tender.

2. Meanwhile, in a small saucepan, combine the remaining ingredients. Bring to a boil. Reduce heat; cover and simmer for 20 minutes, stirring occasionally. Remove from the heat.

3. Carefully open the foil to allow steam to escape. Remove the brisket from foil; let stand for 20 minutes. Thinly slice the meat across the grain. Place in an ungreased 13-in. x 9-in. baking dish. Spoon the sauce over the meat. Cover and bake for 1 hour or until heated through. **Yield:** 12 servings.

Editor's Note: This is a fresh beef brisket, not corned beef.

Nutrition Facts: 5 ounces equals 279 calories, 8 g fat (3 g saturated fat), 80 mg cholesterol, 515 mg sodium, 10 g carbohydrate, trace fiber, 39 g protein. **Diabetic Exchanges:** 5 lean meat, 1/2 starch.

Beef Stir-Fry on a Stick

Prep: 20 min. **Grill:** 15 min.

Gwendolyn Lambert, Frisco City, Alabama

Who says stir-fry has to come from a skillet or wok? A thick, Asian-style sauce coats these beef and vegetable kabobs served over rice. They're full of flavor and always a hit.

1/2 cup hoisin sauce
3 tablespoons water
2 tablespoons canola oil
1 tablespoon soy sauce
1 garlic clove, minced
1/4 to 1/2 teaspoon crushed red pepper flakes
3 cups large fresh broccoli florets
2 medium yellow summer squash, cut into 3/4-inch slices
1 large sweet red pepper, cut into 1-inch pieces
1 pound beef tenderloin, cut into 1-inch cubes
Hot cooked rice

1. For the glaze, in a small bowl, combine the hoisin sauce, water, oil, soy sauce, garlic and pepper flakes.

2. On four metal skewers or soaked wooden skewers, alternately thread the broccoli, squash, red pepper and beef. Brush with 1/3 cup of glaze.

3. Grill, covered, over medium heat or broil 4 in. from the heat for 6-7 minutes on each side or until meat reaches desired doneness and vegetables are tender, basting once with remaining glaze. Serve with rice. **Yield:** 4 servings.

Garden-Style Beef Lasagna

Prep: 25 min. **Cook:** 30 min. + standing

Micaela Miller, Corinth, Texas

Everyone who's sampled this sensational lasagna packed with ground beef and vegetable-filled pasta sauce has raved over it. Plus, they're always surprised to learn that it can be prepared entirely in the microwave. When we're in the mood to change things up a bit, I add a layer of sliced zucchini.

1-1/2 **pounds lean ground beef (90% lean)**
  3/4 **cup chopped onion**
    1 **teaspoon minced garlic**
1-1/2 **cups garden-style pasta sauce**
    1 **can (15 ounces) tomato sauce**
    2 **tablespoons dried parsley flakes,** *divided*
    1 **teaspoon dried oregano**
    2 **cups (16 ounces) 4% cottage cheese**
  1/2 **cup grated Parmesan cheese,** *divided*
    1 **egg**
    1 **teaspoon dried basil**
    6 **no-cook lasagna noodles**
    2 **cups (8 ounces) shredded part-skim mozzarella cheese,** *divided*

1. Crumble beef into a microwave-safe dish. Add onion and garlic; mix well. Cover and microwave on high for 3 minutes; stir. Cook 2-3 minutes longer or until meat is no longer pink. Stir in the pasta sauce, tomato sauce, 1 tablespoon parsley and oregano; cover and microwave for 2 minutes or until heated through. Set aside.

2. In a small bowl, combine cottage cheese, 1/4 cup Parmesan cheese, egg, basil and remaining parsley. Spread 1-1/3 cups prepared meat sauce in a greased microwave-safe 11-in. x 7-in. baking dish.

3. Layer with three noodles, 1 cup cheese mixture and 1/2 cup mozzarella cheese. Repeat layers. Top with remaining meat sauce.

4. Cover loosely and microwave at 50% power for 15-18 minutes or until noodles are tender. Sprinkle with remaining cheeses.

5. Microwave, uncovered, 5 minutes longer or until cheese is melted. Let stand for 15 minutes before serving. **Yield:** 6-8 servings.

Editor's Note: This recipe was tested in a 1,100-watt microwave.

PG. 136

PG. 126

PG. 136

PORK & MORE ENTREES

Whether you want a fancy ham for the holidays, a saucy shrimp dish to serve guests or a meatless mainstay as a quick weeknight dinner, you'll find a wide variety of memorable main courses here.

Waldorf Stuffed Ham

Prep: 35 min. **Bake:** 1-1/4 hours + standing

Colleen Vrooman, Waukesha, Wisconsin

When I wanted to try something new with ham, this recipe popped into my head. It uses apple pie filling and a stuffing mix. I served it to my husband, and he said it's a keeper.

- 1-1/2 cups unsweetened apple juice
- 1/4 cup butter, cubed
- 1 package (6 ounces) pork stuffing mix
- 1 medium tart apple, finely chopped
- 1/4 cup chopped sweet onion
- 1/4 cup chopped celery
- 1/4 cup chopped walnuts
- 1 bone-in fully cooked spiral-sliced ham (8 pounds)
- 1 can (21 ounces) apple pie filling
- 1/4 teaspoon ground cinnamon

1. In a large saucepan, bring apple juice and butter to a boil. Remove from the heat; stir in the stuffing mix, apple, onion, celery and walnuts.

2. Place ham on a rack in a shallow roasting pan. Spoon stuffing by tablespoonfuls between ham slices. Spoon pie filling over ham; sprinkle with cinnamon.

3. Bake, uncovered, at 325° for 1-1/4 to 1-3/4 hours or until a meat thermometer reads 140°. Let stand for 10 minutes before serving. **Yield:** 14-16 servings.

Pear-Stuffed Pork Loin

Prep: 30 min. **Bake:** 1-1/4 hours + standing

Mary Shivers, Ada, Oklahoma

Our two pear trees produce an abundant crop, so I'm always searching for new ways to use that bounty in my menus. This fancy-looking roast incorporates both fresh and dried fruit into a main-course stuffing and glaze.

- 1 boneless whole pork loin roast (3 to 4 pounds)
- 1/2 cup chopped peeled ripe pears
- 1/2 cup chopped dried pears
- 1/2 cup chopped walnuts
- 1/4 cup minced fresh cilantro
- 3 tablespoons honey
- 2 garlic cloves, minced
- 1/4 teaspoon crushed red pepper flakes

GLAZE:
- 1 cup finely chopped peeled ripe pears
- 1/2 cup finely chopped onion
- 1/4 cup maple syrup
- 2 tablespoons Worcestershire sauce
- 2 tablespoons chili sauce
- 1 jalapeno pepper, seeded and finely chopped
- 1/8 teaspoon cayenne pepper

1. Cut a lengthwise slit down the center of roast to within 1/2 in. of bottom. Open roast so it lies flat. On each half, make another lengthwise slit down the center to within 1/2 in. of bottom; open roast and cover with plastic wrap. Flatten to 3/4-in. thickness. Remove plastic wrap.

2. In a small bowl, combine the ripe pears, dried pears, walnuts, cilantro, honey, garlic and red pepper flakes; spread over the roast to within 1 in. of the edges. Roll up from a long side; tie with kitchen string at 2-in. intervals. Place in a shallow roasting pan lined with heavy-duty foil.

3. Combine glaze ingredients; spoon over roast. Bake, uncovered, at 350° for 1-1/4 to 1-1/2 hours or until a meat thermometer reads 160°, basting occasionally with pan drippings. Let stand for 10-15 minutes before slicing. **Yield:** 12 servings.

Editor's Note: When cutting hot peppers, disposable gloves are recommended. Avoid touching your face.

Black Bean Tortilla Pie

Prep: 50 min. **Bake:** 15 min.

Wendy Kelly, Voorheesville, New York

I found a tortilla pie recipe that sounded great, but I wanted something a little bit lighter. My solution was to decrease the cheese and increase the flavor-enhancing herbs. I love the tasty but guilt-free results, and my family does, too.

 This recipe includes Nutrition Facts & Diabetic Exchanges.

1 medium onion, chopped
1 medium green pepper, chopped
1 teaspoon ground cumin
1/4 teaspoon pepper
1 tablespoon olive oil
3 garlic cloves, minced
2 cans (15 ounces *each*) black beans, rinsed and drained
1 can (14-1/2 ounces) vegetable broth
1 package (10 ounces) frozen corn, thawed
4 green onions, thinly sliced
4 flour tortillas (8 inches)
1 cup (4 ounces) shredded reduced-fat cheddar cheese, *divided*

1. In a large skillet, saute the onion, green pepper, cumin and pepper in oil until vegetables are tender. Add the garlic; cook 1 minute longer. Add beans and

broth. Bring to a boil; cook until liquid is reduced to about 1/3 cup. Stir in corn and green onions; remove from the heat.

2. Place one tortilla in a 9-in. springform pan coated with cooking spray. Layer with 1-1/2 cups bean mixture and 1/4 cup cheese. Repeat layers twice. Top with remaining tortilla. Place pan on a baking sheet.

3. Bake, uncovered, at 400° for 15-20 minutes or until heated through. Remove sides of pan. Sprinkle with remaining cheese. Cut into wedges. **Yield:** 6 servings.

Nutrition Facts: 1 wedge equals 353 calories, 9 g fat (3 g saturated fat), 14 mg cholesterol, 842 mg sodium, 53 g carbohydrate, 8 g fiber, 17 g protein. **Diabetic Exchanges:** 3 starch, 1 very lean meat, 1 vegetable, 1 fat.

Cod Delight

Prep/Total Time: 10 min.

Nancy Daugherty, Cortland, Ohio

I used to cook these delightfully seasoned fillets in the oven, but the microwave lets me enjoy them even faster. The colorful cod is a terrific choice for company.

 This recipe includes Nutrition Facts & Diabetic Exchanges.

1 pound cod fillets
1/2 cup chopped tomatoes
1/3 cup finely chopped onion
2 tablespoons water
2 tablespoons canola oil
4-1/2 teaspoons lemon juice
1 teaspoon dried parsley flakes
1/2 teaspoon minced garlic
1/2 teaspoon minced fresh basil
1/8 teaspoon salt
1 teaspoon seafood seasoning

1. Place the cod fillets in a shallow microwave-safe dish. In a small bowl, combine the tomatoes, onion, water, oil, lemon juice, parsley, garlic, basil and salt; spoon over cod. Sprinkle with seafood seasoning.

2. Cover and microwave on high for 6 minutes or until fish flakes easily with a fork. **Yield:** 4 servings.

Editor's Note: This recipe was tested in a 1,100-watt microwave.

Nutrition Facts: 1 serving equals 154 calories, 8 g fat (1 g saturated fat), 43 mg cholesterol, 304 mg sodium, 3 g carbohydrate, 1 g fiber, 18 g protein. **Diabetic Exchanges:** 3 very lean meat, 1 fat.

1/3 cup all-purpose flour
2 cups whole milk
1 cup (4 ounces) shredded cheddar cheese
1/2 cup sour cream
2 cups cubed fully cooked ham
1 jar (4-1/2 ounces) sliced mushrooms, drained
TOPPING:
1 cup soft bread crumbs
1 tablespoon butter, melted

1. Place cauliflower in a large saucepan; cover with 1 in. water. Bring to a boil. Reduce heat; cover and simmer for 5-10 minutes or until tender.

2. Meanwhile, in another large saucepan, melt butter. Stir in flour until smooth; gradually add milk. Bring to a boil; cook and stir for 2 minutes or until thickened. Remove from the heat. Stir in cheese and sour cream until melted.

3. Drain the cauliflower. In a large bowl, combine the cauliflower, ham and mushrooms. Add the prepared cheese sauce and toss to coat. Transfer to a greased 2-qt. baking dish.

4. Combine the topping ingredients; sprinkle over casserole. Bake, uncovered, at 350° for 40-45 minutes or until heated through. **Yield:** 6 servings.

Cauliflower Ham Casserole

Prep: 20 min. **Bake:** 40 min.

Sue Herlund, White Bear Lake, Minnesota

Cauliflower replaces the potatoes in this homey supper, which I've been making for a number of years. My husband requests it whenever we have leftover ham.

4 cups chopped fresh cauliflower
1/4 cup butter, cubed

Crumb Clue

For soft bread crumbs, tear several slices of fresh white, French or whole wheat bread into 1-inch pieces. Place them in a food processor or blender; cover it and push the pulse button several times to make coarse crumbs.

Greek Pizzas

Prep/Total Time: 30 min.

 This recipe includes Nutrition Facts & Diabetic Exchanges.

4 pita breads (6 inches)
1 cup reduced-fat ricotta cheese
1/2 teaspoon garlic powder
1 package (10 ounces) frozen chopped spinach, thawed and squeezed dry
3 medium tomatoes, sliced
3/4 cup crumbled feta cheese
3/4 teaspoon dried basil

1. Place pita breads on a baking sheet. Combine ricotta cheese and garlic powder; spread over pitas. Top with spinach, tomatoes, feta cheese and basil.

2. Bake at 400° for 12-15 minutes or until bread is lightly browned. **Yield:** 4 servings.

Nutrition Facts: 1 pizza equals 320 calories, 7 g fat (4 g saturated fat), 26 mg cholesterol, 642 mg sodium, 46 g carbohydrate, 6 g fiber, 17 g protein.
Diabetic Exchanges: 2 starch, 2 vegetable, 1 lean meat, 1 fat.

DORIS ALLERS PORTAGE, MICHIGAN

Pita breads make crispy, sized-just-right crusts for these individual pizzas. Topped with two kinds of cheese as well as spinach and tomatoes, they're a hit with everyone who tries them.

GRAND PRIZE WINNER

Pork Chili Verde

Prep: 25 min. **Cook:** 6-1/2 hours

Kimberly Burke, Chico, California

Chunks of pork slowly stew with jalapenos, green enchilada sauce, onion and spices in this Southwestern dish. Enjoy it on its own or stuffed in a warm flour tortilla with sour cream, shredded cheddar cheese and ripe olives.

- 1 boneless pork sirloin roast (3 pounds), cut into 1-inch cubes
- 4 medium carrots, sliced
- 1 medium onion, thinly sliced
- 1 cup minced fresh cilantro
- 4 garlic cloves, minced
- 3 tablespoons canola oil
- 1 can (28 ounces) green enchilada sauce
- 2 jalapeno peppers, seeded and chopped
- 1 tablespoon cornstarch
- 1/4 cup cold water
- Hot cooked rice
- Flour tortillas, warmed

1. In a large skillet, saute pork, carrots, onion, cilantro and garlic in oil in batches until pork is browned.

Transfer to a 5-qt. slow cooker. Add enchilada sauce and jalapenos. Cover and cook on low for 6 hours or until meat is tender.

2. In a small bowl, combine the cornstarch and water until smooth; stir into pork mixture. Cover and cook on high for 30 minutes or until thickened. Serve with rice and tortillas. **Yield:** 8 servings.

Editor's Note: When cutting hot peppers, disposable gloves are recommended. Avoid touching your face.

Seafood Fettuccine Alfredo

Prep/Total Time: 30 min.

Jimmy Spellings, Oakland, Tennessee

I like to serve crusty Italian bread alongside this creamy pasta featuring scallops and shrimp. Sprinkled with chopped tomato and parsley, it looks just as good as it tastes.

- 4 ounces uncooked fettuccine
- 1/4 pound uncooked medium shrimp, peeled and deveined
- 1/4 pound sea scallops, halved
- 2 tablespoons olive oil, *divided*
- 1 small shallot, chopped
- 1 garlic clove, minced
- 1/4 cup chicken broth
- 1/4 cup white wine *or additional chicken broth*
- 1 cup heavy whipping cream *or half-and-half cream*
- 1/2 cup grated Parmesan cheese
- 1 Roma tomato, diced
- 2 tablespoons minced fresh parsley

1. Cook the fettuccine according to the package directions. Meanwhile, in a large skillet, saute the shrimp and scallops in 1 tablespoon oil for 3-5 minutes or until shrimp turn pink and scallops are opaque. Remove and keep warm.

2. In the same skillet, saute shallot in remaining oil until tender. Add garlic; cook 1 minute longer. Stir in broth and wine. Bring to a boil. Reduce heat; simmer, uncovered, for 6-8 minutes or until most of the liquid has evaporated. Stir in cream; cook, uncovered, over medium heat for 5 minutes or until thickened.

3. Drain fettuccine; stir into cream sauce. Add shrimp, scallops and cheese; toss to coat. Sprinkle with tomato and parsley. **Yield:** 2 servings.

Italian Sausage with Polenta

Prep: 15 min. **Cook:** 25 min.

Mary Bilyeu, Ann Arbor, Michigan

This skillet combination of turkey sausage and veggies served over homemade polenta is easy to fix and delicious. Rely on this recipe when you want a satisfying weeknight meal.

    1 package (19-1/2 ounces) Italian turkey
      sausage links, casings removed
  1/2 cup chopped red onion
    4 garlic cloves, minced
2-1/2 cups fresh broccoli florets
    2 cans (15 ounces *each*) crushed tomatoes
    2 tablespoons prepared pesto
  1/2 teaspoon crushed red pepper flakes
  1/4 teaspoon pepper
    3 cups reduced-sodium chicken broth
    1 cup cornmeal
Shaved Parmesan cheese, optional

1. In a large nonstick skillet coated with cooking spray, cook sausage and onion over medium heat until meat is no longer pink. Add garlic; cook 1 minute longer. Stir in broccoli. Reduce heat; cover and cook for 5-7 minutes or until broccoli is tender.

2. Stir in tomatoes, pesto, pepper flakes and pepper; bring to a boil. Reduce heat; simmer, uncovered, for 10 minutes.

3. Meanwhile, for polenta, bring broth to a boil in a small heavy saucepan. Reduce heat to a gentle boil; slowly whisk in cornmeal. Continue stirring for 10-12 minutes or until polenta is thickened and has a smooth texture. Serve with sausage mixture. Garnish with cheese if desired. **Yield:** 6 servings.

Curried Shrimp and Apples

Prep/Total Time: 30 min.

Lynda Mack, Neptune Beach, Florida

Seasoned with curry, the apples and shrimp blend wonderfully in this distinctive main course. When I want a change of pace, I make it with chicken instead of shrimp.

 This recipe includes Nutrition Facts & Diabetic Exchanges.

    1 medium onion, chopped
    2 celery ribs, chopped
  1/4 cup butter, cubed
    2 medium apples, sliced
    2 teaspoons all-purpose flour
  3/4 teaspoon curry powder
  3/4 cup water
    1 teaspoon chicken bouillon granules
  3/4 pound uncooked medium shrimp, peeled
      and deveined
Hot cooked rice

1. In a large skillet, saute onion and celery in butter for 2 minutes. Stir in apples; saute 1-2 minutes longer or until crisp-tender.

2. Sprinkle with the flour and curry powder. Gradually whisk in water and bouillon until smooth. Add shrimp; bring to a boil. Reduce heat; simmer for 2-3 minutes or until shrimp turn pink and sauce is thickened. Serve with rice. **Yield:** 4 servings.

Nutrition Facts: 1 cup (prepared with reduced-fat butter; calculated without rice) equals 181 calories, 7 g fat (4 g saturated fat), 146 mg cholesterol, 311 mg sodium, 16 g carbohydrate, 3 g fiber, 16 g protein. **Diabetic Exchanges:** 2 lean meat, 1 vegetable, 1 fruit.

Phyllo-Wrapped Halibut

Prep: 20 min. **Bake:** 20 min.

Carrie Vazzano, Rolling Meadows, Illinois

I came up with this simple fish for my husband. He likes both the phyllo wrapping and the vegetables hidden inside of it. It's great for weeknights and company alike.

 This recipe includes Nutrition Facts.

  4 **cups fresh baby spinach**
3/4 **cup chopped sweet red pepper**
3/4 **teaspoon salt-free lemon-pepper seasoning, divided**
1/2 **teaspoon lemon juice**
  6 **sheets phyllo dough (14 inches x 9 inches)**
  2 **tablespoons reduced-fat butter, melted**
  2 **halibut fillets (4 ounces each)**
1/4 **teaspoon salt**
1/8 **teaspoon pepper**
1/4 **cup shredded part-skim mozzarella cheese**

1. In a large nonstick skillet lightly coated with cooking spray, saute the spinach and red pepper until tender. Add 1/2 teaspoon lemon-pepper and lemon juice. Remove from the heat; cool.

2. Line a baking sheet with foil and coat the foil with cooking spray; set aside. Place one sheet of phyllo dough on a work surface; brush with butter. (Until ready to use, keep phyllo dough covered with plastic wrap and a damp towel to prevent it from drying out.) Layer remaining phyllo over first sheet, brushing each with butter. Cut stack in half widthwise.

3. Place a halibut fillet in the center of each square; sprinkle with salt and pepper. Top with cheese and spinach mixture. Fold sides and bottom edge over fillet and roll up to enclose it; trim end of phyllo if necessary. Brush with remaining butter; sprinkle with remaining lemon-pepper.

4. Place the seam side down on the prepared baking sheet. Bake at 375° for 20-25 minutes or until golden brown. **Yield:** 2 servings.

Editor's Note: This recipe was tested with Land O'Lakes light stick butter.

Nutrition Facts: 1 serving equals 330 calories, 12 g fat (6 g saturated fat), 64 mg cholesterol, 676 mg sodium, 26 g carbohydrate, 4 g fiber, 33 g protein.

Tofu Manicotti

Prep: 25 min. **Bake:** 50 min.

Carolyn Diana, Scottsdale, Arizona

To create an Italian dish that's a little lighter, I borrowed bits and pieces from different recipes, including my mom's lasagna. No one suspects that the creamy, cheesy filling includes tofu. It's easy to prepare, and my kids love it.

 This recipe includes Nutrition Facts & Diabetic Exchanges.

- 2 cups meatless spaghetti sauce
- 1 can (14-1/2 ounces) diced tomatoes, undrained
- 1/3 cup finely shredded zucchini
- 1/4 cup finely shredded carrot
- 1/2 teaspoon Italian seasoning
- 1 package (12.3 ounces) silken firm tofu
- 1 cup (8 ounces) 1% cottage cheese
- 1 cup (4 ounces) shredded part-skim mozzarella cheese
- 1 tablespoon grated Parmesan cheese
- 10 uncooked manicotti shells

1. Combine the spaghetti sauce, tomatoes, zucchini, carrot and Italian seasoning; spread 3/4 cup into a 13-in. x 9-in. baking dish coated with cooking spray.

2. Combine the tofu and cheeses; stuff into uncooked manicotti shells. Place over spaghetti sauce; top with remaining sauce.

3. Cover and bake at 375° for 50-55 minutes or until the noodles are tender. Let stand for 5 minutes before serving. **Yield:** 5 servings.

Nutrition Facts: 2 stuffed manicotti shells equals 319 calories, 7 g fat (3 g saturated fat), 16 mg cholesterol, 885 mg sodium, 42 g carbohydrate, 4 g fiber, 23 g protein. **Diabetic Exchanges:** 3 starch, 2 lean meat.

Creamy Ham 'n' Macaroni

Prep: 20 min. **Bake:** 20 min.

Christy Looper, Colorado Springs, Colorado

Here, traditional macaroni and cheese gets a hearty makeover with the addition of cubed ham and grated Parmesan.

- 2 cups uncooked elbow macaroni
- 1/4 cup butter, cubed
- 1/4 cup all-purpose flour
- 2 cups milk
- 4 teaspoons chicken bouillon granules
- 1/4 teaspoon pepper
- 2 cups (8 ounces) shredded cheddar cheese, *divided*
- 1-1/2 cups cubed fully cooked ham
- 1/4 cup grated Parmesan cheese

1. Cook macaroni according to package directions; drain and set aside. In a large saucepan, melt butter over low heat; whisk in flour until smooth. Whisk in milk, bouillon and pepper. Bring to a boil; cook and stir for 2 minutes or until thickened. Remove from the heat. Stir in 1 cup cheddar cheese, ham, Parmesan cheese and macaroni.

2. Transfer to a greased 2-qt. baking dish. Sprinkle with remaining cheddar cheese. Bake, uncovered, at 350° for 20-25 minutes or until bubbly. Let stand for 5 minutes before serving. **Yield:** 6 servings.

Bacon Shrimp Creole

Prep: 25 min. Cook: 45 min.

Jan Tucker, Virginia Beach, Virginia

This flavor-packed dish is a combination of two Creole recipes I found in my mother's New Orleans cookbooks. The bacon adds heartiness, and the cayenne brings a spicy kick.

 This recipe includes Nutrition Facts & Diabetic Exchanges.

3/4 cup chopped onion
2 celery ribs, chopped
1/2 cup chopped green pepper
2 tablespoons olive oil
3 garlic cloves, minced

1 can (14-1/2 ounces) diced tomatoes, undrained
1 can (8 ounces) tomato sauce
3/4 cup cold water, *divided*
1/4 cup crumbled cooked bacon
1 tablespoon dried parsley flakes
1 teaspoon sugar
1/2 teaspoon salt
1/2 teaspoon dried thyme
1/2 teaspoon curry powder
1/2 teaspoon pepper
1/4 teaspoon cayenne pepper
1 tablespoon all-purpose flour
1-1/2 pounds uncooked medium shrimp, peeled and deveined
3 cups hot cooked long grain rice

1. In a Dutch oven, saute the onion, celery and green pepper in oil until tender. Add garlic; saute 1 minute longer. Add the tomatoes, tomato sauce, 1/2 cup water, bacon, parsley, sugar, salt, thyme, curry powder, pepper and cayenne. Bring to a boil. Reduce heat; cover and simmer for 30 minutes.

2. Combine the flour and remaining water until smooth; gradually stir into the mixture. Bring to a boil; cook and stir for 1-2 minutes or until thickened. Reduce the heat; add the shrimp. Simmer, uncovered, for 5 minutes or until shrimp turn pink. Serve with the rice. **Yield:** 6 servings.

Nutrition Facts: 3/4 cup shrimp creole with 1/2 cup rice equals 292 calories, 7 g fat (1 g saturated fat), 171 mg cholesterol, 814 mg sodium, 33 g carbohydrate, 3 g fiber, 24 g protein. **Diabetic Exchanges:** 3 very lean meat, 2 vegetable, 1-1/2 starch, 1 fat.

Country-Style Pork Medallions

Prep: 20 min. Cook: 20 min.

2 pork tenderloins (1 pound *each*)
6 tablespoons butter, *divided*
2 small onions, sliced and separated into rings
3/4 pound small fresh mushrooms
2 small apples, cored and cut into rings
APPLE CREAM SAUCE:
1 cup apple cider *or* juice
1 package (8 ounces) cream cheese, cubed
1/4 cup apple brandy *or* additional apple cider
1 teaspoon dried basil

1. Cut pork into 1/2-in. slices; flatten to 1/4-in. thickness. In a large skillet over medium-high heat,

cook pork in batches in 3 tablespoons butter until juices run clear. Remove to a serving platter and keep warm.

2. In same skillet, saute the onions and mushrooms in the remaining butter for 4 minutes or until crisp-tender. Add the apples; saute for 3-4 minutes or until vegetables and apples are tender. Arrange over pork.

3. Add cider and cream cheese to the skillet; cook and stir over medium heat for 3 minutes or until cheese is melted and sauce is smooth. Stir in brandy and basil; heat through. Serve with the pork and vegetables. **Yield:** 6 servings.

PAMELA JESSEN CALGARY, ALBERTA

Be prepared to hear rave reviews when you pass around this impressive pork entree featuring fresh mushrooms, apples, onions and a creamy sauce served on the side. I think leftovers would be fantastic in sandwiches, but I've never had any I could try!

GRAND PRIZE WINNER

Sausage Noodle Supper

Prep/Total Time: 25 min.

Mary Jo Miller, Mansfield, Ohio

I can't recall how I came up with this hearty main dish, but it's now one of my menu staples. Using a convenient coleslaw mix and packaged noodles with a flavorful sauce, I can easily get this on the table in less than half an hour. Slices of cheesy garlic toast are great on the side.

- 1 cup thinly sliced fresh carrots
- 3 tablespoons butter
- 1/2 pound smoked sausage, thinly sliced
- 3/4 cup green thinly sliced onions
- 4 cups coleslaw mix
- 2-1/4 cups water
- 1 package (4.9 ounces) quick-cooking noodles and sour cream and chive sauce mix

1. In a large skillet, cook the carrots in the butter for 2 minutes. Add sausage and onions; cook for 2 minutes. Stir in coleslaw mix; cook 1-2 minutes longer. Add water; bring to a boil.

2. Stir in the noodles and sauce mix. Return to a boil; cook and stir for 7-9 minutes or until the noodles are tender, stirring occasionally. Let stand for 2-3 minutes before serving. **Yield:** 3-4 servings.

Spicy Salmon Kabobs

Prep: 15 min. + marinating Grill: 10 min.

Terri Mach, Homer, Alaska

I first made these for a team of archaeologists excavating a site in the Aleutian Islands. We used fresh sockeye salmon, but other varieties of salmon also work well.

- 1-1/2 pounds salmon fillets, cut into 1-1/2-inch cubes
- 1 tablespoon brown sugar
- 1 teaspoon salt
- 1 teaspoon garlic powder
- 1 teaspoon celery seed
- 1 teaspoon pepper
- 1 teaspoon paprika
- 1/2 teaspoon onion powder
- 1/2 teaspoon cayenne pepper
- 1/4 teaspoon chili powder
- 1/8 teaspoon fennel seed, crushed
- 1/8 teaspoon ground cumin

1. Place the salmon in a large resealable plastic bag. Combine the remaining ingredients; sprinkle over the salmon. Seal the bag and toss to coat; refrigerate for 30 minutes.

2. Thread salmon onto six metal or soaked wooden skewers. Grill, covered, over medium heat or broil 4 in. from the heat for 4-6 minutes on each side or until fish flakes easily with a fork. **Yield:** 6 servings.

Sunday Pork Chops

Prep/Total Time: 25 min.

Trisha Kruse, Eagle, Idaho

I love this recipe because it tastes like a real "Sunday" supper, but I don't have to spend my whole Sunday fixing it! Instead, I can go biking, work in my garden or do some other activity all day, then wind up the weekend by serving my family a home-cooked, sit-down dinner in 25 minutes.

- 1 tablespoon brown sugar
- 1/4 teaspoon garlic powder
- 4 bone-in pork loin chops (1 inch thick and 6 ounces *each*)
- 1 tablespoon olive oil
- 1 can (11 ounces) Mexicorn, undrained
- 1-1/3 cups reduced-sodium chicken broth
- 1 package (6 ounces) corn bread stuffing mix
- 2 tablespoons butter

1. Combine the brown sugar and garlic powder; rub over both sides of the pork chops. In a large skillet, brown pork chops in oil over medium heat. Remove from the pan.

2. In the same skillet, combine the Mexicorn, broth, stuffing mix and butter; top with pork chops. Cover and cook for 10-12 minutes or until a meat thermometer reads 160°. **Yield:** 4 servings.

About Olive Oil

Store olive oil tightly capped at room temperature or in the refrigerator for up to 1 year. When chilled, the oil turns cloudy and thick but will return to its original consistency when left at room temperature for a short time.

Cran-Orange Pork Medallions

Prep/Total Time: 30 min.

Julie Wesson, Wilton, Wisconsin

Talk about versatile! This is a longtime favorite in our house just as it is, but I occasionally give the pork a twist with some jalapeno peppers and fresh ginger. I've also prepared it using peach preserves and dried cherries in place of the cranberries.

- 1 pork tenderloin (1 pound), cut into 1-inch slices
- 1/2 teaspoon salt
- 1/2 teaspoon garlic powder
- 1/2 teaspoon ground coriander
- 1/4 teaspoon pepper
- 2 tablespoons olive oil
- 1 medium red onion, chopped
- 1/2 cup orange marmalade
- 1/4 cup orange juice
- 1/4 cup dried cranberries
- 2 tablespoons balsamic vinegar

1. Flatten pork slices to 1/4-in. thickness. Combine the salt, garlic powder, coriander and pepper; sprinkle over both sides of pork.

2. In a large skillet, saute the pork in oil for 3 minutes on each side or until no longer pink. Remove and keep warm.

3. In same skillet, saute the onion in pan juices for 5 minutes or until tender. Stir in marmalade, orange juice, berries and vinegar. Bring to a boil. Reduce heat; return pork to skillet. Simmer, uncovered, for 5 minutes or until sauce is thickened. **Yield:** 4 servings.

Chipotle-Teriyaki Pork Chops

Prep: 25 min. **Grill:** 15 min.

Kathleen Boulanger, Williston, Vermont

These deliciously different pork chops have both Southwestern and Asian character. They're sprinkled with queso fresco (also called queso blanco)—a white, fresh Mexican cheese available in Latin supermarkets and larger grocery stores. If you can't find it, simply substitute Monterey Jack.

1/4 cup lime juice
1/4 cup orange juice
  2 tablespoons soy sauce
  2 tablespoons grated onion
  1 tablespoon teriyaki sauce
  1 chipotle pepper in adobo sauce, drained
  1 garlic clove, peeled
1/8 teaspoon ground ginger
  2 tablespoons ground ancho pepper
  2 tablespoons olive oil
  1 teaspoon salt
1/2 teaspoon dried oregano
1/2 teaspoon coarsely ground pepper
1/4 teaspoon ground cumin
  4 boneless pork loin chops (8 ounces *each*)
1/2 cup queso fresco *or* shredded Monterey Jack cheese

1. For sauce, combine the first eight ingredients in a blender; cover and process until smooth. Transfer to a small bowl; set aside. Combine the ancho pepper, oil, salt, oregano, pepper and cumin; gently rub over both sides of pork chops.

2. Grill the chops, covered, over medium-hot heat for 5-7 minutes on each side or until a meat thermometer reads 160°, basting occasionally with 1/3 cup of the sauce. Sprinkle with queso fresco; grill 2-3 minutes longer or until cheese is softened. Serve with remaining sauce. **Yield:** 4 servings.

Asian Vegetable Pasta

Prep/Total Time: 20 min.

Mitzi Sentiff, Annapolis, Maryland

Peanut butter and chopped peanuts give this Far-East entree plenty of flavor. Red pepper flakes bring a bit of a kick, but brown sugar balances it out with a hint of sweetness.

  4 quarts water
  8 ounces uncooked angel hair pasta
  1 pound fresh asparagus, trimmed and cut into 1-inch pieces
3/4 cup julienned carrots
1/3 cup reduced-fat creamy peanut butter
  3 tablespoons rice vinegar
  3 tablespoons reduced-sodium soy sauce
  2 tablespoons brown sugar
1/2 teaspoon crushed red pepper flakes
1/4 cup unsalted peanuts, chopped

1. In a Dutch oven, bring the water to a boil. Add the pasta and asparagus; cook for 3 minutes. Stir in the carrots; cook for 1 minute or until the pasta is tender. Drain and keep warm.

2. In a small saucepan, combine the peanut butter, vinegar, soy sauce, brown sugar and pepper flakes. Bring to a boil over medium heat, stirring constantly. Pour over pasta mixture; toss to coat. Sprinkle with peanuts. **Yield:** 5 servings.

Pear 'n' Prosciutto Pork Loin

Prep: 50 min. **Bake:** 1-1/2 hours + standing

Anthony Guaetta, Peabody, Massachusetts

This distinctive pork is outstanding served on a bed of mesclun with fresh goat cheese and roasted veggies. Prepare the stuffing with thin deli ham if you don't have prosciutto.

 1 bottle (750 milliliters) sweet white wine
 2 cups water
 2 cups sugar
 2 tablespoons ground ginger
 2 cinnamon sticks (3 inches)
 3 whole cloves
 4 medium Bosc pears, peeled and quartered
 1 boneless whole pork loin roast (3 to 4 pounds)
 3/4 teaspoon salt, *divided*
 1/2 teaspoon pepper, *divided*
 8 thin slices prosciutto (about 4 ounces)
 1/4 cup butter, cubed

1. In a large saucepan, combine the white wine, water, sugar, ginger, cinnamon sticks and cloves; bring to a boil. Reduce heat; simmer, uncovered, for 10 minutes.

Add the pears; cover and simmer for 15-20 minutes or until tender.

2. Using a slotted spoon, carefully remove pears and cool to room temperature. Continue to simmer the poaching liquid, uncovered, for 15-25 minutes or until reduced to 2 cups. Remove and discard the cinnamon sticks and cloves. Cover and refrigerate liquid.

3. Cut a lengthwise slit down center of roast to within 1/2 in. of bottom. Open roast so it lies flat; cover with plastic wrap. Flatten to 3/4-in. thickness. Remove plastic; sprinkle meat with 1/2 teaspoon salt and 1/4 teaspoon pepper. Top with prosciutto and pears. Roll up jelly-roll style, starting with a long side; tie several times with kitchen string.

4. Place roast in a shallow roasting pan lined with heavy-duty foil. Bake, uncovered, at 350° for 1-1/2 to 2 hours or until a meat thermometer reads 160°. Cover and let stand 10-15 minutes before slicing.

5. Pour poaching liquid into a small saucepan. Add the remaining salt and pepper. Bring to a boil. Reduce heat; simmer, uncovered, for 5 minutes. Stir in butter until melted. Serve with meat. **Yield:** 12 servings.

Minted Lamb 'n' Veggie Kabobs

Prep: 30 min. + marinating **Grill:** 10 min.

Michael Rose, Grand Prairie, Texas

Mint leaves give these mouthwatering grilled skewers a burst of refreshing flavor and a delightful aroma. Served with brown rice, the colorful kabobs featuring lamb and a variety of veggies look and taste special enough for company.

- 3 tablespoons olive oil
- 2 tablespoons lemon juice
- 4 garlic cloves, minced
- 2 teaspoons dried basil
- 1 teaspoon dried oregano
- 1 teaspoon pepper
- 1/2 teaspoon salt
- 1/2 teaspoon dried thyme
- 1 pound boneless leg of lamb, cut into 1-inch cubes
- 1 medium sweet red pepper, cut into 1-inch pieces
- 1 medium sweet yellow pepper, cut into 1-inch pieces
- 1 medium zucchini, cut into 1/4-inch slices
- 1 small red onion, cut into chunks
- 16 medium fresh mushrooms
- 1 cup fresh mint leaves

Hot cooked brown rice

1. In a large resealable plastic bag, combine the oil, lemon juice, garlic, basil, oregano, pepper, salt and thyme; add lamb. Seal bag and turn to coat; refrigerate for 30 minutes.

2. On eight metal skewers or soaked wooden skewers, alternately thread the lamb and vegetables with the mint leaves.

3. Grill, covered, over medium heat or broil 4 in. from the heat for 4-5 minutes on each side or until the meat reaches the desired doneness and the vegetables are tender. Serve with rice. **Yield:** 4 servings.

Pronto Pan

Plan to make delicious Spice-Rubbed Ribs on the grill for your next backyard barbecue or other get-together? You can quickly and easily make a drip pan for the grill by shaping heavy-duty aluminum foil into a small pan.

Spice-Rubbed Ribs

Prep: 10 min. **Grill:** 1 hour

Cheryl Ewing, Ellwood City, Pennsylvania

When it comes to grilling, here's the rub I always recommend. Cayenne, oregano, thyme and more create a wonderful blend. Have some left after making ribs? Put it in a shaker and use it another day on roasts, tenderloins or steaks.

- 3 tablespoons paprika
- 2 tablespoons plus 1 teaspoon salt
- 2 tablespoons plus 1 teaspoon garlic powder
- 2 tablespoons cayenne pepper
- 4 teaspoons onion powder
- 4 teaspoons dried oregano
- 4 teaspoons dried thyme
- 4 teaspoons pepper
- 10 pounds pork baby back ribs

1. In a small bowl, combine the seasonings; rub over the ribs.

2. Prepare the grill for indirect heat, using a drip pan. Grill the ribs, covered, over indirect medium heat for 1 hour or until juices run clear and meat is tender, turning occasionally. **Yield:** 10 servings.

Shrimp-Stuffed Sole

Prep/Total Time: 15 min.

Robert Bishop, Lexington, Kentucky

If you like stuffed fish but don't have lots of time to spend in the kitchen, this recipe is the way to go! It's a snap to assemble and cooks in just a few minutes in the microwave. When you want a change of pace, try replacing the sole with chicken.

 This recipe includes Nutrition Facts & Diabetic Exchanges.

> 4 sole fillets, halved lengthwise
> 1 tablespoon lemon juice
> 1/8 teaspoon onion salt *or* onion powder
> 1/4 cup butter, melted, *divided*
> 1 can (6 ounces) small shrimp, rinsed and drained
> 1/3 cup milk
> 1/4 cup finely chopped celery
> 2 teaspoons minced fresh parsley
> 1 cup cubed bread, toasted

Dash paprika

1. Sprinkle fillets with lemon juice and onion salt; set aside. Pour 2 tablespoons butter into an 8-in. square microwave-safe dish. Add the shrimp, milk, celery and parsley. Cover and microwave on high for 1 to 1-1/2 minutes or until celery is tender. Stir in bread cubes.

2. Spoon shrimp mixture onto fillets. Starting with a short side, roll up each and secure with toothpicks.

Place in a greased shallow microwave-safe dish. Brush with remaining butter; sprinkle with paprika.

3. Cover and microwave on high for 4-6 minutes or until the fish flakes easily with a fork. Let fish stand for 5 minutes before serving. Discard the toothpicks. **Yield:** 4 servings.

Editor's Note: This recipe was tested in a 1,100-watt microwave.

Nutrition Facts: 1 serving (prepared with onion powder, reduced-fat butter and fat-free milk) equals 266 calories, 8 g fat (5 g saturated fat), 188 mg cholesterol, 769 mg sodium, 6 g carbohydrate, trace fiber, 41 g protein. **Diabetic Exchanges:** 5 very lean meat, 1-1/2 fat, 1 vegetable.

Spaghetti with Checca Sauce

Prep/Total Time: 20 min.

Angela Strother, New Port Richey, Florida

This cheesy dish is a great meatless choice. If you prefer saucier pasta, add some of the water from cooking the spaghetti.

> 4 ounces uncooked spaghetti
> 2 tablespoons olive oil
> 2 small tomatoes, quartered
> 3/4 cup shredded Parmesan cheese
> 5 fresh basil leaves
> 2 green onions, chopped
> 2 garlic cloves, minced

Dash salt and pepper

> 2 ounces fresh mozzarella cheese, cut into 1/2-inch cubes
> 1/4 cup hot water

1. Cook spaghetti according to package directions. Meanwhile, in a blender, combine the oil, tomatoes, Parmesan cheese, basil, onions, garlic, salt and pepper; cover and process until coarsely chopped.

2. Drain the spaghetti and place in a bowl. Add the tomato mixture, mozzarella cheese and water; toss to coat. **Yield:** 2 servings.

1 egg, lightly beaten
1 cup milk
2 medium onions, chopped
1 medium green pepper, chopped
1 cup soft bread crumbs
1-1/2 pounds ground fully cooked ham
1 pound bulk pork sausage
1 can (14 ounces) whole-berry cranberry sauce
1/4 cup water
1 tablespoon light corn syrup

Cranberry Ham Loaf

Prep: 20 min. **Bake:** 70 min.

Ronald Heffner, Pawleys Island, South Carolina

With a tangy cranberry-sauce topping, this easy-to-fix loaf is festive enough to serve on special occasions. I've found it's also a great way to use up leftover ham.

1. In a large bowl, combine egg, milk, onions, green pepper and bread crumbs. Crumble ham and sausage over mixture and mix well.

2. Pat into an ungreased 9-in. x 5-in. loaf pan (pan will be full). Place on a baking sheet. Bake, uncovered, at 350° for 70-80 minutes or until a meat thermometer reads 160°.

3. In a small saucepan, combine the cranberry sauce, water and corn syrup. Bring to a boil. Reduce heat; simmer, uncovered, for 5 minutes or until thickened. Remove the ham loaf to a serving platter; serve with cranberry sauce. **Yield:** 8 servings.

Stuffed Ham with Raisin Sauce

Prep: 30 min. **Bake:** 1-3/4 hours

1 boneless fully cooked ham (6 to 7 pounds)
1 large onion, chopped
1/4 cup butter, cubed
2 cups corn bread stuffing mix
1-1/2 cups chopped pecans, toasted
1/2 cup minced fresh parsley
1/4 cup egg substitute
2 tablespoons prepared mustard
1/2 cup honey
2 tablespoons orange juice concentrate
RAISIN SAUCE:
1/2 cup packed brown sugar
2 tablespoons all-purpose flour
1/2 teaspoon ground mustard
1/2 cup raisins
1-1/2 cups water
1/4 cup cider vinegar

1. Using a sharp thin-bladed knife and beginning at one end of ham, carefully cut a 2-1/2-in. circle about 6 in. deep; remove cutout. Cut a 1-1/2-in. slice from the end of removed piece; set aside.

2. Continue cutting a 2-1/2-in. tunnel halfway through ham, using a spoon to remove pieces of ham (save for another use). Repeat from opposite end of ham, cutting and removing ham until a tunnel has been cut through entire length of ham.

3. In a small skillet, saute the onion in butter until tender. In a large bowl, combine the stuffing mix, pecans, parsley, egg substitute and mustard. Stir in onion. Stuff ham; cover end openings with reserved ham slices. Place in a shallow roasting pan.

4. Bake, uncovered, at 325° for 1-1/4 hours. In a small saucepan, combine honey and orange juice concentrate; cook and stir for 1-2 minutes or until blended. Brush over ham. Bake 30 minutes longer or until a meat thermometer reads 140°.

5. For the sauce, combine the brown sugar, flour, mustard and raisins in a saucepan. Gradually add the water and cider vinegar. Bring to a boil; cook and stir for 1-2 minutes or until thickened. Serve with ham. **Yield:** 12-14 servings.

Editor's Note: Two fully cooked boneless ham halves can be substituted for the whole ham. Simply hollow out each ham; loosely spoon stuffing into each half, then bake as directed.

JEANNE MILLER BIG SKY, MONTANA

This fancy main course makes a memorable centerpiece for a holiday dinner, but I've prepared it most often for brunch. No matter when it's on the table, it draws raves.

GRAND
PRIZE
WINNER

Spiral Ham with Cranberry Glaze

Prep: 15 min. **Bake:** 3 hours

Patricia Prescott, Manchester, New Hampshire

The sweet, tangy glaze that complements this ham looks so pretty, and the cranberry flavor pairs well with the meat. It's been a tradition in my home for as long as I can remember.

- 1 bone-in fully cooked spiral-sliced ham (8 pounds)
- 1 can (14 ounces) whole-berry cranberry sauce
- 1 package (12 ounces) fresh or frozen cranberries
- 1 jar (12 ounces) red currant jelly
- 1 cup light corn syrup
- 1/2 teaspoon ground ginger

1. Place the ham on a rack in a shallow roasting pan. Cover and bake at 325° for 2-1/2 hours.

2. Meanwhile, for the glaze, combine the remaining ingredients in a saucepan. Bring to a boil. Reduce the heat; simmer, uncovered, until cranberries pop, stirring occasionally. Remove from the heat; set aside.

3. Uncover the ham; bake 30 minutes longer or until a meat thermometer reads 140°, basting twice with 1-1/2 cups glaze. Serve remaining glaze with ham. **Yield:** 12-16 servings.

Golden Sea Bass

Prep/Total Time: 25 min.

Judi Markert, Mentor-on-the-Lake, Ohio

If you've ever had potato-crusted sea bass in a restaurant and wished you could have it at home, try this version. Store-bought mashed potato flakes and an Italian salad dressing mix create a great coating that's a breeze to whip up.

 This recipe includes Nutrition Facts & Diabetic Exchanges.

- 1 cup mashed potato flakes
- 1 envelope Italian salad dressing mix
- 1/4 teaspoon pepper
- 1 egg
- 2 pounds sea bass fillets or halibut steaks
- 2 tablespoons butter, melted

Paprika

1. In a shallow bowl, combine the mashed potato flakes, dressing mix and pepper. In another bowl, beat the egg. Dip the fillets into egg, then coat with potato flake mixture.

2. Place in a single layer in a 15-in. x 10-in. x 1-in. baking pan coated with cooking spray. Drizzle with butter; sprinkle with paprika.

3. Bake, uncovered, at 450° for 10-14 minutes or until fish flakes easily with a fork. **Yield:** 8 servings.

Nutrition Facts: 3 ounces cooked fish equals 180 calories, 6 g fat (3 g saturated fat), 81 mg cholesterol, 451 mg sodium, 8 g carbohydrate, trace fiber, 22 g protein. **Diabetic Exchanges:** 3 very lean meat, 1 fat, 1/2 starch.

Pork Fajita Kabobs

Prep/Total Time: 30 min.

Bea Westphal, Slidell, Louisiana

Here's my favorite way to eat pork loin. The grilled meat and veggies, seasoned with a homemade Southwestern-style spice blend, are appropriately served in a flour tortilla. Just top it all off with some chunky salsa and enjoy!

      2 teaspoons paprika
1-1/2 teaspoons ground cumin
1-1/2 teaspoons dried oregano
      1 teaspoon garlic powder
  1/8 to 1/4 teaspoon crushed red pepper flakes
1-1/2 pounds boneless pork loin chops, cut into
      1-inch cubes
      1 small green pepper, cut into 1-inch pieces
      1 small onion, cut into eight wedges
      8 large fresh mushrooms
     16 grape tomatoes
      8 flour tortillas (8 inches), warmed
  3/4 cup chunky salsa

1. In a large resealable plastic bag, combine paprika, cumin, oregano, garlic powder and pepper flakes; add pork. Seal the bag and toss to coat. On eight metal or soaked wooden skewers, alternately thread the pork, green pepper, onion, mushrooms and tomatoes.

2. Grill the kabobs, covered, over medium heat or broil 4 in. from the heat for 5-8 minutes on each side or until the meat is no longer pink and the vegetables are tender. Place each kabob in a tortilla; remove the skewers and fold the tortillas in half. Serve with salsa. **Yield:** 4 servings.

Shrimp with Style

Prep/Total Time: 25 min.

Cyndi McLaughlin, Pinon Pines, California

I came up with this seafood supper one day using just the food I happened to have in the refrigerator. The sun-dried tomatoes, feta cheese and almonds really complemented the shrimp, and now my family requests this all the time.

      1 package (9 ounces) refrigerated angel hair
        pasta
  1/2 pound sliced fresh mushrooms
      1 cup butter, cubed
1-1/2 teaspoons minced garlic
      1 pound uncooked medium shrimp, peeled and
        deveined
      2 packages (3 ounces *each*) julienned sun-dried
        tomatoes (not packed in oil)
      1 package (2-1/4 ounces) slivered almonds,
        toasted
  1/2 cup crumbled feta cheese
  1/2 cup minced fresh parsley
      3 tablespoons white wine *or* chicken broth
      2 teaspoons lemon juice
  1/2 teaspoon salt
  1/2 teaspoon pepper
  1/2 cup shredded Parmesan cheese

1. Cook the pasta according to the package directions. Meanwhile, in a large skillet, saute the mushrooms in butter for 2 minutes. Add garlic; cook 1 minute longer. Add the shrimp; cook and stir for 5-7 minutes or until shrimp turn pink.

2. Stir in the tomatoes, almonds, feta cheese, parsley, white wine, lemon juice, salt and pepper; cook for 3-5 minutes or until heated through.

3. Drain pasta and place in a serving bowl; top with shrimp mixture and cheese. **Yield:** 5 servings.

1 medium onion, chopped
1/4 cup minced fresh parsley
1-1/2 teaspoons minced fresh basil *or* 1/2 teaspoon dried basil
1-1/2 teaspoons minced fresh oregano *or* 1/2 teaspoon dried oregano
1/4 cup olive oil
3 tablespoons butter
2 garlic cloves, minced
1 can (14-1/2 ounces) chicken broth
1 tablespoon lemon juice
1/2 cup shredded Parmesan cheese

1. Cook the penne pasta according to the package directions. Meanwhile, in a large skillet, saute the ham, red pepper, onion, parsley, basil and oregano in oil and butter for 4-6 minutes or until the ham is browned and the vegetables are tender. Add the garlic; cook 1 minute longer.

2. Stir in the broth and lemon juice. Bring to a boil. Reduce heat; simmer, uncovered, for 10-15 minutes or until liquid is reduced by half. Drain pasta; stir into ham mixture. Sprinkle with cheese. **Yield:** 6 servings.

Pretty Penne Ham Skillet

Prep/Total Time: 30 min.

Kathy Stephan, West Seneca, New York

I enjoy experimenting with herbs and spices in my cooking as a way of cutting down on salt and sugar. Fresh parsley, basil and oregano season this tasty main dish.

1 package (16 ounces) penne pasta
3 cups cubed fully cooked ham
1 large sweet red pepper, diced

Pasta Perfection

To cook pasta more evenly, prevent it from sticking together and avoid boil-overs, always cook pasta in a large kettle or Dutch oven. Unless you have a very large kettle, don't cook more than 2 pounds of pasta at a time.

Sausage Spinach Bake

Prep: 20 min. **Bake:** 35 min.

1 package (6 ounces) savory herb-flavored stuffing mix
1/2 pound bulk pork sausage
1/4 cup chopped green onions
1/2 teaspoon minced garlic
1 package (10 ounces) frozen chopped spinach, thawed and squeezed dry
1-1/2 cups (6 ounces) shredded Monterey Jack cheese
1-1/2 cups half-and-half cream
3 eggs
2 tablespoons grated Parmesan cheese

1. Prepare the stuffing according to the package directions. Meanwhile, crumble sausage into a large skillet; add onions; cook over medium heat until meat is no longer pink. Add garlic; cook 1 minute longer. Drain.

2. In a large bowl, combine the stuffing, sausage mixture and spinach. Transfer to a greased 13-in. x 9-in. baking dish; sprinkle with the Monterey Jack cheese. In a small bowl, combine cream and eggs; pour over sausage mixture.

3. Bake casserole at 400° for 30 minutes or until a thermometer reads 160°. Sprinkle with Parmesan cheese; bake 5 minutes longer or until bubbly. **Yield:** 12 servings.

KATHLEEN GRANT SWAN LAKE, MONTANA

A friend gave me the recipe for this creamy and cheesy casserole, which takes advantage of a packaged stuffing mix and frozen spinach. The hearty bake is great all by itself for dinner… and can even make a great contribution to a brunch buffet.

GRAND
PRIZE
WINNER

Salmon with Sweet Salsa

Prep/Total Time: 15 min.

Rebecca Reece, Henderson, Nevada

I didn't eat salmon for years...then I tasted it one night at a formal dinner, where it was served with a sweet topping that I really liked. After experimenting in my own kitchen, I came up with this sweet-spicy combo that has just five ingredients. It's great with a side of fried rice.

    4 salmon fillets (6 ounces *each*)
    4 teaspoons Creole seasoning
    2 tablespoons olive oil
 3/4 cup salsa
 1/2 cup apricot preserves

1. Sprinkle one side of the salmon fillets with Creole seasoning. In a large skillet, cook salmon, seasoned side down, in oil over medium-high heat for 2 minutes. Turn salmon; reduce heat to medium and cook 8-10 minutes longer or until fish flakes easily with a fork.

2. Meanwhile, in a small bowl, combine salsa and preserves. Serve with salmon. **Yield:** 4 servings.

Editor's Note: The following spices may be substituted for 1 teaspoon Creole seasoning: 1/4 teaspoon each salt, garlic powder and paprika; and a pinch each of dried thyme, ground cumin and cayenne pepper.

Pork Tenderloin with Mango Relish

Prep: 15 min. Bake: 45 min.

Gloria Bradley, Naperville, Illinois

Colorful mango relish is a refreshing counterpoint to the heat in the meat rub that peps up this roasted pork tenderloin. It turns out juicy and delicious every time.

 1-1/2 teaspoons ground coriander
     1 teaspoon ground cumin
   1/2 teaspoon salt
   1/2 teaspoon sugar
   1/2 teaspoon ground chipotle pepper
   1/2 teaspoon smoked Spanish paprika
     2 pork tenderloins (3/4 pound *each*)
MANGO RELISH:
     1 medium mango, peeled and chopped
     2 plum tomatoes, seeded and chopped
   1/3 cup chopped onion
   1/3 cup chopped seeded peeled cucumber
   1/4 cup minced fresh cilantro
     1 jalapeno pepper, seeded and chopped
     3 tablespoons lime juice

1. In a small bowl, combine the first six ingredients. Set aside 1/2 teaspoon for relish; rub remaining spice mixture over tenderloins. Place in a lightly greased 13-in. x 9-in. baking pan. Bake, uncovered, at 350° for 45-50 minutes or until a meat thermometer reads 160°. Let stand for 5 minutes.

2. Meanwhile, in a small bowl, combine the mango, tomatoes, onion, cucumber, cilantro and jalapeno. Combine lime juice and reserved spice mixture; add to mango mixture and toss to coat. Slice pork; serve with relish. **Yield:** 6 servings.

Editor's Note: When cutting hot peppers, disposable gloves are recommended. Avoid touching your face.

Crawfish Fettuccine

Prep: 30 min. **Cook:** 30 min.

Carolyn Lejeune, Welsh, Louisiana

I've lived in this close-knit community all my life and really enjoy cooking Cajun favorites—especially those with seafood. Alongside a green salad and garlic bread, this dish is ideal for family gatherings. The recipe can easily be doubled for a larger crowd...and if you'd prefer less spice, simply remove the seeds from the jalapeno pepper before chopping it.

- 1 large onion, chopped
- 1 medium sweet red pepper, chopped
- 2/3 cup sliced green onions
- 1 celery rib, chopped
- 1-1/4 cups butter, cubed
- 1 garlic clove, minced
- 1/4 cup all-purpose flour
- 8 ounces process cheese (Velveeta), cubed
- 1 cup half-and-half cream
- 1 tablespoon chopped jalapeno pepper
- 1/2 teaspoon salt
- 8 ounces uncooked fettuccine
- 1-1/2 pounds frozen cooked crawfish tails, thawed *or* cooked medium shrimp, peeled and deveined

1. In a Dutch oven, saute the onion, red pepper, green onions and celery in butter for 5 minutes or until vegetables are crisp-tender. Add garlic; cook 1 minute longer. Stir in the flour until blended; cook and stir for 2 minutes. Add the cheese, cream, jalapeno and salt; cook and stir for 10 minutes or until the mixture is thickened and the cheese is melted.

2. Meanwhile, cook fettuccine according to package directions; drain. Stir fettuccine and crawfish into the vegetable mixture. Cook, uncovered, over medium heat for 10 minutes or until heated through, stirring occasionally. **Yield:** 8 servings.

Editor's Note: When cutting hot peppers, disposable gloves are recommended. Avoid touching your face.

Asian Pork Kabobs

Prep: 10 min. + marinating **Grill:** 10 min.

Trisha Kruse, Eagle, Idaho

These Asian-inspired skewers get a tongue-tingling kick from hot pepper sauce and make a complete meal with rice. Feel free to thread the kabobs with different vegetables.

- 1/4 cup teriyaki sauce
- 2 tablespoons balsamic vinegar
- 2 tablespoons sesame oil
- 2 tablespoons honey
- 2 teaspoons sriracha Asian hot chili sauce *or* 1 teaspoon hot pepper sauce
- 1 pound pork tenderloin, cut into 1-inch cubes
- 1 medium onion, quartered
- 1 medium sweet red pepper, cut into 2-inch pieces

1. In a small bowl, combine teriyaki sauce, balsamic vinegar, oil, honey and hot pepper sauce. Pour 1/3 cup marinade into a large resealable plastic bag; add the pork. Seal the bag and turn to coat; refrigerate for at least 2 hours. Cover and refrigerate the remaining marinade for basting.

2. Drain and discard the marinade from pork. On four metal or soaked wooden skewers, alternately thread the pork, onion and red pepper.

3. Grill the kabobs, covered, over medium heat for 10-15 minutes or until vegetables are tender and meat is no longer pink, turning occasionally and basting frequently with reserved marinade. **Yield:** 4 servings.

Zippy Raspberry Roast Pork

Prep: 20 min. **Bake:** 1-1/4 hours + standing

Kim Pettipas, Oromocto, New Brunswick

Rosemary, sage, thyme and garlic blend for the mouthwatering pork rub in this main course. The raspberry sauce gets a slight kick from chipotle peppers but complements the meat well.

 This recipe includes Nutrition Facts & Diabetic Exchanges.

- 1 boneless whole pork loin roast (3-1/2 pounds)
- 4 teaspoons olive oil, *divided*
- 1 tablespoon minced fresh rosemary *or* 1 teaspoon dried rosemary, crushed
- 1 tablespoon minced fresh sage *or* 1 teaspoon rubbed sage
- 1 tablespoon minced fresh thyme *or* 1 teaspoon dried thyme
- 4 garlic cloves, peeled
- 1 teaspoon salt
- 1/2 teaspoon pepper

SAUCE:
- 1/2 cup chopped onion
- 3 garlic cloves, minced
- 2 teaspoons olive oil
- 4 cups fresh raspberries
- 3/4 cup sugar
- 1/2 cup raspberry vinegar
- 2 teaspoons minced chipotle pepper in adobo sauce
- 1/2 teaspoon salt

1. In a large nonstick skillet, brown the roast on all sides in 3 teaspoons oil. Place on a rack in a shallow roasting pan. In a food processor, combine rosemary, sage, thyme, garlic, salt, pepper and remaining oil; cover and process until smooth. Rub over roast. Bake, uncovered, at 350° for 70 minutes.

2. Meanwhile, in a large saucepan, saute onion and garlic in oil until tender. Add the raspberries, sugar, vinegar, chipotle pepper and salt. Bring to a boil. Reduce heat; simmer, uncovered, for 10 minutes or until sauce is reduced to 2 cups. Press through a sieve; discard seeds.

3. Brush 2 tablespoons of sauce over pork. Bake 5-15 minutes longer or until a meat thermometer reads 160°. Let stand for 10 minutes before slicing. Serve with remaining sauce. **Yield:** 12 servings.

Nutrition Facts: 3 ounces cooked pork with 3-1/2 teaspoons sauce equals 262 calories, 9 g fat (3 g saturated fat), 66 mg cholesterol, 341 mg sodium, 19 g carbohydrate, 3 g fiber, 26 g protein. **Diabetic Exchanges:** 3 lean meat, 1 starch, 1/2 fat.

Herb-Crusted Pork Roast

Prep: 25 min. **Bake:** 2 hours + standing

Mary Ann Lee, Clifton Park, New York

To me, there's nothing like a pork roast that's well seasoned, pan-seared and baked to perfection. This version gets a flavor boost from a cheesy herbal crust and simple reduction sauce.

- 1 teaspoon ground mustard
- 1 teaspoon lemon-herb seasoning
- 1 teaspoon salt
- 1/2 teaspoon pepper
- 1 bone-in pork loin roast (4 pounds)
- 2 tablespoons plus 1/4 cup olive oil, *divided*
- 1 tablespoon Dijon mustard
- 1-1/2 cups soft bread crumbs
- 1/2 cup grated Parmesan cheese
- 1/4 cup minced fresh basil *or* 4 teaspoons dried basil
- 2 teaspoons minced fresh thyme
- 2 teaspoons minced fresh rosemary
- 2 garlic cloves, minced
- 1 cup white wine *or* chicken broth

1. In a small bowl, combine the ground mustard, herb seasoning, salt and pepper; rub over roast. In a large skillet, brown roast in 2 tablespoons oil. Place roast fat side up on a rack in a shallow roasting pan. Brush the top with Dijon mustard. Combine the bread crumbs, cheese, basil, thyme, rosemary, garlic and remaining oil; press onto roast.

2. Bake, uncovered, at 350° for 2 to 2-1/4 hours or until a meat thermometer reads 160°. Place roast on a warm serving platter. Let stand for 10-15 minutes before slicing.

3. Stir wine into the roasting pan, scraping to loosen browned bits. Pour into a saucepan. Bring to a boil over medium-high heat; cook until reduced by half. Serve with roast. **Yield:** 14 servings.

Almond Pork Chops with Honey Mustard

Prep/Total Time: 25 min.

Lily Julow, Gainesville, Florida

I love how the crunchy smoked almonds and honey-sweetened mustard enhance these tender chops. I frequently double the recipe because one serving never seems to be enough for my gang of grown children and grandchildren!

- 1/2 cup smoked almonds
- 1/2 cup dry bread crumbs
- 2 eggs
- 1/3 cup all-purpose flour
- 1/4 teaspoon salt
- 1/8 teaspoon pepper
- 4 boneless pork loin chops (1 inch thick and 6 ounces *each*)
- 2 tablespoons olive oil
- 2 tablespoons butter
- 1/2 cup reduced-fat mayonnaise
- 1/4 cup honey
- 2 tablespoons Dijon mustard

1. In a food processor, process the almonds until finely chopped. Transfer to a shallow bowl; add the bread crumbs. In another bowl, beat the eggs. In a large resealable plastic bag, combine flour, salt and pepper. Add pork chops, one at a time, and shake to coat. Dip in eggs, then coat with almond mixture.

2. In a large skillet over medium heat, cook chops in oil and butter for 5 minutes on each side or until a meat thermometer reads 160°. Meanwhile, in a small bowl, combine the mayonnaise, honey and mustard. Serve with pork chops. **Yield:** 4 servings.

Spicy Ham 'n' Broccoli Pasta

Prep/Total Time: 25 min.

Valerie Smith, Aston, Pennsylvania

I love pasta but get tired of preparing it with the usual tomato sauce. My family always raves about the deliciously different combination of cubed deli ham, broccoli and ripe olives in this simple meal-in-one. It goes together in less than half an hour and pairs perfectly with crusty garlic bread.

- 8 ounces uncooked bow tie pasta
- 2-1/2 cups frozen broccoli florets
- 1 medium onion, halved and thinly sliced
- 1 teaspoon minced garlic
- 2 cups cubed deli ham
- 1 can (2-1/4 ounces) sliced ripe olives, drained
- 1/4 cup olive oil
- 1/2 teaspoon salt
- 1/2 teaspoon Italian seasoning
- 1/2 teaspoon crushed red pepper flakes
- 1/2 cup grated Parmesan cheese

1. In a large saucepan, cook pasta according to the package directions, adding the broccoli, onion and garlic during the last 5-7 minutes. Cook until pasta and broccoli are tender; drain. In a large serving bowl, combine the ham, olives and pasta mixture.

2. In a small bowl, whisk the oil, salt, Italian seasoning and pepper flakes. Pour over pasta mixture. Sprinkle with cheese; toss to coat. **Yield:** 4-5 servings.

Cajun Shrimp Skewers

Prep: 20 min. + marinating Grill: 5 min.

Dwayne Veretto, Roswell, New Mexico

This recipe gives shrimp a one-two punch of flavor thanks to both a homemade marinade and a spicy Cajun butter sauce. The skewers can be served not only as a special entree, but also as a hearty appetizer. You'll love them either way!

- 3/4 cup canola oil
- 1 medium onion, finely chopped
- 2 tablespoons Cajun seasoning
- 6 garlic cloves, minced
- 2 teaspoons ground cumin
- 1 teaspoon minced fresh rosemary
- 1 teaspoon minced fresh thyme
- 2 pounds uncooked large shrimp, peeled and deveined

CAJUN BUTTER:
- 1 cup butter, cubed
- 1 teaspoon minced fresh basil
- 1 teaspoon minced fresh tarragon
- 1 teaspoon Cajun seasoning
- 1/2 teaspoon garlic powder
- 3 drops hot pepper sauce

1. In a small bowl, combine the first seven ingredients. Place the shrimp in a large resealable plastic bag; add half of the marinade. Seal the bag and turn to coat; refrigerate for 1-2 hours. Cover and refrigerate the remaining marinade for basting.

2. In a small saucepan, combine the Cajun butter ingredients; heat until butter is melted. Keep warm.

3. Drain and discard the marinade. Thread shrimp onto eight metal or soaked wooden skewers. Grill, uncovered, over medium heat for 2-4 minutes on each side or until shrimp turn pink, basting once with the reserved marinade. Serve with butter. **Yield:** 8 servings.

Easy Shrimp Creole

Prep/Total Time: 25 min.

Jean Gauthier, Rives Junction, Michigan

I came across this fuss-free seafood recipe in a magazine years ago and changed it a little to suit my taste. Using convenience products such as canned tomato soup and store-bought salsa, I can get this dish on the table in just 25 minutes. Every time I serve it to guests, it gets rave reviews.

- 3/4 cup chopped onion
- 3/4 cup chopped celery
- 3/4 cup chopped green pepper
- 2 tablespoons canola oil
- 1 can (10-3/4 ounces) condensed tomato soup, undiluted
- 1 cup tomato juice
- 1/4 cup water
- 1/4 cup salsa
- 2 tablespoons lemon juice
- 1 tablespoon minced fresh parsley
- 2 teaspoons chili powder
- 1-1/4 teaspoons garlic powder
- 1/4 teaspoon pepper
- 1 pound cooked medium shrimp, peeled and deveined

Hot cooked rice

1. In a large skillet, saute the onion, celery and green pepper in oil for 6-7 minutes or until crisp-tender. Stir in the soup, tomato juice, water, salsa, lemon juice, parsley, chili powder, garlic powder and pepper. Bring to a boil. Reduce heat to medium; cover and cook for 6-8 minutes or until heated through.

2. Add the shrimp; cook, uncovered, for 3-4 minutes or until heated through. Serve shrimp with rice. **Yield:** 5 servings.

Pasta with Chorizo And Spinach

Prep/Total Time: 20 min.

Athena Russell, Florence, South Carolina

When I get home from work, I like dinner preparation to go quickly. This zippy all-in-one supper is one of our favorites. It looks and tastes great but is a cinch to make.

- 1-1/4 cups uncooked penne pasta
- 4 teaspoons olive oil
- 1/3 pound uncooked chorizo *or* bulk spicy pork sausage
- 1 small onion, thinly sliced
- 4 ounces sliced fresh mushrooms
- 1/3 cup water-packed artichoke hearts, rinsed, drained and quartered
- 1/3 cup chopped oil-packed sun-dried tomatoes, drained
- 1 garlic clove, minced
- 1/4 teaspoon dried oregano
- 1/8 teaspoon salt
- 1/8 teaspoon pepper
- 3 cups chopped fresh spinach
- 2 tablespoons grated Parmesan cheese

1. Cook the pasta according to package directions. Meanwhile, heat oil in a large skillet; crumble chorizo into the pan. Add the onion, mushrooms, artichokes, tomatoes, garlic, oregano, salt and pepper. Cook and stir over medium heat until chorizo is fully cooked and vegetables are tender.

2. Add spinach; cook and stir for 1-2 minutes or until wilted. Drain pasta; top with chorizo mixture. Sprinkle with cheese. **Yield:** 2 servings.

PG. 159

PG. 162

PG. 161

SIDES, BREADS & CONDIMENTS

A contest–winning main course calls for side dishes that are just as special. Look here for memorable choices such as White Cheddar Scalloped Potatoes, Appalachian Corn Bread and Almond Pear Chutney.

PG. 162

Green Onion Cornmeal Muffins

Prep/Total Time: 30 min.

Naomi Rogers, Essex, Connecticut

Corn bread and corn muffins are popular in New England. This recipe gets a bit of a twist from green onions and sour cream, and the aroma during baking is wonderful. I like to pair these golden-brown bites with soups and stews.

  1 cup all-purpose flour
3/4 cup yellow cornmeal
  3 tablespoons brown sugar
  3 teaspoons baking powder
1/4 teaspoon salt
  1 egg, lightly beaten
  1 cup (8 ounces) sour cream
1/3 cup milk
  2 tablespoons butter, melted
1/4 cup chopped green onions

1. In a large bowl, combine the flour, cornmeal, brown sugar, baking powder and salt. In a small bowl, combine the egg, sour cream, milk, butter and onions; stir into dry ingredients just until moistened.

2. Fill greased or paper-lined muffin cups three-fourths full. Bake at 400° for 18-20 minutes or until a toothpick inserted near the center comes out clean. Cool for 5 minutes before removing from pan to a wire rack. Serve warm. **Yield:** 1 dozen.

Spicy Corn on the Cob

Prep/Total Time: 15 min.

Glenda Ardoin, Hessmer, Louisiana

Here in Louisiana, many of our regional specialties are hot—even our vegetables. This sweet corn is a summer staple and gets zip from a little jalapeno and cumin.

 | This recipe includes Nutrition Facts & Diabetic Exchanges.

  2 large ears sweet corn
  1 tablespoon olive oil
  1 tablespoon butter
  1 jalapeno pepper, seeded and minced
1/4 teaspoon ground cumin
1/4 teaspoon pepper

1. Fill a large saucepan half full with water; bring to a boil. Add corn; cover and cook for 5-7 minutes or until tender.

2. Meanwhile, in a small saucepan, heat oil and butter over low heat until butter is melted. Stir in the jalapeno, cumin and pepper. Drain corn; brush with butter mixture. **Yield:** 2 servings.

Editor's Note: When cutting hot peppers, disposable gloves are recommended. Avoid touching your face.

Nutrition Facts: 1 ear of corn equals 191 calories, 14 g fat (5 g saturated fat), 15 mg cholesterol, 72 mg sodium, 18 g carbohydrate, 3 g fiber, 3 g protein. **Diabetic Exchanges:** 2 fat, 1 starch.

Asparagus with Lemon Sauce

Prep/Total Time: 15 min.

Janice Gerbitz, Woodland, California

We didn't have an oven or stove in our first years of marriage, so we relied heavily on our microwave. This asparagus in a creamy lemon sauce was always a favorite. Garnished with fresh lemon wedges, it's a special addition to any menu.

3 cups cut fresh asparagus (2-inch pieces)
1 can (8 ounces) sliced water chestnuts, drained
1/4 cup cream cheese, softened
2 tablespoons water
2 tablespoons milk
1/2 teaspoon grated lemon peel
1 tablespoon sliced almonds, toasted

1. Place asparagus and water chestnuts in a shallow microwave-safe dish; add 1/2 in. of water. Cover and microwave on high for 6-8 minutes or until asparagus is crisp-tender; drain and keep warm.

2. In a small microwave-safe bowl, combine the cream cheese, water, milk and grated lemon peel. Cover and microwave on high for 1 to 1-1/2 minutes or until heated through, stirring occasionally. Pour over the asparagus mixture; sprinkle with the almonds. **Yield:** 4 servings.

Editor's Note: This recipe was tested in a 1,100-watt microwave.

White Cheddar Scalloped Potatoes

Prep: 40 min. **Bake:** 70 min.

Hope Toole, Muscle Shoals, Alabama

This recipe for scalloped potatoes has evolved over the years. After I added the thyme, ham and sour cream, my husband declared, "This is it!" Serve it as a hearty side dish…or even as an entree accompanied by a salad and French bread.

1 medium onion, finely chopped
1/4 cup butter, cubed
1/4 cup all-purpose flour
1 teaspoon dried parsley flakes
1 teaspoon salt
1/2 teaspoon pepper
1/2 teaspoon dried thyme
3 cups milk
1 can (10-3/4 ounces) condensed cream of mushroom soup, undiluted
1 cup (8 ounces) sour cream
8 cups thinly sliced peeled potatoes
3-1/2 cups cubed fully cooked ham
2 cups (8 ounces) shredded white cheddar cheese

1. In a large saucepan, saute onion in butter until tender. Stir in the flour, parsley, salt, pepper and thyme until blended. Gradually add milk. Bring to a boil; cook and stir for 2 minutes or until thickened. Stir in the soup. Remove from the heat; stir in sour cream until blended.

2. In a large bowl, combine the potatoes and ham. In a greased 13-in. x 9-in. baking dish, layer half of the potato mixture, cheddar cheese and white sauce. Repeat layers.

3. Cover and bake at 375° for 30 minutes. Uncover; bake 40-50 minutes longer or until the potatoes are tender. **Yield:** 6-8 servings.

Tangy Baked Beans

Prep: 10 min. **Bake:** 25 min.

Dean Copeland, Ochlocknee, Georgia

Sized just right for two people, these jazzed-up canned beans make a home-style dish that's guaranteed to please.

- 2 bacon strips, cut into 1-inch pieces
- 2 tablespoons strong brewed coffee
- 4 teaspoons brown sugar
- 1 teaspoon cider vinegar
- 1/4 teaspoon ground mustard
- 1/8 teaspoon salt
- 1 can (8.3 ounces) baked beans, undrained
- 1/2 cup chopped onion

1. In a small skillet, cook bacon over medium heat until partially cooked but not crisp. Meanwhile, in a small saucepan, combine coffee, sugar, vinegar, mustard and salt. Bring to a boil; cook and stir for 2-3 minutes or until sugar is dissolved. Stir in beans and onion.

2. Drain bacon on paper towels. Divide bean mixture between two 6-oz. ramekins or custard cups coated with cooking spray. Top with bacon. Bake at 350° for 25-30 minutes or until bubbly. **Yield:** 2 servings.

Coffee Clue

Like to use coffee in your cooking or baking? Unopened vacuum-packed cans or packages of beans or ground coffee can be stored in your pantry for up to 1 year.

Sweet Potato Fries

Prep: 15 min. **Bake:** 25 min.

- 2 tablespoons beaten egg
- 1 tablespoon water
- 1/3 cup dry bread crumbs
- 2 tablespoons grated Parmesan cheese
- 1/4 teaspoon cayenne pepper
- 1/4 teaspoon pepper
- 1 large sweet potato (14 ounces), peeled
- 2 teaspoons olive oil

MANGO CHUTNEY MAYONNAISE:
- 1/4 cup mayonnaise
- 2 tablespoons mango chutney
- 1/4 teaspoon curry powder

Dash salt
- 2 teaspoons minced fresh parsley, optional

1. In a shallow bowl, whisk egg and water. In a resealable plastic bag, combine the bread crumbs, cheese, cayenne and pepper. Cut sweet potato into 1/4-in. strips. Add to egg mixture, a few at a time, and toss to coat. Add to the crumb mixture, a few at a time; seal bag and shake to coat.

2. Arrange potato strips in a single layer on a baking sheet coated with cooking spray; drizzle with oil. Bake at 450° for 25-30 minutes or until golden brown and crisp, turning occasionally.

3. In a small bowl, combine the mayonnaise, chutney, curry powder and salt. If desired, sprinkle parsley over fries. Serve with mango chutney mayonnaise. **Yield:** 2 servings.

KELLY MCWHERTER HOUSTON, TEXAS

Nutritious sweet potatoes bring added flavor to these extra-crunchy fries. Served with the accompanying mayo-chutney dip, this super side could easily double as a party appetizer.

Pistachio Cranberry Orzo

Prep/Total Time: 20 min.

Barbara Spitzer, Lodi, California

This recipe was originally an entree with chicken and linguini. Now, I keep changing the ingredients to go with whatever else I'm serving for dinner, but my husband prefers this version.

- 1/3 cup uncooked orzo pasta
- 1 shallot, finely chopped
- 2 teaspoons olive oil
- 2 teaspoons butter
- 1/4 cup pistachios, chopped
- 1/4 cup dried cranberries
- 1/4 cup heavy whipping cream
- 1/4 cup chicken broth
- 3 tablespoons marsala wine *or additional chicken broth*
- **Dash salt and pepper**

1. Cook orzo according to the package directions. Meanwhile, in a nonstick skillet, saute shallot in oil and butter for 1 minute. Add the pistachios; saute for 1-2 minutes or until lightly browned.

2. Stir in the cranberries, cream, broth and wine. Cook over medium heat for 3-4 minutes or until thickened. Drain orzo; add to cranberry mixture. Season with salt and pepper. **Yield:** 2 servings.

Chili-Topped Sweet Potatoes

Prep: 15 min. Cook: 40 min.

Jill Nerbas, St. Albert, Alberta

After creating my own thick and chunky chili, I realized it would make a fun topping for sweet potatoes. This comforting dish is a great way to warm up on cold nights.

 This recipe includes Nutrition Facts & Diabetic Exchanges.

- 8 medium sweet potatoes
- 2 medium green peppers, chopped
- 2 medium onions, chopped
- 1 tablespoon chili powder
- 2 teaspoons ground cumin
- 1 teaspoon ground coriander
- 1/2 teaspoon salt
- 1/4 teaspoon pepper
- 1 teaspoon olive oil
- 2 garlic cloves, minced
- 1 can (28 ounces) diced tomatoes, undrained
- 1 can (15 ounces) black beans, rinsed and drained
- 1 cup frozen corn, thawed
- 1/4 cup minced fresh parsley

1. Scrub sweet potatoes and pierce with a fork. Bake at 400° for 35-40 minutes or until tender.

2. Meanwhile, in a large nonstick skillet coated with cooking spray, cook the green peppers, onions, chili powder, cumin, coriander, salt and pepper in oil for 10 minutes. Add garlic; cook 1 minute longer. Stir in the tomatoes and beans. Bring to a boil. Reduce heat; simmer, uncovered, for 20 minutes. Stir in corn and parsley; simmer 5 minutes longer.

3. Cut the sweet potatoes in half; top with chili. **Yield:** 8 servings.

Nutrition Facts: 1 sweet potato with 2/3 cup chili equals 233 calories, 1 g fat (trace saturated fat), 0 cholesterol, 400 mg sodium, 51 g carbohydrate, 10 g fiber, 7 g protein. **Diabetic Exchanges:** 2-1/2 starch, 2 vegetable.

Curried Butternut Squash Kabobs

Prep: 30 min. + cooling **Grill:** 10 min.

Mary Relyea, Canastota, New York

These baked squash cubes get terrific flavor not only from the grill, but also from a mild curry butter. The impressive orange kabobs add interest to more traditional summer entrees.

 This recipe includes Nutrition Facts & Diabetic Exchanges.

> 1 butternut squash (2 pounds), peeled, seeded and cut into 1-inch cubes
> 3 tablespoons butter, melted
> 1 teaspoon curry powder
> 1/4 teaspoon salt

1. Place squash in a greased 13-in. x 9-in. baking dish. Combine the butter, curry powder and salt; drizzle over squash and toss to coat.

2. Bake, uncovered, at 450° for 20-25 minutes or until tender and lightly browned, stirring twice. Cool on a wire rack.

3. On 12 metal or soaked wooden skewers, thread squash cubes. Grill, covered, over medium heat for 3-5 minutes on each side or until heated through. **Yield:** 12 servings.

Nutrition Facts: 1/2 cup (prepared with reduced-fat butter) equals 42 calories, 2 g fat (1 g saturated fat), 5 mg cholesterol, 69 mg sodium, 8 g carbohydrate, 2 g fiber, 1 g protein. **Diabetic Exchanges:** 1/2 starch, 1/2 fat.

Tangy Rhubarb Chutney

Prep: 25 min. **Cook:** 40 min. + chilling

Barbara Estabrook, Rhinelander, Wisconsin

My mother-in-law gave me a wonderful chutney recipe that I like to experiment with by substituting fruits. This variation is a bit different, but I love the combination of pears, onion and rhubarb. And the longer it sets, the better it tastes!

> 3 cups chopped fresh *or* frozen rhubarb
> 1 cup packed brown sugar
> 1 cup white balsamic vinegar
> 1 cup finely chopped onion
> 3/4 cup golden raisins
> 1 tablespoon Worcestershire sauce
> 2 teaspoons minced fresh gingerroot
> 1 teaspoon salt
> 3/4 teaspoon curry powder
> 1/4 teaspoon ground nutmeg
> 2 medium pears, peeled and diced
> 2 tablespoons minced fresh mint

1. In a large saucepan, combine the rhubarb, brown sugar, vinegar, onion, raisins, Worcestershire sauce, ginger, salt, curry and nutmeg. Cook and stir until the mixture comes to a boil. Reduce heat; simmer, uncovered, for 25-30 minutes or until the rhubarb is tender, stirring occasionally.

2. Add the pears. Simmer, uncovered, 10-15 minutes longer or until the pears are tender. Cool to room temperature. Stir in mint. Transfer to a large bowl. Cover and refrigerate for at least 6 hours before serving. May be stored in the refrigerator up to 1 week. **Yield:** 4 cups.

Orange Rhubarb Spread

Prep: 5 min. Cook: 20 min. + standing

Betty Nyenhuis, Oostburg, Wisconsin

This tangy spread is easy to make and tastes especially good slathered on hot, buttered cinnamon toast.

- 4 cups diced fresh *or* frozen rhubarb
- 2 cups water
- 1 can (6 ounces) frozen orange juice concentrate, thawed
- 1 package (1-3/4 ounces) powdered fruit pectin
- 4 cups sugar

1. In a large saucepan, bring rhubarb and water to a boil. Reduce heat; simmer, uncovered, for 7-8 minutes or until rhubarb is tender. Drain and reserve cooking liquid. Cool rhubarb and liquid to room temperature.

2. Place the rhubarb in a blender; cover and process until pureed. Transfer to a 4-cup measuring cup; add enough reserved cooking liquid to measure 2-1/3 cups. Return to the saucepan.

3. Add orange juice concentrate and pectin; bring to a full rolling boil, stirring constantly. Stir in sugar.

Return to a full rolling boil; boil and stir for 1 minute. Remove from the heat; skim off foam.

4. Pour into jars or freezer containers; cool to room temperature, about 1 hour. Cover and let stand overnight or until set, but not longer than 24 hours. Refrigerate or freeze. Refrigerate for up to 3 weeks and freeze for up to 12 months. **Yield:** 5 half-pints.

Fried Green Tomatoes

Prep: 30 min. Cook: 25 min.

Ingrid Parker, Hattiesburg, Mississippi

Homemade salsa is a zippy addition to these golden tomatoes. They can be enjoyed either as a side or as an appetizer.

- 1/2 cup all-purpose flour
- 1 teaspoon sugar
- 1 teaspoon salt
- 3/4 teaspoon cayenne pepper
- 1 egg
- 1 tablespoon fat-free milk
- 1 cup cornflake crumbs
- 4 medium green tomatoes, cut into 1/2-inch slices
- 1/4 cup canola oil

FRESH TOMATO SALSA:
- 5 medium red tomatoes, seeded and chopped
- 1/2 cup minced fresh cilantro
- 1/4 cup chopped onion
- 2 jalapeno peppers, seeded and chopped
- 4-1/2 teaspoons lime juice
- 2 teaspoons sugar
- 1 garlic clove, minced
- 1/4 teaspoon salt
- 1/4 teaspoon pepper

1. In a shallow bowl, combine the flour, sugar, salt and cayenne. In another shallow bowl, beat egg and milk. Place the cornflake crumbs in a third bowl. Pat green tomato slices dry. Coat with flour mixture, dip into egg mixture, then coat with crumbs.

2. In a large nonstick skillet, heat 4 teaspoons oil over medium heat. Fry tomato slices, four at a time, for 3-4 minutes on each side or until golden brown, adding more oil as needed. Drain on paper towels.

3. Place the fried tomatoes on an ungreased baking sheet. Bake at 375° for 4-5 minutes or until tender. Meanwhile, in a large bowl, combine salsa ingredients. Serve with the fried tomatoes. **Yield:** 6 servings.

Editor's Note: When cutting hot peppers, disposable gloves are recommended. Avoid touching your face.

Cranberry Cornmeal Dressing

Prep: 30 min. **Bake:** 40 min.

Corinne Portteus, Albuquerque, New Mexico

This moist dressing is perfect when paired with a main course of poultry or even pork. The sweet-tart flavor from the dried cranberries really complements the Italian turkey sausage.

 This recipe includes Nutrition Facts & Diabetic Exchanges.

- 3 **cups reduced-sodium chicken broth,** *divided*
- 1/2 **cup yellow cornmeal**
- 1/2 **teaspoon salt**
- 1/2 **teaspoon white pepper**
- 1/2 **pound Italian turkey sausage links, casings removed**
- 1 **large onion, diced**
- 1 **large fennel bulb, diced (about 1 cup)**
- 1 **garlic clove, minced**
- 1 **egg yolk**
- 4 **cups soft French or Italian bread crumbs**
- 3/4 **cup dried cranberries**
- 2 **tablespoons minced fresh parsley**
- 1 **tablespoon balsamic vinegar**
- 1 **teaspoon minced fresh sage**
- 1 **teaspoon minced fresh savory**
- 1/4 **teaspoon ground nutmeg**

1. In a small bowl, whisk 1 cup broth, cornmeal, salt and pepper until smooth. In a large saucepan, bring the remaining broth to a boil. Add the cornmeal mixture, stirring constantly. Return to a boil; cook and stir for 3 minutes or until thickened. Remove from the heat; set aside.

2. Crumble the sausage into a large nonstick skillet, add onion and fennel. Cook over medium heat until sausage is no longer pink. Add garlic; cook 1 minute longer; drain. Stir in egg yolk and cornmeal mixture. Add the bread crumbs, cranberries, parsley, vinegar, sage, savory and nutmeg.

3. Transfer the dressing to a 1-1/2-qt. baking dish coated with cooking spray. Cover and bake at 350° for 40-45 minutes or until a thermometer reads 160°. **Yield:** 8 servings.

Nutrition Facts: 2/3 cup equals 205 calories, 4 g fat (1 g saturated fat), 42 mg cholesterol, 695 mg sodium, 33 g carbohydrate, 3 g fiber, 9 g protein. **Diabetic Exchanges:** 2 starch, 1 lean meat.

Thai-Style Green Beans

Prep/Total Time: 20 min.

Candace McMenamin, Lexington, South Carolina

Peanut butter, soy sauce and hoisin sauce accent this fast and fabulous bean dish that's sized just right for two.

- 1 **tablespoon reduced-sodium soy sauce**
- 1 **tablespoon hoisin sauce**
- 1 **tablespoon creamy peanut butter**
- 1/8 **teaspoon crushed red pepper flakes**
- 1 **tablespoon chopped shallot**
- 1 **teaspoon minced fresh gingerroot**
- 1 **tablespoon canola oil**
- 1/2 **pound fresh green beans, trimmed**

Minced fresh cilantro and chopped dry roasted peanuts, optional

1. In a small bowl, combine soy sauce, hoisin sauce, peanut butter and red pepper flakes; set aside.

2. In a small skillet, saute the shallot and ginger in oil over medium heat for 2 minutes or until crisp-tender. Add the green beans; cook and stir for 3 minutes or until crisp-tender.

3. Add reserved sauce; toss to coat. Sprinkle with cilantro and peanuts if desired. **Yield:** 2 servings.

Italian Herb Muffins

Prep: 20 min. Bake: 15 min.

Cyndee Page, Reno, Nevada

My husband likes to have garlic bread with spaghetti. While preparing that main course for dinner one day, I realized I was out of bread and thought, "Why not make an herb muffin instead?" I came up with this recipe featuring garlic powder, Italian seasoning and Parmesan. It was a hit!

     2 cups all-purpose flour
     2 tablespoons grated Parmesan cheese
     1 tablespoon sugar
     1 tablespoon Italian seasoning
     3 teaspoons baking powder
     1 teaspoon salt
     1 egg
    3/4 cup 2% milk
    1/2 cup canola oil
    1/4 cup butter, softened
    1/2 teaspoon garlic powder

1. In a large bowl, combine the flour, cheese, sugar, Italian seasoning, baking powder and salt. In another bowl, combine the egg, milk and oil; stir into dry ingredients just until moistened.

2. Fill greased or paper-lined muffin cups three-fourths full. Bake at 400° for 15-20 minutes or until a toothpick

inserted near the center comes out clean. Cool for 5 minutes before removing from pan to a wire rack.

3. In a small bowl, combine the butter and garlic powder. Serve with warm muffins. **Yield:** 10 muffins.

Buttery Garlic Potatoes

Prep/Total Time: 15 min.

Heidi Iacovetto, Phippsburg, Colorado

Everyone in our house loves oven-roasted potatoes. But I work full-time, so once I get home and start dinner, I usually don't have time to make them. My solution was to whip up this quick and delicious recipe in the microwave using just six ingredients, and it's become a family favorite.

     6 small red potatoes, quartered
    1/4 cup butter, melted
     1 teaspoon seasoned salt
     1 teaspoon paprika
     1 teaspoon dried parsley flakes
     1 teaspoon minced garlic

1. Place the potatoes in a 2-qt. microwave-safe dish. In a small bowl, combine the butter, seasoned salt, paprika, parsley and garlic; pour over the potatoes and toss to coat.

2. Microwave, uncovered, on high for 8-10 minutes or until potatoes are tender, stirring frequently. **Yield:** 4 servings.

Editor's Note: This recipe was tested in a 1,100-watt microwave.

Appalachian Corn Bread

Prep: 15 min. **Bake:** 20 min.

Anne Wiehler, Farmington, Pennsylvania

We live on the westernmost ridge of the Appalachians and get abundant rain and sunshine. The climate allows our children to grow a super-sweet crop of corn, which we are always happy to include in our menus. This cheesy bread, flecked with chives and onion, is just one of the ways we enjoy that harvest.

        2 tablespoons chopped onion
        4 tablespoons canola oil, *divided*
        1 cup all-purpose flour
        1 cup cornmeal
        2 tablespoons sugar
        4 teaspoons baking powder
    1/2 teaspoon salt
        2 eggs
        1 cup milk
    1/2 cup fresh *or* frozen corn, thawed
    1/3 cup shredded cheddar cheese
    1/4 cup salsa
        2 tablespoons minced chives

1. In a small saucepan, saute the onion in 1 tablespoon oil until tender; set aside.

2. In a large bowl, combine the flour, cornmeal, sugar, baking powder and salt. In another bowl, whisk the eggs, milk and remaining oil. Stir in the corn, cheddar cheese, salsa, chives and reserved onion. Stir into the dry ingredients just until combined.

3. Transfer batter to a greased 9-in. square baking pan. Bake at 425° for 20-25 minutes or until a

toothpick inserted near the center comes out clean and the top is lightly browned. Cut bread into squares; serve warm. **Yield:** 9 servings.

Almond Pear Chutney

Prep: 15 min. **Cook:** 30 min.

Michaela Rosenthal, Woodland Hills, California

This chunky condiment featuring orange slices, almonds and ginger is great with an entree of chicken, turkey or pork. You can prepare the chutney a couple of days in advance, too.

        4 cups chopped peeled ripe pears
        1 small unpeeled navel orange, halved and
            thinly sliced
    1/2 cup water
        2 teaspoons lemon juice
    1-1/2 cups sugar
    1/4 teaspoon ground cinnamon
    1/3 cup coarsely chopped unblanched almonds,
            toasted
        2 tablespoons chopped crystallized ginger

1. In a large saucepan, combine the pears, orange, water and lemon juice. Bring to a boil, stirring constantly. Reduce heat; simmer, uncovered, for 10 minutes.

2. Stir in sugar and cinnamon. Bring to a boil. Reduce heat; simmer, uncovered, for 15-20 minutes or until thickened, stirring occasionally.

3. Remove from the heat; stir in almonds and ginger. Serve warm or cold. May be refrigerated for up to 1 week. **Yield:** 3 cups.

Blueberry Quick Bread

Prep: 25 min. **Bake:** 50 min. + cooling

Lois Everest, Goshen, Indiana

This yummy blueberry bread recipe won a blue ribbon at our state fair. I think the crushed pineapple and coconut are the ingredients that make this recipe stand out. It yields two loaves so you can freeze one for a future treat.

 This recipe includes Nutrition Facts & Diabetic Exchanges.

> 2/3 cup butter, softened
> 1-1/4 cups sugar blend
> 2 eggs

> 4 egg whites
> 1-1/2 teaspoons lemon juice
> 3 cups all-purpose flour
> 3-3/4 teaspoons baking powder
> 1/2 teaspoon salt
> 1/2 cup fat-free milk
> 2 cups fresh *or* frozen blueberries
> 1 cup canned unsweetened crushed pineapple, drained
> 1/2 cup chopped pecans *or* walnuts
> 1/2 cup flaked coconut

1. In a large bowl, cream butter and sugar blend until light and fluffy. Beat in the eggs, egg whites and lemon juice. Combine the flour, baking powder and salt; gradually add to creamed mixture alternately with milk, beating well after each addition. Fold in the blueberries, pineapple, pecans and coconut.

2. Transfer to two 8-in. x 4-in. loaf pans coated with cooking spray. Bake at 350° for 50-60 minutes or until a toothpick inserted near the center comes out clean. Cool for 10 minutes before removing from pans to wire racks. **Yield:** 2 loaves (12 slices each).

Editor's Note: This recipe was tested with Splenda sugar blend. If using frozen blueberries, do not thaw before adding to batter.

Nutrition Facts: 1 slice equals 193 calories, 8 g fat (4 g saturated fat), 31 mg cholesterol, 186 mg sodium, 27 g carbohydrate, 1 g fiber, 3 g protein. **Diabetic Exchanges:** 1-1/2 starch, 1-1/2 fat.

Spiced Cranberry Sauce

Prep: 5 min. **Cook:** 30 min. + chilling

Allison Thompson, Lansing, Michigan

While this special cranberry sauce is simmering, the wonderful fragrance of the spices brings back happy memories of when my mother made it for the holidays. My husband and three sons are glad I'm carrying on her tradition!

> 1 package (12 ounces) fresh *or* frozen cranberries
> 1-3/4 cups sugar
> 1/2 cup water
> 1/2 teaspoon ground cinnamon
> 1/2 teaspoon ground allspice
> 1/8 teaspoon salt
> 1/8 teaspoon ground ginger
> 1/8 teaspoon ground cloves

In a large saucepan, combine all ingredients. Bring to a boil. Reduce heat; simmer, uncovered, until the cranberries pop and the mixture is thickened, about 30 minutes. Cool. Transfer to a serving bowl; cover and refrigerate until chilled. **Yield:** 2 cups.

German-Style Mashed Potatoes

Prep: 20 min. **Cook:** 20 min.

Alena Horn, Austin, Texas

Comforting and filling, this tangy favorite will warm up any meal—especially one featuring German dishes. The potatoes are a fitting accompaniment to sausages such as bratwurst.

- 3 pounds red potatoes, peeled and cubed
- 2 large tart apples, peeled and chopped
- 4 bacon strips, diced
- 2 medium onions, sliced
- 1 tablespoon sugar
- 1 tablespoon cider vinegar
- 3/4 teaspoon salt

1. Place potatoes in a large saucepan and cover with water. Bring to a boil. Reduce heat; cover and cook for 10 minutes. Add apples; cook 10 minutes longer or until potatoes and apples are tender.

2. Meanwhile, in a large skillet, cook the bacon over medium heat until crisp. Using a slotted spoon, remove to paper towels; drain, reserving 1 tablespoon drippings. In the drippings, saute onions until lightly browned.

3. Drain potatoes and apples. Add sugar, vinegar and salt; mash slightly. Transfer to a serving bowl. Top with onions and bacon. **Yield:** 7 servings.

Feta 'n' Chive Muffins

Prep: 15 min. **Bake:** 20 min.

Angela Buchanan, Boulder, Colorado

This is a variation on a savory muffin my husband has made for years. It has a light texture—almost like a popover—and tastes best eaten hot right from the oven.

 This recipe includes Nutrition Facts & Diabetic Exchanges.

- 1-1/2 cups all-purpose flour
- 3 teaspoons baking powder
- 1/4 teaspoon salt
- 2 eggs
- 1 cup milk
- 2 tablespoons butter, melted
- 1/2 cup crumbled feta cheese
- 3 tablespoons minced chives

1. In a large bowl, combine the flour, baking powder and salt. In another bowl, combine the eggs, milk and butter; stir into dry ingredients just until moistened. Fold in the feta cheese and chives.

2. Fill greased or paper-lined muffin cups two-thirds full. Bake at 400° for 18-22 minutes or until a toothpick

inserted near the center comes out clean. Cool for 5 minutes before removing from pan to a wire rack. Serve warm. Refrigerate leftovers. **Yield:** 1 dozen.

Nutrition Facts: 1 muffin equals 105 calories, 4 g fat (2 g saturated fat), 43 mg cholesterol, 235 mg sodium, 13 g carbohydrate, 1 g fiber, 4 g protein. **Diabetic Exchanges:** 1 starch, 1/2 fat.

PG. 168

PG. 175

PG. 170

COOKIES, BARS & CANDY

Have an empty cookie jar, treat tray or candy dish? They're no match for this chapter! You'll have dozens of delights when you whip up Mocha Truffles, Dipped Gingersnaps or any of the other recipes here.

PG. 170

Chunky Fruit 'n' Nut Fudge

Prep: 30 min. + standing

Allene Bary-Cooper, Wichita Falls, Texas

The possibilities for varying this rich fudge are endless, but the version here is my favorite. Besides featuring five types of chips, it's loaded with dried cranberries, dried cherries and cashews. Every bite is packed with flavor and crunch.

- 1 package (11 ounces) dried cherries
- 1 cup dried cranberries
- 1-1/2 teaspoons plus 3/4 cup butter, softened, divided
- 1 can (14 ounces) sweetened condensed milk
- 1 package (12 ounces) miniature semisweet chocolate chips
- 1 package (11-1/2 ounces) milk chocolate chips
- 1 package (10 to 11 ounces) butterscotch chips
- 1 package (10 ounces) peanut butter chips
- 3 tablespoons heavy whipping cream
- 1 jar (7 ounces) marshmallow creme
- 1/2 teaspoon almond *or* rum extract
- 1-1/2 cups unsalted cashew halves
- 1 package (11-1/2 ounces) semisweet chocolate chunks

1. In a large bowl, combine cherries and cranberries. Add enough warm water to cover; set aside. Line a 15-in. x 10-in. x 1-in. pan with foil and grease the foil with 1-1/2 teaspoons butter; set aside.

2. In a large heavy saucepan, melt remaining butter. Stir in the milk, chips and cream. Cook and stir over low heat for 15-20 minutes or until chips are melted and mixture is smooth and blended (mixture will first appear separated, but continue stirring until fully blended). Remove from the heat; stir in marshmallow creme and extract.

3. Drain cherries and cranberries; pat dry with paper towels. Stir the fruit, cashews and chocolate chunks into chocolate mixture. Spread into prepared pan. Let stand at room temperature until set.

4. Using foil, lift fudge out of pan. Discard foil; cut fudge into 1-in. squares. **Yield:** 6-3/4 pounds.

Chewy Date Nut Bars

Prep: 15 min. **Bake:** 35 min. + cooling

Linda Hutmacher, Teutopolis, Illinois

You'll need just six basic ingredients, including a convenient packaged cake mix, to bake a pan of these chewy goodies chock-full of chopped nuts and dates. It's my husband's favorite snack, and he loves to bring it to work.

- 1 package (18-1/4 ounces) yellow cake mix
- 3/4 cup packed brown sugar
- 3/4 cup butter, melted
- 2 eggs
- 2 cups chopped dates
- 2 cups chopped walnuts

1. In a large bowl, combine cake mix and brown sugar. Add butter and eggs; beat on low speed for 30 seconds. Beat on medium for 2 minutes. Combine dates and walnuts; stir into batter (batter will be stiff).

2. Spread into a greased 13-in. x 9-in. baking pan. Bake at 350° for 35-45 minutes or until edges are golden brown. Cool on a wire rack for 10 minutes. Run a knife around the sides of pan to loosen; cool completely before cutting. **Yield:** 3 dozen.

Cookies 'n' Cream Brownies

Prep: 15 min. **Bake:** 25 min. + cooling

Darlene Brenden, Salem, Oregon

Forget the frosting on these brownies—the marbled top is too pretty to cover up! Plus, that yummy cream cheese layer makes these taste like they're already frosted. Whip up a few dozen for your family and watch eyes light up.

- 1 **package (8 ounces) cream cheese, softened**
- 1/4 **cup sugar**
- 1 **egg**
- 1/2 **teaspoon vanilla extract**

BROWNIE LAYER:
- 1/2 **cup butter, melted**
- 1/2 **cup sugar**
- 1/2 **cup packed brown sugar**
- 1/2 **cup baking cocoa**
- 2 **eggs**
- 1/2 **cup all-purpose flour**
- 1 **teaspoon baking powder**
- 1 **teaspoon vanilla extract**
- 12 **cream-filled chocolate sandwich cookies, crushed**

1. In a small bowl, beat the cream cheese, sugar, egg and vanilla until smooth; set aside. For brownie layer, combine the butter, sugars and cocoa in a large bowl; blend well. Add the eggs, one at a time, beating well after each addition. Combine flour and baking powder; stir into the cocoa mixture. Stir in the vanilla and cookie crumbs.

2. Pour the batter into a greased 11-in. x 7-in. baking pan. Spoon the cream cheese mixture over the batter; cut through the batter with a knife to swirl. Bake at 350° for 25-30 minutes or until a toothpick inserted near the center comes out with moist crumbs. Cool completely on a wire rack. Cut into bars. Store in refrigerator. **Yield:** 2 dozen.

Iced Cinnamon Chip Cookies

Prep: 30 min. **Bake:** 10 min./batch + cooling

Katie Jean Boyd, Roachdale, Indiana

My mother helped me prepare my first batch of cookies when I was just 8 years old, and I still enjoy baking them. I like to take these treats to get-togethers and give them as gifts. The cinnamon chips and soft vanilla icing make them special.

- 1 **cup butter, softened**
- 3/4 **cup sugar**
- 3/4 **cup packed brown sugar**
- 2 **eggs**
- 1 **teaspoon vanilla extract**
- 3 **cups all-purpose flour**
- 1 **teaspoon baking soda**
- 1 **teaspoon salt**
- 1 **package (10 ounces) cinnamon baking chips**

ICING:
- 1/4 **cup butter, melted**
- 1/4 **cup shortening**
- 1-1/4 **cups confectioners' sugar**
- 1 **tablespoon milk**
- 3/4 **teaspoon vanilla extract**

1. In a large bowl, cream butter and sugars until light and fluffy. Beat in eggs and vanilla. Combine the flour, baking soda and salt; gradually add to creamed mixture and mix well. Fold in cinnamon chips.

2. Drop cookie dough by rounded tablespoonfuls 2 in. apart onto ungreased baking sheets. Bake at 350° for 10-12 minutes or until golden brown. Remove to wire racks to cool.

3. In a small bowl, combine icing ingredients; beat on high speed for 1-2 minutes or until fluffy. Spread over cooled cookies. **Yield:** about 3-1/2 dozen.

Hazelnut Shortbread

Prep: 15 min. + chilling
Bake: 15 min./batch + cooling

Karen Morrell, Canby, Oregon

Traditional shortbread contains only flour, sugar and butter, resulting in a rich and crumbly cookie. This variation gets extra flavor from the hazelnuts and maple syrup. Add a drizzle of chocolate candy coating for a festive touch.

> 1 cup butter, softened
> 1/2 cup sugar
> 2 tablespoons maple syrup *or* honey
> 2 teaspoons vanilla extract
> 2 cups all-purpose flour
> 1-1/4 cups finely chopped hazelnuts
> 1/2 cup *each* white, red, green, yellow and dark chocolate candy coating disks

1. In a large bowl, cream butter and sugar until light and fluffy. Add syrup and vanilla. Beat in flour just until combined; fold in nuts. Shape into two 1-1/2-in. rolls; wrap tightly in waxed paper. Chill for 2 hours or until firm.

2. Cut the dough into 1/4-in. slices and place 2 in. apart on ungreased baking sheets. Bake at 325° for 14-16 minutes or until edges begin to brown. Remove to wire racks to cool.

3. In separate microwave-safe bowls, melt candy coating disks; stir until smooth. Drizzle over cookies. Let stand until set. **Yield:** 6 dozen.

Mocha Truffles

Prep: 25 min. + chilling

> 2 packages (12 ounces *each*) semisweet chocolate chips
> 1 package (8 ounces) cream cheese, softened
> 3 tablespoons instant coffee granules
> 2 teaspoons water
> 1 pound dark chocolate candy coating, coarsely chopped
> White candy coating, optional

1. In a microwave-safe bowl, melt chocolate chips; stir until smooth. Add the cream cheese, coffee and water. Chill until firm enough to shape. Shape into 1-in. balls and place on waxed paper-lined baking sheet. Chill for 1-2 hours or until firm.

2. In a microwave, melt chocolate coating; stir until smooth. Dip balls in chocolate; allow excess to drip off. Place on waxed paper; let stand until set. Melt white coating and drizzle over truffles if desired. **Yield:** about 5-1/2 dozen.

Freezer Convenience

Plan to make truffles for a party or other special occasion? Save time on the day of your event by working ahead! Truffles can be frozen for several months before they are dipped in chocolate. Just thaw them in the refrigerator before dipping.

STACY ABELL OLATHE, KANSAS

When it comes to a sweet treat, it's hard to top these melt-in-your-mouth truffles accented with the flavor of coffee. Whenever I make them for my family or friends, the little candies are quickly devoured. No one ever guesses how easy they are to prepare!

GRAND PRIZE WINNER

Frosted Rhubarb Cookies

Prep: 30 min. **Bake:** 10 min./batch + cooling

Shauna Schneyder, Idaho Falls, Idaho

We have two prolific rhubarb plants, so I'm always looking for new ways to put our bountiful harvest to good use. A friend of mine gave me the recipe for these soft cookies accented with coconut and spread with a cream-cheese frosting.

    1 **cup shortening**
1-1/2 **cups packed brown sugar**
    2 **eggs**
    3 **cups all-purpose flour**
    1 **teaspoon baking soda**
 1/2 **teaspoon salt**
1-1/2 **cups diced fresh or frozen rhubarb**
 3/4 **cup flaked coconut**
FROSTING:
    1 **package (3 ounces) cream cheese, softened**
    1 **tablespoon butter, softened**
1-1/2 **cups confectioners' sugar**
    3 **teaspoons vanilla extract**

1. In a large bowl, cream shortening and brown sugar until light and fluffy. Beat in eggs. Combine the flour, baking soda and salt; gradually add to creamed mixture and mix well. Fold in rhubarb and coconut.

2. Drop by rounded tablespoonfuls 2 in. apart onto greased baking sheets. Bake at 350° for 10-14 minutes or until golden brown. Cool for 1 minute before removing to wire racks to cool completely.

3. For frosting, in a small bowl, beat cream cheese and butter until fluffy. Beat in the confectioners' sugar and vanilla. Spread over cookies. **Yield:** 4 dozen.

Editor's Note: If using frozen rhubarb, measure rhubarb while still frozen, then thaw completely. Drain in a colander, but do not press liquid out.

Orange Chocolate Meltaways

Prep: 30 min. + chilling

Lori Kostecki, Wausau, Wisconsin

I don't have a lot of time to spend in the kitchen, but when I do cook, I like to get "fancy." In this case, "fancy" doesn't mean difficult. The terrific combination of rich chocolate and orange flavor makes these some of the best truffles I've ever had…and they're easier to make than they look.

    1 **package (11-1/2 ounces) milk chocolate chips**
    1 **cup (6 ounces) semisweet chocolate chips**
 3/4 **cup heavy whipping cream**
    1 **teaspoon grated orange peel**
2-1/2 **teaspoons orange extract**
1-1/2 **cups finely chopped toasted pecans**
COATING:
    1 **cup (6 ounces) milk chocolate chips**
    2 **tablespoons shortening**

1. Place the chocolate chips in a bowl; set aside. In a saucepan, bring heavy whipping cream and orange peel to a gentle boil; immediately pour over chips. Let stand for 1 minute; whisk until smooth. Add extract. Cover and chill for 35 minutes or until mixture begins to thicken.

2. Beat the mixture for 10-15 seconds or just until it lightens in color (do not overbeat). Spoon rounded teaspoonfuls onto waxed paper-lined baking sheets. Cover and chill for 5 minutes.

3. Gently shape into balls; roll half in pecans. In a microwave; melt chocolate and shortening; stir until smooth. Dip remaining balls in chocolate; allow excess to drip off. Place on waxed paper; let stand until set. Store in the refrigerator. **Yield:** 6 dozen.

Chocolate Mint Wafers

Prep: 30 min. + chilling
Bake: 5 min./batch + cooling

Annette Esau, Durham, Ontario

You can rest assured that a batch of these chocolaty sandwich cookies featuring a cool mint filling won't last long. They're irresistible piled high on a pretty glass plate.

　　2/3 cup butter, softened
　　1/2 cup sugar
　　1/2 cup packed brown sugar
　　1/4 cup whole milk
　　　1 egg
　　　2 cups all-purpose flour
　　3/4 cup baking cocoa
　　　1 teaspoon baking powder
　　1/2 teaspoon baking soda
　　1/4 teaspoon salt
FILLING:
2-3/4 cups confectioners' sugar
　　1/4 cup half-and-half cream
　　1/4 teaspoon peppermint extract
　　1/4 teaspoon salt
Green food coloring

1. In a large bowl, cream butter and sugars until light and fluffy. Beat in milk and egg. Combine the flour, cocoa, baking powder, baking soda and salt; gradually add to creamed mixture and mix well. Cover and refrigerate for 2 hours or until firm.

2. On a lightly floured surface, roll out the cookie dough to 1/8-in. thickness. Cut with a 1-1/2-in. cookie cutter and place 1 in. apart on greased baking sheets. Bake at 375° for 5-6 minutes or until the edges are lightly browned. Remove the cookies to wire racks to cool completely.

3. Combine filling ingredients; spread on the bottom of half of the cookies and top with the remaining cookies. **Yield:** about 7-1/2 dozen.

Chewy Apple Oatmeal Cookies

Prep: 20 min.　**Bake:** 10 min./batch

Jan Marshall, Fenton, Missouri

My family members have always been fans of oatmeal raisin cookies, but I wanted to try something new with that classic recipe. We also enjoy apples, so I thought of mixing dried fruit into the dough. Everyone loved them!

　　1 cup butter, softened
　　1 cup packed brown sugar
　1/2 cup sugar
　　2 eggs
　　1 teaspoon vanilla extract
1-1/2 cups all-purpose flour
　　2 teaspoons ground cinnamon
　　1 teaspoon baking soda
　1/4 teaspoon salt
　　3 cups old-fashioned oats
　1/2 cup chopped dried apples

1. In a large bowl, cream the butter and sugars until light and fluffy. Beat in the eggs and vanilla. Combine the flour, cinnamon, baking soda and salt; gradually

add to the creamed mixture and mix well. Stir in the oats and dried apples.

2. Drop by rounded tablespoonfuls 2 in. apart onto ungreased baking sheets. Bake at 350° for 10-12 minutes or until golden brown. Let stand for 1 minute before removing to wire racks. **Yield:** 4 dozen.

Cookies, Bars & Candy　**173**

Chocolate Dipped Brownies

Prep: 30 min. + freezing **Bake:** 35 min. + cooling

Jackie Archer, Clinton, Iowa

My family members refer to these as "the world's chocolatiest brownies" and are happy to gobble them up whenever I make them. Sprinkled with nuts, jimmies or nonpareils, they're a festive part of a Christmas cookie tray or bake sale.

> 3/4 cup sugar
> 1/3 cup butter, cubed
> 2 tablespoons water
> 4 cups (24 ounces) semisweet chocolate chips, divided
> 1 teaspoon vanilla extract
> 2 eggs
> 3/4 cup all-purpose flour
> 1/2 teaspoon salt
> 1/4 teaspoon baking soda
> 2 tablespoons shortening
> Chopped pecans, jimmies *and/or* nonpareils, optional

1. In a large saucepan, bring the sugar, butter and water to a boil over medium heat. Remove from the heat; stir in 1 cup chocolate chips and vanilla until smooth. Cool for 5 minutes. Add eggs, one at a time, beating well after each addition. Combine the flour, salt and baking soda; stir into chocolate mixture. Stir in 1 cup chocolate chips.

2. Pour the batter into a greased 9-in. square baking pan. Bake at 325° for 35 minutes or until set. Cool completely on a wire rack. Place in the freezer for 30-40 minutes or until firm (do not freeze completely). Cut into bars.

3. In a microwave-safe bowl, melt the remaining chips with shortening; stir until smooth. Using a small fork, dip the brownies to completely coat; shake off excess. Place on waxed paper-lined baking sheets. Sprinkle with pecans, jimmies and/or nonpareils if desired. Let stand until set. Store in an airtight container. **Yield:** 3 dozen.

Any-Occasion Treat

Chocolate Dipped Brownies make a festive treat not only for Christmastime, but also for other holidays. Simply decorate them to suit the occasion. For example, use orange and purple sprinkles for a Halloween party.

Walnut Bars

Prep: 15 min. **Bake:** 45 min. + cooling

Chante Jones, Alturas, California

In California, walnuts seem to grow everywhere. I grew up on a walnut acre, and when I use them in my baking, it brings back memories of my family and harvesttime. These sensational treats with a lemon glaze are a favorite.

- 1/2 cup butter, softened
- 1/4 cup sugar
- 1 egg
- 1/2 teaspoon vanilla extract
- 1-1/4 cups all-purpose flour
- 1/2 teaspoon salt

FILLING:
- 2 eggs
- 1-1/2 cups packed brown sugar
- 2 tablespoons all-purpose flour
- 1 teaspoon vanilla extract
- 1/2 teaspoon salt
- 1/2 teaspoon baking powder
- 1-1/2 cups chopped walnuts

LEMON GLAZE:
- 1-1/2 cups confectioners' sugar
- 2 to 3 tablespoons lemon juice

1. In a small bowl, cream butter and sugar until light and fluffy. Beat in egg and vanilla. Combine flour and salt; gradually add to creamed mixture and mix well.

2. Press onto the bottom of a greased 13-in. x 9-in. baking pan. Bake at 350° for 20 minutes or until edges are lightly browned.

3. For the filling, in a small bowl, combine the eggs, brown sugar, flour, vanilla, salt and baking powder. Stir in walnuts. Spread over crust.

4. Bake for 25 minutes or until filling is golden brown. Cool on a wire rack.

5. Combine the confectioners' sugar and enough lemon juice to achieve desired consistency; spread over filling. Let stand until set before cutting. **Yield:** 2-1/2 dozen.

Anise Butter Cookies

Prep: 30 min. **Bake:** 40 min.

Mari Lynn Van Ginkle, Sandia Park, New Mexico

There are many variations of this recipe, which has been passed down through the generations, but I love this one. The cookies are yummy dunked in milk or all by themselves.

- 2 cups butter, softened
- 1-3/4 cups sugar, *divided*
- 2 eggs
- 1/4 cup thawed orange juice concentrate
- 4 teaspoons aniseed, crushed
- 6 cups all-purpose flour
- 3 teaspoons baking powder
- 1/2 teaspoon salt
- 1 teaspoon ground cinnamon

1. In a large bowl, cream the butter and 1-1/2 cups sugar until light and fluffy. Add eggs, one at a time, beating well after each addition. Beat in orange juice concentrate and aniseed. Combine the flour, baking powder and salt; gradually add to creamed mixture and mix well.

2. On a lightly floured surface, roll out the cookie dough to 1/4-in. thickness. Cut with a floured 2-1/2-in. round cookie cutter. Place 1 in. apart on ungreased baking sheets.

3. Combine the cinnamon and remaining sugar; sprinkle over cookies. Bake at 350° for 12-15 minutes or until golden brown. Remove the cookies to wire racks. **Yield:** 5 dozen.

Triple-Chocolate Brownie Cookies

Prep: 25 min. + chilling
Bake: 10 min./batch + cooling

Linda Robinson, New Braunfels, Texas

Our family of chocolate lovers gets three times as excited when these extra-rich cookies come out of the oven. They have the texture and taste of a scrumptious fudge brownie and are finished off with a tempting drizzle.

> 4 ounces unsweetened chocolate, chopped
> 3/4 cup butter, cubed
> 4 eggs
> 2 cups sugar
> 1-1/2 cups all-purpose flour
> 1/2 cup baking cocoa
> 2 teaspoons baking powder
> 1/2 teaspoon salt
> 2 cups (12 ounces) semisweet chocolate chips, divided
> 2 teaspoons shortening

1. In a microwave, melt chocolate and butter; stir until smooth. Cool slightly. In a large bowl, beat eggs and sugar. Stir in chocolate mixture. Combine the flour, cocoa, baking powder and salt; gradually add to chocolate mixture and mix well. Stir in 1-1/2 cups chocolate chips.

2. Cover and refrigerate cookie dough for 2 hours or until easy to handle.

3. Drop by tablespoonfuls 2 in. apart onto greased baking sheets. Bake at 350° for 7-9 minutes or until edges are set and tops are slightly cracked. Cool for 2 minutes before removing from pans to wire racks to cool completely.

4. In a microwave, melt the remaining chips and shortening; stir until smooth. Drizzle over cookies. Let stand for 30 minutes or until chocolate is set. Store in an airtight container. **Yield:** 6 dozen.

Chocolate Meringue Stars

Prep: 25 min. **Bake:** 30 min./batch + cooling

Edna Lee, Greeley, Colorado

These light, delicate and chewy cookies make for very merry munching during the Christmas season or anytime. It's difficult to keep the kids away from these dipped stars long enough to get any on our holiday cookie tray!

> 3 egg whites
> 3/4 teaspoon vanilla extract
> 3/4 cup sugar
> 1/4 cup baking cocoa
> **GLAZE:**
> 3 ounces semisweet chocolate, chopped
> 1 tablespoon shortening

1. In a large bowl, beat egg whites and vanilla until soft peaks form. Gradually add the sugar, about 2 tablespoons at a time, beating until stiff peaks form. Gently fold in cocoa.

2. Insert a #8b large open star tip into a pastry bag; fill half full with meringue. Pipe stars, about 1-1/4 in. in diameter, or drop by rounded teaspoonfuls onto parchment paper-lined baking sheets.

3. Bake at 300° for 30-35 minutes or until lightly browned. Remove from paper; cool on wire racks.

4. In a microwave, melt chocolate and shortening; stir until smooth. Dip cookies halfway into glaze; allow excess to drip off. Place on waxed paper; let stand until set. **Yield:** about 4 dozen.

Fudge-Topped Brownies

Prep: 25 min. **Bake:** 25 min. + freezing

Judy Olson, Whitecourt, Alberta

Why have only brownies or fudge when you can combine the two? These exquisite half-and-half goodies are the ultimate delight for sweet tooths and perfect to put in gift tins.

- 1 cup butter
- 4 ounces unsweetened chocolate, chopped
- 2 cups sugar
- 2 teaspoons vanilla extract
- 4 eggs
- 1-1/2 cups all-purpose flour
- 1 teaspoon baking powder
- 1/2 teaspoon salt
- 1 cup chopped walnuts

TOPPING:
- 4-1/2 cups sugar
- 1 can (12 ounces) evaporated milk
- 1/2 cup butter, cubed
- 1 package (12 ounces) semisweet chocolate chips
- 1 package (11-1/2 ounces) milk chocolate chips
- 1 jar (7 ounces) marshmallow creme
- 2 teaspoons vanilla extract
- 2 cups chopped walnuts

1. In a heavy saucepan or microwave, melt butter and chocolate; stir until smooth. Remove from the heat; blend in sugar and vanilla. Add eggs; mix well. Combine the flour, baking powder and salt; add to chocolate mixture. Stir in walnuts. Pour into a greased 13-in. x 9-in. baking pan. Bake at 350° for 25-30 minutes or until top springs back when lightly touched. Cool on a wire rack while preparing topping.

2. Combine the sugar, milk and butter in a large heavy saucepan; bring to a boil over medium heat. Reduce heat; simmer, uncovered, for 5 minutes, stirring constantly. Remove from the heat. Stir in the chocolate chips, marshmallow creme and vanilla until smooth. Add walnuts. Spread over warm brownies. Freeze for 3 hours or until firm. Cut into 1-in. squares. Store in the refrigerator. **Yield:** about 10 dozen.

Dipped Gingersnaps

Prep: 20 min. **Bake:** 10 min./batch + cooling

Laura Kimball, West Jordan, Utah

I really enjoy giving time-tested treats like these soft, chewy gingersnaps as gifts. Dipping them in melted white baking chips makes a yummy treat even more special.

- 2 cups sugar
- 1-1/2 cups canola oil
- 2 eggs
- 1/2 cup molasses
- 4 cups all-purpose flour
- 4 teaspoons baking soda
- 3 teaspoons ground ginger
- 2 teaspoons ground cinnamon
- 1 teaspoon salt

Additional sugar
- 2 packages (10 to 12 ounces *each*) white baking chips
- 1/4 cup shortening

1. In a large bowl, combine sugar and oil. Beat in eggs. Stir in molasses. Combine the flour, baking soda, ginger, cinnamon and salt; gradually add to creamed mixture and mix well.

2. Shape into 3/4-in. balls and roll in sugar. Place 2 in. apart on ungreased baking sheets. Bake at 350° for 10-12 minutes or until cookie springs back when touched lightly. Remove to wire racks to cool.

3. In a microwave, melt chips and shortening; stir until smooth. Dip cookies halfway into the melted chips; allow excess to drip off. Place on waxed paper; let stand until set. **Yield:** about 14-1/2 dozen.

Mocha Truffle Cookies

Prep: 15 min. Bake: 10 min. + cooling

Pamela Jessen, Calgary, Alberta

Looking for the perfect treat to chase away the winter doldrums? Invite a friend over on some chilly afternoon to share a hot beverage and a plateful of these tempting goodies. Crisp on the outside and gooey on the inside, the mocha-flavored cookies will be especially popular with anyone who likes coffee.

　1/4 cup butter, cubed
　1/4 cup semisweet chocolate chips
1-1/2 teaspoons instant coffee granules
　1/3 cup sugar
　1/3 cup packed brown sugar
　　1 egg, lightly beaten
　　1 teaspoon vanilla extract
　　1 cup all-purpose flour
　　2 tablespoons plus 2 teaspoons baking cocoa
　1/4 teaspoon baking powder
　1/8 teaspoon salt
　1/3 cup English toffee bits *or* almond brickle chips
　　1 ounce milk chocolate, melted

1. In a microwave-safe bowl, melt the butter and chocolate; stir until smooth. Stir in coffee granules until dissolved; cool for 5 minutes. Transfer to a small bowl. Add the sugars, egg and vanilla.

2. Combine the flour, cocoa, baking powder and salt; add to the chocolate mixture and mix well. Stir in the toffee bits.

3. Drop by rounded tablespoonfuls 2 in. apart onto a baking sheet lightly coated with cooking spray.

4. Bake at 350° for 8-10 minutes or until set. Cool for 1 minute before removing cookies to a wire rack to cool completely. Drizzle with the melted chocolate. **Yield:** 15 cookies.

Chocolate Caramel Cookies

Prep: 25 min. Bake: 10 min.

Melissa Vannoy, Childress, Texas

This is my go-to recipe when I need something to sell at a bake sale or bazaar. Each delightfully sweet cookie is dipped in chopped pecans before baking and features a fun surprise in the center—a chocolate-and-caramel candy.

　　1 cup butter, softened
　　1 cup plus 1 tablespoon sugar, *divided*
　　1 cup packed brown sugar
　　2 eggs
　　2 teaspoons vanilla extract
2-1/2 cups all-purpose flour
　3/4 cup baking cocoa
　　1 teaspoon baking soda
　　1 cup chopped pecans, *divided*
　　1 package (13 ounces) Rolo candies

1. In a large bowl, cream butter, 1 cup sugar and brown sugar. Beat in eggs and vanilla. Combine flour, cocoa and baking soda; gradually add to creamed mixture just until combined. Stir in 1/2 cup pecans.

2. Shape dough by tablespoonfuls around each candy. In a small bowl, combine remaining pecans and sugar; dip each cookie halfway.

3. Place with nut side up on ungreased baking sheets. Bake at 375° for 7-10 minutes or until top is slightly cracked. Cool for 3 minutes; remove to wire racks to cool completely. **Yield:** about 5 dozen.

Simply Sweet

Light brown sugar has a delicate flavor, while dark brown sugar has a stronger, more intense molasses flavor. Light and dark brown sugar can be used interchangeably in recipes depending on your personal preference.

Rocky Road Brownies

Prep: 10 min. **Bake:** 40 min. + cooling

Donna Sawatzky, Piedmont, Oklahoma

Years ago, my girlfriend and I combined our favorite brownie recipes. With the addition of miniature marshmallows and chocolate chips, the result was a chocoholic's dream.

      1 ounce unsweetened chocolate
  1/4 cup butter, cubed
      1 egg, lightly beaten
  1/2 cup sugar
  1/2 teaspoon vanilla extract
  1/4 cup all-purpose flour
  1/8 teaspoon salt
  1/2 cup miniature marshmallows
  1/3 cup miniature semisweet chocolate
         chips
  1/3 cup chopped pecans

1. In a microwave, melt the unsweetened chocolate and butter; stir until smooth. Cool slightly. In a large bowl, beat the egg and sugar. Stir in the vanilla and chocolate mixture.

2. Combine flour and salt; gradually add chocolate mixture. Stir in the marshmallows, chocolate chips and pecans.

3. Spread into an 8-in. x 4-in. loaf pan coated with cooking spray. Bake at 350° for 40-45 minutes or until brownies begin to pull away from sides of pan. Cool on a wire rack. **Yield:** 6 servings.

Pinwheel Cookies

Prep: 25 min. + chilling **Bake:** 10 min.

Paulette Morgan, Moorhead, Minnesota

The smiles on the faces of family and friends enjoying these spirals makes preparing them well worth the effort. I spread the dough with a rich chocolate-and-orange filling.

      1 cup butter, softened
      1 package (3 ounces) cream cheese, softened
      1 cup sugar
      1 egg
      1 tablespoon grated orange peel
      1 teaspoon vanilla extract
  3-1/2 cups all-purpose flour
      1 teaspoon salt
FILLING:
      1 cup (6 ounces) semisweet chocolate chips
      1 package (3 ounces) cream cheese, softened
  1/2 cup confectioners' sugar
  1/4 cup orange juice

1. In a large bowl, cream the butter, cream cheese and sugar until light and fluffy. Beat in the egg, orange peel and vanilla. Combine flour and salt; gradually add to the creamed mixture and mix well. Cover and chill for 4 hours or until firm.

2. Meanwhile, combine all filling ingredients in a small saucepan. Cook and stir over low heat until smooth; set aside to cool.

3. On a floured surface, divide dough in half; roll each half into a 12-in. x 10-in. rectangle. Spread with filling. Carefully roll up into a tight jelly roll and wrap in waxed paper. Chill overnight.

4. Unwrap and cut into 1/4-in. slices. Place 2 in. apart on ungreased baking sheets. Bake at 375° for 8-10 minutes or until lightly browned. Remove to wire racks to cool. **Yield:** about 8 dozen.

PG. 192

PG. 199

PG. 182

CAKES & PIES

Oohs and aahs are guaranteed when you surprise your family and friends with any of these freshly baked favorites...from creamy Spring Breeze Cheesecake Pie to luscious Pumpkin Cake with Caramel Sauce.

PG. 191

Chippy Macaroon Angel Cake

Prep: 25 min. + standing **Bake:** 50 min. + cooling

Joyce Platfoot, Wapakoneta, Ohio

I love to bake breads and desserts for our large family. This homemade angel food cake, filled with coconut and chocolate chips, is as light as a cloud. And it's pretty with the sweetened whipped cream frosting piped next to each slice.

1-1/2 cups egg whites (about 10)
1-1/2 cups confectioners' sugar
   1 cup cake flour
1-1/2 teaspoons cream of tartar
   1 teaspoon almond extract
   1 teaspoon vanilla extract
  1/4 teaspoon salt
   1 cup sugar
   1 cup (6 ounces) miniature semisweet chocolate
    chips
  1/2 cup flaked coconut
TOPPING:
   1 cup heavy whipping cream
   2 tablespoons confectioners' sugar
  1/2 cup flaked coconut, toasted

1. Place egg whites in a large bowl; let stand at room temperature for 30 minutes. Sift confectioners' sugar and flour together twice; set aside.

2. Add the cream of tartar, extracts and salt to egg whites; beat on medium speed until soft peaks form. Gradually add sugar, 1 tablespoon at a time, beating on high until glossy peaks form and sugar is dissolved. Gradually fold in flour mixture, about 1/2 cup at a time. Fold in chocolate chips and coconut.

3. Gently spoon into an ungreased 10-in. tube pan. Cut through batter with a knife to remove air pockets. Bake on the lowest oven rack at 325° for 50-55 minutes or until top springs back when lightly touched and cracks feel dry. Immediately invert baking pan; cool completely.

4. For the topping, in a large bowl, beat the heavy whipping cream until it begins to thicken. Add the confectioners' sugar; beat until stiff peaks form. Serve with the cake; sprinkle with coconut. Refrigerate any leftover topping. **Yield:** 12-16 servings.

Cinnamon-Sugar Rhubarb Cake

Prep: 30 min. **Bake:** 40 min.

Marlys Haber, White, South Dakota

Always a crowd-pleaser, this snack-like treat is loaded with rhubarb and sprinkled with a sweet cinnamon-sugar topping. Everyone will be asking for the recipe…and another piece!

- 1/2 cup shortening
- 1 cup packed brown sugar
- 1 cup sugar, *divided*
- 1 egg
- 1 teaspoon vanilla extract
- 2 cups all-purpose flour
- 1 teaspoon baking soda
- 1/2 teaspoon salt
- 1 cup buttermilk
- 2 cups diced fresh or frozen rhubarb
- 1 teaspoon ground cinnamon

1. In a large bowl, cream the shortening, brown sugar and 1/2 cup sugar until light and fluffy. Add the egg and vanilla; beat for 2 minutes. Combine the flour, baking soda and salt; add to the creamed mixture alternately with the buttermilk, beating well after each addition. Stir in rhubarb.

2. Pour into a greased 13-in. x 9-in. baking dish. Combine the cinnamon and remaining sugar; sprinkle

over batter. Bake at 350° for 40-45 minutes or until a toothpick inserted near the center comes out clean. Serve warm. **Yield:** 12-16 servings.

Editor's Note: If using frozen rhubarb, measure rhubarb while still frozen, then thaw completely. Drain in a colander, but do not press liquid out.

Cherry Cream Pie

Prep: 40 min. + chilling

Carol Wencka, Greenfield, Wisconsin

A popular vacation destination in Wisconsin, Door County is known for its abundance of cherry orchards, and that's where this recipe originated. The delectable pie features a nutty crumb crust, real whipped cream and, of course, cherry pie filling.

CRUST:
- 1 cup all-purpose flour
- 1 cup finely chopped walnuts
- 1/2 cup butter, softened
- 1/4 cup packed brown sugar

FILLING:
- 1 package (8 ounces) cream cheese, softened
- 1 cup confectioners' sugar
- 1/4 teaspoon almond extract
- 1/2 cup heavy whipping cream, whipped
- 1 can (21 ounces) cherry pie filling

1. In a small bowl, combine the flour, walnuts, butter and brown sugar. Transfer to a 13-in. x 9-in. baking pan. Bake at 375° for 15 minutes, stirring once. Set aside 1 cup of crumbs. While warm, press the remaining crumbs into a greased 9-in. pie plate, firmly pressing onto the bottom and up the sides of plate. Chill crust for 30 minutes.

2. In a small bowl, beat cream cheese, confectioners' sugar and almond extract until smooth. Spread over bottom of crust. Gently fold whipped cream into the pie filling; spread over cream cheese layer. Sprinkle with reserved crumbs. Chill for at least 4 hours before serving. **Yield:** 6-8 servings.

Potluck Apple Pie

Prep: 35 min. **Bake:** 1 hour

Alma Lynne Gravel, Trappe, Pennsylvania

I experimented and came up with this crumb-topped dessert made in a jelly roll pan. It's the perfect apple pie for a large group and always disappears in a hurry.

2-1/4 cups all-purpose flour, *divided*
  1/4 cup water
Pinch salt
    1 cup shortening
FILLING:
  1/2 cup maple syrup, *divided*
    3 pounds tart apples (8 to 9 medium), peeled
      and thinly sliced
1-1/4 cups sugar

  1/4 cup lemon juice
    2 teaspoons ground cinnamon
    1 teaspoon vanilla extract
TOPPING:
    1 cup all-purpose flour
  1/2 cup packed brown sugar
  1/2 cup cold butter, cubed
    1 cup chopped pecans

1. In a small bowl, combine 1/4 cup flour and water until smooth; set aside. In a large bowl, combine salt and remaining flour; cut in shortening until mixture resembles coarse crumbs. Add reserved flour mixture; knead gently until dough forms a ball.

2. Press dough onto the bottom and up the sides of an ungreased 15-in. x 10-in. x 1-in. baking pan.

3. Spread 1/4 cup maple syrup over the crust. Arrange apples over maple syrup. Combine the sugar, lemon juice, cinnamon, vanilla and remaining syrup; drizzle over apples.

4. For the topping, combine the flour and sugar in a bowl; cut in the butter until the mixture resembles coarse crumbs. Stir in the pecans. Sprinkle over filling. Bake at 350° for 1 hour or until apples are tender. **Yield:** 18-24 servings.

Editor's Note: The pastry can be easily pressed into the pan by placing a large sheet of plastic wrap on top of the dough.

Lemon Delight Cake

Prep: 35 min. **Bake:** 40 min. + cooling

    1 package (18-1/4 ounces) lemon cake
      mix
1-1/3 cups water
  3/4 cup egg substitute
  1/3 cup unsweetened applesauce
    3 tablespoons poppy seeds
FILLING:
    1 package (8 ounces) reduced-fat cream
      cheese
  1/2 cup confectioners' sugar
    1 can (15-3/4 ounces) lemon pie
      filling
TOPPING:
  1/3 cup packed brown sugar
  1/4 cup chopped pecans
    3 tablespoons all-purpose flour
4-1/2 teaspoons butter, melted
  1/2 teaspoon ground cinnamon
  1/8 teaspoon vanilla extract

GLAZE:
  1/2 cup confectioners' sugar
    4 teaspoons lemon juice

1. In a large bowl, combine the first five ingredients; beat on low speed for 30 seconds. Beat on medium for 2 minutes. Coat a 13-in. x 9-in. baking pan with cooking spray and dust with flour; spread half of the batter into pan.

2. In a large bowl, beat the cream cheese and confectioners' sugar until smooth. Stir in pie filling. Drop by teaspoonfuls and gently spread over batter. Top with remaining batter.

3. Combine topping ingredients; sprinkle over batter. Bake at 350° for 40-45 minutes or until a toothpick inserted near the center comes out clean. Cool on a wire rack.

4. Combine glaze ingredients; drizzle over cake. Refrigerate leftovers. **Yield:** 18 servings.

LYDIA MASON BRAINERD, MINNESOTA

When I needed to bring a treat to work for my coworkers, I decided to try combining four different recipes I had on hand. The result was this moist, lemony cake. A boxed mix makes it easy, but the creamy filling and buttery topping make it memorable.

GRAND PRIZE WINNER

Macaroon Apple Pie

Prep: 15 min. **Bake:** 50 min.

Frances Musser, Newmanstown, Pennsylvania

I came across this recipe in a rural newspaper years ago, and it's become one of my favorite desserts. I like to serve it warm from the oven with a scoop of vanilla ice cream.

    1-1/2 cups all-purpose flour
      1/2 teaspoon salt
      1/2 cup shortening
      2 to 3 tablespoons cold water
FILLING:
        4 cups sliced peeled tart apples
      1/2 cup sugar
      1/4 teaspoon ground cinnamon
TOPPING:
      1/2 cup all-purpose flour
      1/2 cup sugar
      1/2 teaspoon baking powder
      1/4 teaspoon salt
        1 egg
        2 tablespoons butter, melted
      1/2 teaspoon vanilla extract
      1/4 cup flaked coconut

1. In a large bowl, combine the flour and salt; cut in shortening until crumbly. Gradually add cold water, tossing with a fork until a ball forms.

2. Roll out pastry to fit a 9-in. pie plate; flute edges. Toss apples with sugar and cinnamon; pour into crust. Bake at 375° for 20 minutes.

3. Meanwhile, in a small bowl, combine the first four topping ingredients. Stir in the egg, butter and vanilla until smooth. Add coconut. Spoon over hot apples, carefully spreading to cover. Bake 30 minutes longer or until apples are tender. **Yield:** 6-8 servings.

Fudgy Pecan Pie

Prep: 30 min. + chilling **Bake:** 40 min. + chilling

Ellen Arndt, Cologne, Minnesota

Here's a pie that looks too good to eat...but don't let that stop you! It features two decadent layers of chocolate filling.

        1 unbaked pastry shell (9 inches)
        4 ounces German sweet chocolate, chopped
      1/4 cup butter
        1 can (14 ounces) sweetened condensed milk
      1/2 cup water
        2 eggs, lightly beaten
        1 teaspoon vanilla extract

      1/4 teaspoon salt
      1/2 cup chopped pecans
FILLING:
        1 cup cold milk
        1 package (3.9 ounces) instant chocolate
           pudding mix
        1 cup whipped topping
TOPPING:
        1 cup heavy whipping cream
        1 tablespoon confectioners' sugar
        1 teaspoon vanilla extract

1. Line unpricked pastry shell with a double thickness of heavy-duty foil. Bake at 450° for 5 minutes. Remove foil and set shell aside. Reduce heat to 375°.

2. In a heavy saucepan, melt chocolate and butter. Remove from the heat; stir in milk and water. Add a small amount of hot chocolate mixture to eggs; return all to the pan. Stir in vanilla and salt. Pour into shell; sprinkle with nuts. Cover edges with foil. Bake for 35 minutes or until a knife inserted near the center comes out clean. Remove to a wire rack to cool completely.

3. In a bowl, whisk milk and chocolate pudding mix for 2 minutes. Fold in whipped topping. Spread over nut layer; cover and refrigerate.

4. In a bowl, beat the cream until soft peaks form. Add the sugar and vanilla; beat until stiff peaks form. Spread over pudding layer. Refrigerate until set, about 4 hours. **Yield:** 6-8 servings.

Rhubarb Upside-Down Cake

Prep: 30 min. **Bake:** 40 min. + cooling

Joyce Rowe, Stratham, New Hampshire

This light and airy yellow cake is moist but not too sweet, and the caramelized topping adds tangy flavor. It's a wonderful way to enjoy homegrown rhubarb.

  2/3 **cup packed brown sugar**
    3 **tablespoons butter, melted**
2-1/4 **cups diced fresh *or* frozen rhubarb**
4-1/2 **teaspoons sugar**
BATTER:
    6 **tablespoons butter, softened**
  3/4 **cup sugar**
    2 **eggs, *separated***
    1 **teaspoon vanilla extract**
    1 **cup plus 2 tablespoons all-purpose flour**
1-1/2 **teaspoons baking powder**
  1/2 **teaspoon salt**
  1/4 **cup milk**
  1/4 **teaspoon cream of tartar**
Whipped cream, optional

1. In a small bowl, combine brown sugar and butter. Spread into a greased 9-in. round baking pan. Layer with rhubarb; sprinkle with sugar. Set aside.

2. In a large bowl, cream the butter and sugar until light and fluffy. Beat in egg yolks and vanilla. Combine the flour, baking powder and salt; add to creamed

mixture alternately with the milk, beating well after each addition.

3. In a small bowl, beat egg whites and cream of tartar on medium speed until stiff peaks form. Gradually fold into creamed mixture, about 1/2 cup at a time. Gently spoon over rhubarb (pan will be full, about 1/4 in. from the top of pan).

4. Bake at 325° for 50-60 minutes or until cake springs back when lightly touched. Cool for 10 minutes before inverting cake onto a serving plate. Serve warm with whipped cream if desired. **Yield:** 10-12 servings.

Editor's Note: If using frozen rhubarb, measure rhubarb while still frozen, then thaw completely. Drain in a colander, but do not press liquid out.

Double Peanut Pie

Prep: 10 min. **Bake:** 30 min. + cooling

Vivian Cleeton, Richmond, Virginia

Peanuts are grown in our area, and I always look for ways to use local products. I created this recipe for a national pie contest and won second place for my state.

  2 **eggs**
1/3 **cup creamy peanut butter**
1/3 **cup sugar**
1/3 **cup light corn syrup**
1/3 **cup dark corn syrup**
1/3 **cup butter, melted**
  1 **teaspoon vanilla extract**
  1 **cup salted peanuts**
  1 **unbaked pastry shell (9 inches)**
Whipped cream *or* ice cream, optional

1. In a large bowl, lightly beat eggs. Gradually add the peanut butter, sugar, corn syrups, butter and vanilla until well blended. Fold in peanuts.

2. Pour into the crust. Bake at 375° for 30-35 minutes or until set. Cool. Serve with whipped cream or ice cream if desired. **Yield:** 6-8 servings.

Cranberry Pear Cake

Prep: 40 min. **Bake:** 45 min. + cooling

Jeanne Holt, Saint Paul, Minnesota

If you want a change-of-pace cake that's full of autumn flavor, try this pairing of cranberries and pears. The nutty filling and glaze topping elevate it from a coffee cake to a fancy dessert. You'll want to serve it for all of your special fall occasions.

    1 **cup packed brown sugar**
3/4 **cup chopped pecans**
1/3 **cup chopped dried cranberries**
    1 **teaspoon apple pie spice**
BATTER:
1/2 **cup butter, softened**
    1 **cup sugar**
    3 **eggs**
    1 **teaspoon vanilla extract**
    2 **cups all-purpose flour**
    2 **teaspoons baking powder**
    1 **teaspoon baking soda**
1/2 **teaspoon salt**
    1 **cup (8 ounces) sour cream**
    2 **cups chopped peeled ripe pears**
GLAZE:
    1 **cup confectioners' sugar**

    5 **teaspoons 2% milk**
4-1/2 **teaspoons butter, melted**
  1/4 **teaspoon apple pie spice**
  1/4 **teaspoon vanilla extract**

1. In a small bowl, combine the brown sugar, pecans, dried cranberries and apple pie spice; set the mixture aside.

2. In a large bowl, cream the butter and sugar until light and fluffy. Add the eggs, one at a time, beating well after each addition. Beat in the vanilla. Combine the flour, baking powder, baking soda and salt; add to the creamed mixture alternately with the sour cream just until combined. Fold in the pears.

3. Pour half of the cake batter into a greased and floured 10-in. fluted tube pan. Sprinkle with half of the pecan mixture; top with the remaining batter and pecan mixture.

4. Bake at 350° for 45-50 minutes or until a toothpick inserted near the center comes out clean. Cool for 10 minutes before removing from pan to a wire rack to cool completely.

5. In a small bowl, whisk the glaze ingredients until smooth; drizzle the glaze over the cooled cake. **Yield:** 12-14 servings.

Chocolate Angel Cake

Prep: 25 min. **Bake:** 35 min. + cooling

Joyce Shiffler, Colorado Springs, Colorado

When I first got married, I could barely boil water! My dear mother-in-law taught me how to make her specialty—the lightest angel food cakes you've ever tasted. This tantalizing chocolate variation is easy yet impressive.

1-1/2 cups egg whites (about 10)
1-1/2 cups confectioners' sugar
  1 cup cake flour
  1/4 cup baking cocoa
1-1/2 teaspoons cream of tartar
  1/2 teaspoon salt
  1 cup sugar
FROSTING:
1-1/2 cups heavy whipping cream
  1/2 cup sugar
  1/4 cup baking cocoa
  1/2 teaspoon salt
  1/2 teaspoon vanilla extract
Chocolate leaves, optional

1. Place egg whites in a large bowl; let stand at room temperature for 30 minutes. Sift together confectioners' sugar, flour and cocoa three times; set aside.

2. Add cream of tartar and salt to egg whites; beat on medium speed until soft peaks form. Gradually add sugar, about 2 tablespoons at a time, beating on high until stiff

glossy peaks form and sugar is dissolved. Gradually fold in flour mixture, about 1/2 cup at a time.

3. Spoon into an ungreased 10-in. tube pan. Carefully run a metal spatula or knife through batter to remove air pockets. Bake on the lowest oven rack at 375° for 35-40 minutes or until lightly browned and entire top appears dry. Immediately invert pan; cool completely, about 1 hour.

4. Run a knife around side and center tube of pan. Remove cake to a serving plate.

5. In a large bowl, combine the first five frosting ingredients; cover and chill for 1 hour. Beat until stiff peaks form.

6. Spread frosting over the top and sides of cake. Store in refrigerator. Garnish with chocolate leaves if desired. **Yield:** 12-16 servings.

Cream Cheese Pound Cake

Prep: 10 min. **Bake:** 1-1/2 hours + cooling

Mrs. Michael Ewanek, Hastings, Pennsylvania

After chatting with a woman who came to my rummage sale, I sent her some of my favorite zucchini recipes. In return, she mailed me the recipe for this rich treat.

1-1/2 cups butter, softened
  1 package (8 ounces) cream cheese, softened
2-1/3 cups sugar

  6 eggs
  1 teaspoon vanilla extract
  3 cups all-purpose flour

1. In a large bowl, cream the butter, cream cheese and sugar until light and fluffy, about 5 minutes. Add the eggs, one at a time, beating well after each addition. Beat in the vanilla. Gradually add flour, beating just until blended.

2. Pour batter into a greased and floured 10-in. tube pan. Bake at 300° for 1-1/2 hours or until a toothpick inserted near the center comes out clean. Cool for 10 minutes before removing from pan to a wire rack to cool completely. **Yield:** 12-16 servings.

Fruit Finish

Have frozen berries? Use them to make a fruit sauce for Cream Cheese Pound Cake. Softer and juicier than fresh berries, frozen ones are ideal to use in a sauce for cakes or in other recipes where extra juice is a bonus.

Macadamia Fudge Cake

Prep: 30 min. + cooling **Bake:** 30 min. + cooling

Marguerite Gough, Salida, Colorado

Our daughter and her husband run a cookie factory in Hawaii. After she sent us a big supply of macadamia nuts, I came up with this fudgy cake for special dinners.

 1/2 cup butter, softened
 3/4 cup sugar
   1 egg
 3/4 cup sour cream
 1/2 teaspoon vanilla extract
   1 cup all-purpose flour
 1/4 cup baking cocoa
1-1/2 teaspoons instant coffee granules
 1/2 teaspoon baking powder
 1/2 teaspoon baking soda
 1/4 teaspoon salt
TOPPING:
   1 cup (6 ounces) semisweet chocolate chips
 2/3 cup heavy whipping cream
 1/2 cup sugar
   2 tablespoons butter
   2 tablespoons corn syrup
   1 teaspoon vanilla extract
1-1/2 cups coarsely chopped macadamia nuts *or* almonds

1. In a large bowl, cream butter and sugar until light and fluffy. Beat in egg. Beat in sour cream and vanilla.

Combine flour, cocoa, coffee, baking powder, baking soda and salt; add to creamed mixture and mix well.

2. Pour batter into a greased and floured 9-in. round baking pan. Bake at 350° for 30 minutes or until a toothpick inserted near the center comes out clean. Cool for 10 minutes before removing from pan to a wire rack to cool completely.

3. For the topping, combine chocolate chips, cream, sugar, butter and corn syrup in a saucepan; bring to a boil, stirring constantly. Reduce heat to medium; cook and stir for 7 minutes.

4. Remove from the heat; stir in the vanilla. Cool for 10-15 minutes. Beat with a wooden spoon until slightly thickened, about 4-5 minutes. Stir in nuts. Place the cake on a serving plate; pour topping over cake. **Yield:** 8-10 servings.

Triple Fruit Pie

Prep: 15 min. **Bake:** 50 min.

Jeanne Freybler, Grand Rapids, Michigan

When it comes to pies, my goal is to make mine as good as my mom's. I created this recipe to use up fruit in my freezer. The first time I served it, my family begged for seconds.

1-1/4 cups *each* fresh blueberries, raspberries and chopped rhubarb
 1/2 teaspoon almond extract
1-1/4 cups sugar
 1/4 cup quick-cooking tapioca
 1/4 teaspoon ground nutmeg
 1/4 teaspoon salt
Pastry for double-crust pie (9 inches)
   1 tablespoon lemon juice

1. In a large bowl, combine the fruits and extract; toss to coat. In another bowl, combine sugar, tapioca, nutmeg and salt. Add to fruit; stir gently. Let stand for 15 minutes.

2. Line a 9-in. pie plate with bottom crust; trim pastry even with edge. Stir lemon juice into fruit mixture; spoon into the crust. Roll out remaining pastry; make a lattice crust. Seal and flute edges.

3. Bake at 400° for 20 minutes. Reduce heat to 350°; bake 30 minutes longer or until the crust is golden brown and the filling is bubbly. **Yield:** 6-8 servings.

Editor's Note: Frozen berries and rhubarb may be substituted for fresh; thaw and drain before using.

Tiny Texas Sheet Cakes

Prep: 25 min. **Bake:** 20 min. + cooling

Hope Meece, Ambia, Indiana

These moist cakes boast chocolate flavor as big as Texas itself. They freeze well unfrosted and always bring compliments.

- 1/4 cup butter, cubed
- 1/4 cup water
- 1 tablespoon baking cocoa
- 1/2 cup all-purpose flour
- 1/2 cup sugar
- 1/2 teaspoon baking powder
- 1/4 teaspoon ground cinnamon
- Dash salt
- 2 tablespoons beaten egg
- 2 tablespoons 2% milk

FROSTING:
- 2 tablespoons butter
- 4-1/2 teaspoons 2% milk
- 1 tablespoon baking cocoa
- 3/4 cup confectioners' sugar
- 1/4 teaspoon vanilla extract
- 2 tablespoons chopped pecans, toasted, optional

1. In a large saucepan, bring the butter, water and cocoa just to a boil. Immediately remove from the heat. Combine flour, sugar, baking powder, cinnamon

and salt; stir into the butter mixture. Add egg and milk; mix well.

2. Pour into two 5-3/4-in. x 3-in. x 2-in. loaf pans coated with cooking spray. Bake at 350° for 20-25 minutes or until a toothpick inserted near the center comes out clean. Cool for 10 minutes before removing from pans to a wire rack to cool completely.

3. In a small microwave-safe bowl, melt butter; add milk and cocoa. Microwave on high for 30 seconds. Whisk in the confectioners' sugar and vanilla until smooth. Spread over cakes. Sprinkle with pecans if desired. **Yield:** 4 servings.

Editor's Note: This recipe was tested in a 1,100-watt microwave.

Pumpkin Cake with Caramel Sauce

Prep: 20 min. **Bake:** 35 min. + cooling

Roberta Peck, Fort Hill, Pennsylvania

This variation of a traditional spice cake features pumpkin and is draped with a luscious caramel sauce. Yum!

- 2 cups all-purpose flour
- 2 cups sugar
- 2 teaspoons ground cinnamon
- 1 teaspoon baking soda
- 1 teaspoon ground nutmeg
- 1/2 teaspoon salt
- 4 eggs
- 1 can (15 ounces) solid-pack pumpkin
- 1 cup canola oil

CARAMEL SAUCE:
- 1-1/2 cups packed brown sugar
- 3 tablespoons all-purpose flour
- Dash salt
- 1-1/4 cups water
- 2 tablespoons butter
- 1/2 teaspoon vanilla extract

1. In a large bowl, combine the flour, sugar, cinnamon, baking soda, nutmeg and salt. In another bowl, beat the eggs, pumpkin and oil until smooth; add to the dry ingredients. Mix until well blended, about 1 minute.

2. Pour the cake batter into a greased 13-in. x 9-in. baking pan. Bake at 350° for 40-45 minutes or until a toothpick inserted near the center comes out clean. Cool on a wire rack.

3. For sauce, combine the brown sugar, flour and salt in a small saucepan. Stir in water and butter; bring to a boil over medium heat. Boil for 3 minutes, stirring constantly. Remove from the heat; stir in vanilla. Cut cake into squares and serve with warm sauce. **Yield:** 12-16 servings.

Peach Melba Mountain

Prep: 45 min. + chilling **Bake:** 35 min. + cooling

Sally Sibthorpe, Shelby Township, Michigan

I've competed in several state fair cooking contests, and this is one of my best entries. It tastes just as good as it looks.

1 package (16 ounces) angel food cake mix
1 package (3 ounces) peach *or* orange gelatin
1 cup boiling water
1 package (8 ounces) cream cheese, softened
1 teaspoon almond extract
1 carton (12 ounces) frozen whipped topping, thawed
1 cup sliced almonds, toasted, *divided*
3 cups sliced peeled fresh peaches
3 cups fresh raspberries

1. Prepare and bake cake according to package directions, using an ungreased 10-in. tube pan. Immediately invert pan; cool completely, about 1 hour.

2. Meanwhile, in a small bowl, dissolve the gelatin in boiling water; cool. In a large bowl, beat cream cheese and extract until fluffy. Gradually beat in gelatin. Fold in whipped topping and 3/4 cup almonds. Cover and refrigerate for 30 minutes.

3. Run a knife around side and center tube of pan. Remove cake. Cut into three horizontal layers. Place bottom layer on a serving plate; spread with a third of the cream mixture. Top with 1 cup of peaches and 1 cup of berries. Repeat layers. Sprinkle with remaining almonds. Chill for at least 30 minutes before serving. Refrigerate leftovers. **Yield:** 12-14 servings.

Mocha Chip Pie

Prep: 35 min. + chilling

Sheila Watson, Stettler, Alberta

This luscious mocha pie is chocolaty from top to bottom. The only difficult thing about preparing it is waiting for it to set! You and your family will want to dig right in.

1-1/2 cups chocolate wafer crumbs
 1/4 cup butter, softened
   1 envelope unflavored gelatin
 1/2 cup milk
 1/2 cup plus 1 tablespoon sugar, *divided*
 1/2 cup strong brewed coffee
 1/4 cup water
 1/4 teaspoon salt
   2 ounces unsweetened chocolate, melted and cooled
   1 teaspoon vanilla extract
   2 cups heavy whipping cream, *divided*
Toasted sliced almonds, optional

1. In a small bowl, combine wafer crumbs and butter. Press onto the bottom and up the sides of a greased 9-in. pie plate. Bake at 375° for 5-7 minutes or until lightly browned. Cool on a wire rack.

2. In a small saucepan, sprinkle gelatin over milk; let stand for 1 minute. Cook and stir over low heat until gelatin is completely dissolved. Add 1/2 cup sugar, coffee, water and salt; cook and stir for 5 minutes or until sugar is dissolved. Remove from the heat; stir in melted chocolate and vanilla. Transfer to a large bowl; cover and refrigerate until slightly thickened, stirring occasionally.

3. In a small bowl, beat 1 cup cream until stiff peaks form; fold into chocolate mixture. Spread evenly into crust. Refrigerate for 4 hours or until set.

4. Just before serving, in a small bowl, beat remaining cream until it begins to thicken. Add remaining sugar; beat until stiff peaks form. Pipe over pie. Garnish with nuts if desired. Refrigerate leftovers. **Yield:** 8 servings.

Rhubarb-Ribbon Brunch Cake

Prep: 30 min. **Bake:** 1 hour + cooling

Mary Blenk, Cumberland, Maine

My father has always had a flourishing patch of rhubarb, and I wanted to try to create a recipe using his endless supply. This one can be enjoyed either as a coffee cake for brunch or as an elegant finish to a special meal.

3/4 cup sugar
3 tablespoons cornstarch
1/4 teaspoon ground cinnamon
1/8 teaspoon ground nutmeg
1/3 cup cold water
2-1/2 cups sliced fresh *or* frozen rhubarb
3 to 4 drops red food coloring, optional

BATTER:
2-1/4 cups all-purpose flour
3/4 cup sugar
3/4 cup cold butter, cubed
1/2 teaspoon baking powder
1/2 teaspoon baking soda
1/2 teaspoon salt
1 egg, lightly beaten
3/4 cup (6 ounces) vanilla yogurt
1 teaspoon vanilla extract

TOPPING:
1 egg, lightly beaten
8 ounces Mascarpone cheese
1/4 cup sugar
1/2 cup chopped pecans
1/4 cup flaked coconut

1. In a large saucepan, combine the sugar, cornstarch, cinnamon, nutmeg and cold water until smooth. Add the rhubarb. Bring to a boil; cook and stir for 2 minutes or until thickened. Add the food coloring if desired. Set aside.

2. In a large bowl, combine flour and sugar; cut in butter until the mixture resembles coarse crumbs. Set aside 1 cup for the topping. Add the baking powder, baking soda and salt to the remaining crumb mixture. In a small bowl, combine the egg, yogurt and vanilla; stir into batter until smooth. Spread into a greased 9-in. springform pan.

3. Combine the egg, Mascarpone cheese and sugar; spoon over the batter. Top with rhubarb mixture. Add pecans and coconut to the reserved crumb mixture; sprinkle over top.

4. Bake at 350° for 60-65 minutes or until a toothpick inserted near the center comes out clean. Cool on a wire rack for 20 minutes; remove sides of pan. Cool completely. **Yield:** 12 servings.

Editor's Note: If using frozen rhubarb, measure rhubarb while still frozen, then thaw completely. Drain in a colander, but do not press liquid out.

Fresh Blueberry Pie

Prep: 20 min. + chilling

R. Ricks, Kalamazoo, Michigan

We live in blueberry-growing country, and this is a wonderful way to showcase the bountiful crop. A neighbor of ours made this pie for us several years ago and shared the recipe. Just add a dollop of whipped cream for the perfect finishing touch.

> 3/4 cup sugar
> 3 tablespoons cornstarch
> 1/8 teaspoon salt
> 1/4 cup water
> 4 cups fresh blueberries, *divided*
> 1 graham cracker crust (9 inches)
> Whipped cream

1. In a large saucepan, combine the sugar, cornstarch and salt. Gradually add water, stirring until smooth. Stir in 2 cups of blueberries. Bring to a boil; cook and stir for 1-2 minutes or until thickened. Remove from the heat; cool to room temperature.

2. Spoon remaining blueberries into the crust; top with cooled blueberry mixture. Cover and refrigerate for 1-2 hours or until chilled. Serve pie with whipped cream. **Yield:** 6-8 servings.

Vanilla Custard Pie

Prep: 30 min. **Bake:** 15 min. + chilling

Bernard Parys, Ixonia, Wisconsin

My grandmother passed down this recipe to my mother, who in turn gave it to me. Now my daughter likes to make it for her family. With a homemade graham cracker crust, custard filling and fluffy meringue topping, this was one of my favorite treats when I was a kid, and it still is today.

> 1-1/4 cups graham cracker crumbs
> 3 tablespoons brown sugar
> 1/3 cup butter, melted
> **FILLING:**
> 1/2 cup sugar
> 1/4 cup all-purpose flour
> 1/2 teaspoon salt
> 2 cups milk
> 2 egg yolks, lightly beaten
> 2 teaspoons vanilla extract
> **MERINGUE:**
> 2 egg whites
> 1/4 teaspoon vanilla extract
> 1/8 teaspoon cream of tartar
> 1/4 cup sugar
> 1/4 cup graham cracker crumbs

1. Combine the graham cracker crumbs, brown sugar and butter; press onto the bottom and up the sides of an ungreased 9-in. pie plate. Bake at 350° for 8-10 minutes or until lightly browned. Cool the crust on a wire rack.

2. In a small saucepan, combine the sugar, flour and salt. Stir in milk until smooth. Cook and stir over medium-high heat until thickened and bubbly. Reduce heat; cook and stir 2 minutes longer. Remove from the heat. Stir a small amount of hot filling into egg yolks; return all to the pan. Bring to a gentle boil, stirring constantly; cook and stir 2 minutes longer. Remove from the heat. Gently stir in vanilla. Pour into crust.

3. In a small bowl, beat the egg whites, vanilla and cream of tartar on medium speed until soft peaks form. Gradually beat in the sugar, 1 tablespoon at a time, on high until stiff peaks form. Spread over the hot filling, sealing the edges to the crust. Sprinkle with graham cracker crumbs.

4. Bake at 350° for 15 minutes or until golden brown. Cool on a wire rack for 1 hour. Refrigerate for at least 3 hours before serving. **Yield:** 8 servings.

Lemon Meringue Angel Cake

Prep: 40 min. + standing **Bake:** 35 min. + cooling

Sharon Kurtz, Emmaus, Pennsylvania

I've been told this is the best angel food cake around. It has a tongue-tingling layer of lemon curd in the center.

- 12 **egg whites**
- 1-1/2 **cups sugar,** *divided*
- 1 **cup cake flour**
- 2 **teaspoons cream of tartar**
- 1-1/2 **teaspoons vanilla extract**
- 1/4 **teaspoon salt**
- 1 **jar (10 ounces) lemon curd**

MERINGUE TOPPING:
- 4 **egg whites**
- 3/4 **teaspoon cream of tartar**
- 1/2 **cup sugar**

1. Place egg whites in a large bowl; let stand at room temperature for 30 minutes. Sift 1/2 cup sugar and flour together twice; set aside.

2. Add the cream of tartar, vanilla and salt to the egg whites; beat on medium speed until soft peaks form. Gradually beat in the remaining sugar, 2 tablespoons at a time, on high until stiff glossy peaks form and sugar is dissolved. Gradually fold in flour mixture, about 1/2 cup at a time.

3. Gently spoon the batter into an ungreased 10-in. tube pan. Cut through batter with a knife to remove air pockets. Bake on lowest oven rack at 350° for 35-40 minutes or until golden brown and entire top appears dry. Immediately invert pan; cool completely, about 1 hour.

4. Run a knife around side and center tube of pan. Remove cake; split into two horizontal layers. Place the cake bottom on an ovenproof plate. Spread with lemon curd; replace cake top.

5. For the meringue, in a small bowl, beat egg whites and cream of tartar on medium until soft peaks form. Gradually beat in sugar, 1 tablespoon at a time, on high until stiff glossy peaks form and sugar is dissolved. Spread over top and sides of cake. Bake at 350° for 15-18 minutes or until golden brown. Refrigerate leftovers. **Yield:** 14 servings.

Caramel Crunch Cake

Prep: 15 min. **Bake:** 35 min. + cooling

Heather Dollins, Poplar Bluff, Missouri

I love how this eye-catching dessert comes together with little more than a boxed mix, water and egg whites. The crushed candy bars make a fun and crunchy addition on top.

- 1 **package (18-1/4 ounces) devil's food cake mix**
- 1-1/3 **cups water**
- 5 **egg whites**
- 1 **can (14 ounces) fat-free sweetened condensed milk**
- 1/2 **cup fat-free caramel ice cream topping**
- 5 **fun-size Butterfinger candy bars, crushed**
- 1 **carton (8 ounces) frozen fat-free whipped topping, thawed**

1. In a large bowl, combine the cake mix, water and egg whites; beat on low speed for 30 seconds. Beat on medium for 2 minutes. Pour into a 13-in. x 9-in. baking pan coated with cooking spray.

2. Bake at 350° for 35-40 minutes or until a toothpick inserted near the center comes out clean. Cool on a wire rack.

3. With a meat fork or wooden skewer, poke holes about 2 in. apart into the cake. Slowly pour sweetened condensed milk and caramel ice cream topping over cake; sprinkle with two-thirds of the crushed candy bars. Spread with whipped topping; sprinkle with remaining candy bars. Refrigerate until serving. **Yield:** 18 servings.

Butter Pecan Cake

Prep: 40 min. **Bake:** 25 min. + cooling

Becky Miller, Tallahassee, Florida

Pecans and butter give this impressive three-layer cake the same irresistible flavor as the popular flavor of ice cream.

2-2/3 cups chopped pecans
1-1/4 cups butter, softened, *divided*
    2 cups sugar
    4 eggs
    2 teaspoons vanilla extract
    3 cups all-purpose flour
    2 teaspoons baking powder
  1/2 teaspoon salt
    1 cup milk
FROSTING:
    1 cup butter, softened
    8 to 8-1/2 cups confectioners' sugar

    1 can (5 ounces) evaporated milk
    2 teaspoons vanilla extract

1. Place pecans and 1/4 cup butter in a baking pan. Bake at 350° for 20-25 minutes or until toasted, stirring frequently; set aside.

2. In a large bowl, cream sugar and remaining butter until light and fluffy. Add eggs, one at a time, beating well after each addition. Stir in vanilla. Combine the flour, baking powder and salt; add to the creamed mixture alternately with milk, beating well after each addition. Stir in 1-1/3 cups of toasted pecans.

3. Pour into three greased and floured 9-in. round baking pans. Bake at 350° for 25-30 minutes or until a toothpick inserted near the center comes out clean. Cool for 10 minutes before removing from pans to wire racks to cool completely.

4. For frosting, cream butter and confectioners' sugar in a large bowl. Add the milk and vanilla; beat until smooth. Stir in the remaining toasted pecans. Spread the frosting between layers and over top and sides of cake. **Yield:** 12-16 servings.

Tender Treats

Adding dry and wet ingredients alternately to cake batter helps to keep gluten from forming. Gluten can result in a tough cake texture. Excessive beating will also toughen cakes.

Chunky Apple Cake

Prep: 20 min. **Bake:** 40 min. + cooling

  1/2 cup butter, softened
    2 cups sugar
    2 eggs
  1/2 teaspoon vanilla extract
    2 cups all-purpose flour
1-1/2 teaspoons ground cinnamon
    1 teaspoon ground nutmeg
  1/2 teaspoon salt
  1/2 teaspoon baking soda
    6 cups chopped peeled tart apples
BUTTERSCOTCH SAUCE:
  1/2 cup packed brown sugar
  1/4 cup butter, cubed
  1/2 cup heavy whipping cream

1. In a large bowl, cream butter and sugar until light and fluffy. Add eggs, one at a time, beating well after each addition. Beat in vanilla. Combine the flour, cinnamon, nutmeg, salt and baking soda; gradually add to creamed mixture and mix well (batter will be stiff). Stir in apples.

2. Spread batter into a greased 13-in. x 9-in. baking dish. Bake at 350° for 40-45 minutes or until the top is lightly browned and springs back when lightly touched. Cool for 30 minutes before serving.

3. Meanwhile, in a small saucepan, combine the brown sugar and butter. Cook over medium heat until butter is melted.

4. Gradually add the heavy whipping cream. Bring to a slow boil over medium heat, stirring constantly. Remove from the heat. Serve the sauce with the cake. **Yield:** 12-14 servings.

DEBI BENSON BAKERSFIELD, CALIFORNIA

This tender, moist treat is full of the old-fashioned comfort everyone craves. It's loaded with chunks of tart apples, and the yummy brown sugar sauce makes it even more special.

GRAND
PRIZE
WINNER

Cranberry Pear Crisp Pie

Prep: 25 min. **Bake:** 55 min. + cooling

Priscilla Gilbert, Indian Harbour Beach, Florida

Filled with a bubbling combination of cranberries and pears, this crumb-topped pie is a scrumptious change of pace for your Thanksgiving or Christmas feast.

- 5 cups sliced peeled fresh pears
- 1 tablespoon lemon juice
- 1 teaspoon vanilla extract
- 1-2/3 cups fresh or frozen cranberries
- 1/2 cup packed brown sugar
- 1/3 cup all-purpose flour
- 1 unbaked pastry shell (9 inches)

TOPPING:
- 1/4 cup all-purpose flour
- 1/4 cup quick-cooking oats
- 3 tablespoons packed brown sugar
- 3/4 teaspoon ground cinnamon
- 2 tablespoons cold butter

1. Place the pears in a large bowl; sprinkle with lemon juice and vanilla. Add the cranberries. Combine the brown sugar and flour; sprinkle over fruit and gently toss to coat. Spoon into pastry shell.

2. In a small bowl, combine the flour, oats, brown sugar and cinnamon. Cut in butter until crumbly. Sprinkle over filling.

3. Cover the edges of pastry loosely with foil. Bake at 375° for 30 minutes. Remove foil; bake 25-30 minutes longer or until the filling is bubbly. Cool on a wire rack. **Yield:** 8 servings.

Oatmeal Cake with Broiled Frosting

Prep: 30 min. **Bake:** 30 min.

Pat Van Cleve, Winston-Salem, North Carolina

With a homemade coconut frosting that's broiled to a golden brown, this tender snack cake is terrific. Enjoy it not only as a dessert after dinner, but also as a special morning treat.

- 1 cup quick-cooking oats
- 1-1/2 cups boiling water
- 1 cup sugar
- 1 cup packed brown sugar
- 1/2 cup unsweetened applesauce
- 2 eggs, lightly beaten
- 1-1/2 cups all-purpose flour
- 2 teaspoons baking powder
- 2 teaspoons ground cinnamon
- 1 teaspoon salt
- 1/2 teaspoon baking soda
- 1/4 teaspoon ground nutmeg

FROSTING:
- 1 cup flaked coconut
- 1/2 cup packed brown sugar
- 1/2 cup chopped walnuts
- 1/4 cup fat-free half-and-half
- 2 tablespoons butter, melted
- 1/2 teaspoon vanilla extract

1. In a small bowl, combine oats and water; let stand for 20 minutes. In a large bowl, combine the sugars, applesauce and eggs. Add the oat mixture; mix well. Combine the flour, baking powder, cinnamon, salt, baking soda and nutmeg; gradually add to batter and mix well.

2. Pour cake batter into a 13-in. x 9-in. baking pan coated with cooking spray. Bake at 350° for 25-30 minutes or until a toothpick inserted near the center comes out clean.

3. In a large bowl, combine the frosting ingredients; spread over the hot cake. Broil 6 in. from the heat for 1-2 minutes or until lightly browned and bubbly. **Yield:** 15 servings.

Spring Breeze Cheesecake Pie

Prep: 30 min. + chilling Cook: 15 min. + cooling

Deanna Taylor, Ainsworth, Nebraska

I combined two of my favorites—cheesecake and rhubarb—to create this rich and creamy pie topped with a colorful sauce. Everyone who tastes it raves about it.

    1 package (8 ounces) cream cheese, softened
  1/3 cup sugar
    1 cup (8 ounces) sour cream
    2 teaspoons vanilla extract
    1 carton (8 ounces) frozen whipped topping, thawed
    1 graham cracker crust (9 inches)
TOPPING:
    3 cups chopped fresh *or* frozen rhubarb
  1/3 cup sugar
  1/8 teaspoon ground cinnamon
    1 tablespoon cornstarch
    2 tablespoons cold water

1. In a small bowl, beat cream cheese until smooth. Gradually beat in sugar. Beat in sour cream and vanilla. Set aside 1/2 cup whipped topping for garnish; cover and refrigerate. Beat 1/2 cup whipped topping into cream cheese mixture; fold in remaining whipped topping. Spoon into the crust. Cover and refrigerate for at least 2 hours.

2. For the topping, in a large saucepan, bring the rhubarb, sugar and cinnamon to a boil. Reduce the heat; simmer, uncovered, for 5-8 minutes or until the rhubarb is tender.

3. In a small bowl, combine cornstarch and cold water until smooth. Gradually stir into rhubarb mixture. Return to a boil; cook and stir for 1-2 minutes or until thickened. Cool to room temperature.

4. Cut pie into slices; top with rhubarb sauce and reserved whipped topping. **Yield:** 6-8 servings.

Ready for Rhubarb

Planning to make scrumptious Spring Breeze Cheesecake Pie—and wondering how much rhubarb will give you the amount needed for the topping? One pound of rhubarb will yield approximately 3 cups chopped.

Fresh Raspberry Pie

Prep: 15 min. + chilling Cook: 5 min. + cooling

Patricia Staudt, Marble Rock, Iowa

Just-picked raspberries are the stars of this simple but wonderful recipe that uses only six ingredients. There's nothing to distract from the tangy berry flavor and gorgeous ruby-red color.

 This recipe includes Nutrition Facts & Diabetic Exchange.

  1/4 cup sugar
    1 tablespoon cornstarch
    1 cup water
    1 package (3 ounces) raspberry gelatin
    4 cups fresh raspberries
    1 graham cracker crust (9 inches)

1. In a small saucepan, combine the sugar, cornstarch and water until smooth. Bring to a boil, stirring constantly. Cook and stir for 2 minutes or until thickened. Remove from the heat; stir in gelatin until dissolved. Cool for 15 minutes.

2. Place the raspberries in the crust; slowly pour the gelatin mixture over raspberries. Chill until set, about 3 hours. **Yield:** 6-8 servings.

Nutrition Facts: 1 piece equals 162 calories, 1 g fat, 0 cholesterol, 118 mg sodium, 31 g carbohydrate, 4 g fiber, 2 g protein. **Diabetic Exchange:** 2 starch.

Rhubarb Meringue Pie

Prep: 50 min. + chilling **Bake:** 65 min. + cooling

Elaine Sampson, Colesburg, Iowa

My husband's grandmother was a wonderful baker but didn't always share her secrets, so we are fortunate to have her recipe for rhubarb cream pie. I embellished it a bit by adding one of my favorite crusts and a never-fail meringue.

3/4 **cup all-purpose flour**
1/4 **teaspoon salt**
1/4 **teaspoon sugar**
1/4 **cup shortening**
    1 **tablespoon beaten egg**
1/4 **teaspoon white vinegar**
    3 **to 4-1/2 teaspoons cold water**
FILLING:
    3 **cups chopped fresh *or* frozen rhubarb**
    1 **cup sugar**
    2 **tablespoons all-purpose flour**
Dash salt
    3 **egg yolks**
    1 **cup heavy whipping cream**
MERINGUE:
    4 **teaspoons plus 1/3 cup sugar, *divided***
    2 **teaspoons cornstarch**
1/3 **cup water**
    3 **egg whites**
1/8 **teaspoon cream of tartar**

1. In a small bowl, combine flour, salt and sugar; cut in shortening until crumbly. Combine egg and vinegar; sprinkle over crumb mixture. Gradually add the water, tossing with a fork until a ball forms. Cover and chill for 1 hour or until easy to handle.

2. On a lightly floured surface, roll out pastry to fit a 9-in. pie plate. Trim to 1/2 in. beyond edge of plate; flute edges.

3. Place rhubarb in crust. Whisk the sugar, flour, salt, egg yolks and cream; pour over rhubarb. Bake at 350° for 50-60 minutes or until a knife comes out clean.

4. In a small saucepan, combine 4 teaspoons sugar and cornstarch. Gradually stir in the water. Bring to a boil, stirring constantly; cook for 1-2 minutes or until thickened. Cool to room temperature.

5. In a small bowl, beat egg whites and cream of tartar until frothy. Add cornstarch mixture; beat on high until soft peaks form. Gradually beat in remaining sugar, 1 tablespoon at a time, on high until stiff glossy peaks form and sugar is dissolved.

6. Spread evenly over hot filling, sealing edges to crust. Bake for 15 minutes or until meringue is golden brown. Cool on a wire rack for 1 hour. Store in the refrigerator. **Yield:** 6-8 servings.

Editor's Note: If using frozen rhubarb, measure rhubarb while still frozen, then thaw completely. Drain in a colander, but do not press liquid out.

Apple-Topped Cake

Prep: 25 min. **Bake:** 50 min. + cooling

David Heppner, Brandon, Florida

With plenty of apples, walnuts and cinnamon, this dessert is so good with a cup of coffee on a brisk autumn day. Baking the cake in a springform pan helps ensure great results.

 This recipe includes Nutrition Facts & Diabetic Exchanges.

- 3 tablespoons butter, softened
- 3/4 cup sugar
- 1 egg
- 1 egg white
- 1 cup vanilla yogurt
- 1/3 cup unsweetened applesauce
- 2 tablespoons canola oil
- 2 teaspoons vanilla extract
- 2 cups all-purpose flour
- 1 teaspoon baking powder
- 1/2 teaspoon baking soda
- 1/2 teaspoon salt
- 1-1/2 cups chopped peeled apples
- 2 tablespoons chopped walnuts
- 1 tablespoon brown sugar
- 1/2 teaspoon ground cinnamon
- 1/8 teaspoon ground allspice

1. In a large bowl, beat the butter and sugar until crumbly, about 2 minutes. Add the egg, egg white, yogurt, applesauce, oil and vanilla; beat until smooth. Combine the dry ingredients; add to butter mixture, beating just until moistened.

2. Pour batter into a 9-in. springform pan coated with cooking spray. Sprinkle with apples and walnuts. Combine the brown sugar, cinnamon and allspice; sprinkle over top.

3. Bake at 375° for 47-52 minutes or until a toothpick inserted near the center comes out clean. Cool on a wire rack. Run a knife around the edge of the pan to loosen. Remove the sides of the pan. Refrigerate leftovers. **Yield:** 10 servings.

Nutrition Facts: 1 piece equals 268 calories, 9 g fat (3 g saturated fat), 33 mg cholesterol, 285 mg sodium, 43 g carbohydrate, 1 g fiber, 5 g protein. **Diabetic Exchanges:** 3 starch, 1-1/2 fat.

Walnut Apple Bundt Cake

Prep: 15 min. **Bake:** 50 min.

Donna Gonda, North Canton, Ohio

At the campground where my husband and I have our trailer, the campers hold an auction of baked goods. I contributed this moist bundt cake last year, and it brought in the highest bid!

- 3 eggs
- 1 cup canola oil
- 1 tablespoon vanilla extract
- 2 cups shredded peeled tart apples
- 2 cups sugar
- 3 cups all-purpose flour
- 1 tablespoon ground cinnamon
- 1 teaspoon baking soda
- 1 teaspoon salt
- 3/4 teaspoon ground nutmeg
- 1/2 teaspoon baking powder
- 1 cup chopped walnuts
- 2 tablespoons confectioners' sugar
- 2 tablespoons brown sugar

1. In a large bowl, beat eggs, oil and vanilla. Add apples and sugar; beat for 1 minute. Combine flour, cinnamon, baking soda, salt, nutmeg and baking powder; add to apple mixture until blended. Stir in nuts.

2. Pour batter into a greased and floured 10-in. fluted tube pan. Bake at 325° for 50-60 minutes or until a toothpick inserted near the center comes out clean. Cool for 10 minutes before removing from pan to a wire rack to cool completely.

3. Combine confectioners' sugar and brown sugar; sprinkle over cake. **Yield:** 15 servings.

PG. 222

PG. 218

PG. 222

JUST DESSERTS

From White Chocolate Raspberry Cheesecake and Toffee-Crunch Coffee Sundaes to Peanut Butter Ice Cream and Caramel Apple Crisp, these tempting treats are sure to please every sweet tooth at the table.

PG. 206

Colorful Frozen Yogurt

Prep: 20 min. + freezing

Tiffany Blepp, Olathe, Kansas

Here's a pretty, refreshing treat for a hot day. Blending berries and peaches into purchased vanilla frozen yogurt is so easy and creates three different flavors. I serve the honey-topped scoops in martini glasses with mint leaves for garnishes.

        3 pints low-fat vanilla frozen yogurt, softened, *divided*
1-1/2 cups frozen unsweetened sliced peaches, thawed
1-1/4 cups frozen unsweetened blueberries, thawed
1-1/4 cups frozen unsweetened strawberries, thawed
      12 teaspoons honey

1. Place one pint of frozen yogurt in a blender; add the peaches. Cover and process until smooth. Transfer to a freezer-safe container; cover and freeze. Repeat twice, making a batch of blueberry frozen yogurt and a batch of strawberry frozen yogurt.

2. Using a small scoop or melon baller, scoop each flavor of yogurt onto a waxed paper-lined baking sheet. Freeze until firm.

3. For each serving, place two scoops of each flavor in individual dessert dishes. Drizzle each with 1 teaspoon honey. **Yield:** 12 servings.

Editor's Note: We used a melon baller to make the small scoops of frozen yogurt.

Blueberry Cream Dessert

Prep: 20 min. + chilling

Susan Kruspe, Shortsville, New York

I enjoy serving this cool, crumb-topped dessert for spring and summer luncheons and as a light finish to dinner. Feel free to replace the blueberries with another fruit, such as strawberries, oranges, raspberries or whatever is in season.

        1 cup (8 ounces) sour cream
    3/4 cup (6 ounces) blueberry yogurt
        1 envelope unflavored gelatin
    3/4 cup cold water
    3/4 cup sugar, *divided*
    1/2 teaspoon vanilla extract
1-1/4 cups graham cracker crumbs
        6 tablespoons butter, melted
        1 cup fresh blueberries
    1/2 cup heavy whipping cream, whipped

1. In a small bowl, combine sour cream and yogurt; set aside. In a small saucepan, sprinkle the gelatin over the cold water; let stand for 1 minute. Add 1/2 cup sugar. Cook and stir over low heat until the gelatin is completely dissolved.

2. Remove from the heat; stir in the vanilla and sour cream mixture until blended. Transfer to a large bowl. Chill until partially set.

3. Meanwhile, in a small bowl, combine the graham cracker crumbs, butter and remaining sugar; set aside 1/4 cup for topping. Press the remaining crumb mixture into an ungreased 8-in. square dish; set aside.

4. Stir the blueberries into the gelatin mixture; fold in the whipped cream. Spoon into crust. Sprinkle with reserved crumb mixture. Chill until set. Refrigerate leftovers. **Yield:** 9 servings.

White Chocolate Raspberry Cheesecake

Prep: 25 min. **Bake:** 1 hour 20 min. + chilling

Wendy Barkman, Breezewood, Pennsylvania

As a dairy farmer's wife, I cook with a lot of dairy products. This swirled cheesecake is beautiful and decadent.

1-1/2 cups graham cracker crumbs
1/4 cup sugar
1/3 cup butter, melted
FILLING:
   3 packages (8 ounces *each*) cream cheese, softened
3/4 cup sugar
1/3 cup sour cream
   3 tablespoons all-purpose flour
   1 teaspoon vanilla extract
   3 eggs, lightly beaten
   1 package (10 to 12 ounces) white baking chips
1/4 cup seedless raspberry jam

1. In a small bowl, combine graham cracker crumbs, sugar and butter. Press onto the bottom of a greased 9-in. springform pan; set aside.

2. In a large bowl, beat cream cheese and sugar until smooth. Beat in the sour cream, flour and vanilla. Add eggs; beat on low speed just until combined. Fold in the chips. Pour over crust.

3. In a microwave, melt the raspberry jam; stir until smooth. Drop by teaspoonfuls over batter; cut through batter with a knife to swirl.

4. Place pan on a double thickness of heavy-duty foil (about 16 in. square). Securely wrap foil around pan. Place in a large baking pan; add 1 in. of hot water to larger pan.

5. Bake at 325° for 80-85 minutes or until center is just set. Cool on a wire rack for 10 minutes. Carefully run a knife around edge of pan to loosen; cool 1 hour longer. Cover and refrigerate overnight. Remove sides of pan. **Yield:** 12 servings.

Toffee-Crunch Coffee Sundaes

Prep/Total Time: 15 min.

Beth Royals, Richmond, Virginia

I came up with these yummy sundaes one day when I wanted to make hot fudge sauce for guests but didn't have any heavy whipping cream. The result was a hit!

   1 cup (6 ounces) semisweet chocolate chips
   1 quart coffee ice cream, *divided*
   1 tablespoon light corn syrup
1/2 cup chopped Heath candy bars (about 1-1/2 bars)
Whipped cream
Additional chopped Heath candy bars, optional

1. In a microwave-safe bowl, combine the chocolate chips, 1/2 cup ice cream and corn syrup. Microwave on high for 45 seconds or until smooth.

2. Spoon 1/3 cup ice cream into each of four parfait glasses. Top each with 2 tablespoons chocolate sauce and 1 tablespoon chopped candy bars. Repeat layers. Top with the remaining ice cream. Garnish with the whipped cream and additional candy bars if desired. **Yield:** 4 servings.

Watermelon Berry Sorbet

Prep: 30 min. + freezing

Jill Swavely, Green Lane, Pennsylvania

Strawberries, watermelon and three other ingredients are all you'll need to make this frosty refresher that's virtually fat-free. A friend gave me the recipe, promising it was the ultimate in summer desserts. I couldn't agree more!

 This recipe includes Nutrition Facts & Diabetic Exchanges.

- 1 cup water
- 1/2 cup sugar
- 2 cups cubed seedless watermelon
- 2 cups fresh strawberries, hulled
- 1 tablespoon minced fresh mint

1. In a small heavy saucepan, bring the water and sugar to a boil. Cook and stir until sugar is dissolved. Remove from the heat; cool slightly.

2. Place the watermelon and strawberries in a blender; add sugar syrup. Cover and process for 2-3 minutes or until smooth. Strain and discard the seeds and pulp. Transfer the puree to a 13-in. x 9-in. dish. Freeze for 1 hour or until edges begin to firm.

3. Stir in the mint. Freeze 2 hours longer or until firm. Just before serving, transfer the sorbet to a blender; cover and process for 2-3 minutes or until smooth. **Yield:** 6 servings.

Nutrition Facts: 1/2 cup equals 95 calories, trace fat (trace saturated fat), 0 cholesterol, 3 mg sodium, 25 g carbohydrate, 2 g fiber, 1 g protein. **Diabetic Exchanges:** 1 starch, 1/2 fruit.

Berry Nectarine Buckle

Prep: 25 min. **Bake:** 35 min.

 This recipe includes Nutrition Facts & Diabetic Exchanges.

- 1/3 cup all-purpose flour
- 1/3 cup packed brown sugar
- 1 teaspoon ground cinnamon
- 3 tablespoons cold butter

BATTER:
- 6 tablespoons butter, softened
- 3/4 cup plus 1 tablespoon sugar, *divided*
- 2 eggs
- 1-1/2 teaspoons vanilla extract
- 2-1/4 cups all-purpose flour
- 2-1/2 teaspoons baking powder
- 1/2 teaspoon salt
- 1/2 cup fat-free milk
- 1 cup fresh blueberries
- 1 pound medium nectarines, peeled, sliced and patted dry or 1 package (16 ounces) frozen unsweetened sliced peaches, thawed and patted dry
- 1/2 cup fresh raspberries
- 1/2 cup fresh blackberries

1. For topping, in a small bowl, combine the flour, brown sugar and cinnamon; cut in the butter until crumbly. Set aside.

2. In a large bowl, cream the butter and 3/4 cup sugar until light and fluffy. Add eggs, one at a time, beating well after each addition. Beat in vanilla. Combine the flour, baking powder and salt; add to the creamed mixture alternately with milk, beating well after each addition. Set aside 3/4 cup batter. Fold blueberries into remaining batter.

3. Spoon into a 13-in. x 9-in. baking dish coated with cooking spray. Arrange the nectarines on top; sprinkle with remaining sugar. Drop reserved batter by teaspoonfuls over nectarines. Sprinkle with the raspberries, blackberries and reserved topping.

4. Bake at 350° for 35-40 minutes or until a toothpick inserted near the center comes out clean. Serve warm. **Yield:** 20 servings.

Nutrition Facts: 1 piece equals 177 calories, 6 g fat (3 g saturated fat), 35 mg cholesterol, 172 mg sodium, 28 g carbohydrate, 1 g fiber, 3 g protein. **Diabetic Exchanges:** 2 starch, 1 fat.

LISA SJURSEN-DARLING SCOTTSVILLE, NEW YORK

Craving comfort food? We love the combination of blueberries, raspberries, blackberries and nectarines in this delightfully old-fashioned treat. A warm-from-the-oven piece is great all by itself, but we enjoy it even more served with low-fat frozen yogurt.

GRAND PRIZE WINNER

Chocolate Caramel Cheesecake

Prep: 35 min. **Bake:** 30 min. + chilling

Tamara Trouten, Fort Wayne, Indiana

Layers of caramel and pecans really complement the chocolate in this lightened-up cheesecake. Save time on the day of your meal by preparing this the night before.

- 6 whole reduced-fat graham crackers, crushed
- 3 tablespoons butter, melted
- 25 caramels
- 1/4 cup fat-free evaporated milk
- 1/4 cup chopped pecans
- 2 packages (8 ounces *each*) reduced-fat cream cheese
- 1/3 cup sugar
- 1/3 cup semisweet chocolate chips, melted and cooled
- 2 eggs, lightly beaten

1. In a small bowl, combine graham cracker crumbs and butter. Press onto the bottom of a 9-in. springform pan coated with cooking spray. Place on a baking sheet. Bake at 350° for 5-10 minutes or until set. Cool on a wire rack.

2. In a small saucepan over low heat, stir the caramels and evaporated milk until smooth. Pour over crust. Sprinkle with pecans.

3. In a large bowl, beat cream cheese and sugar until smooth. Beat in melted chocolate. Add eggs; beat on low speed just until combined. Pour over the caramel layer. Place pan on baking sheet.

4. Bake at 350° for 30-35 minutes or until the center is almost set. Cool on a wire rack for 10 minutes. Carefully run a knife around edge of pan to loosen; cool 1 hour longer.

5. Chill for 4 hours or overnight. Remove the sides of pan. Refrigerate leftovers. **Yield:** 12 servings.

Cranberry Mousse

Prep: 20 min. + chilling

Pauline Tucker, Baldwinville, Massachusetts

We live about 100 miles from Cape Cod, an area known for its cranberries. When we spent a weekend there, we toured the Cranberry World Visitors Center, which is where I discovered this recipe. I whipped up the creamy mousse for our fellowship group at church, and everyone raved about it. No one could believe that it's made with just four ingredients.

- 1 can (14 ounces) jellied cranberry sauce
- 1 cup cranberry juice
- 1 package (3 ounces) cranberry or raspberry gelatin
- 1 cup heavy whipping cream, whipped

1. In a large saucepan, bring the cranberry sauce and juice to a boil; cook and stir until smooth. Stir in the gelatin until dissolved. Cool slightly; transfer to a bowl. Refrigerate for 1 hour or until the mixture begins to thicken.

2. Fold in the whipped cream. Spoon the mousse into dessert dishes. Chill for 3-4 hours or until firm. **Yield:** 6 servings.

Mocha Fondue

Prep/Total Time: 20 min.

Karen Boehner, Glen Elder, Kansas

At our friends' 25th anniversary party, several couples had a lot of fun concocting this warm chocolate sauce. For the dippers, try pound cake, strawberries, bananas and pineapple chunks... or even marshmallows, pretzels and vanilla wafers.

- **2 cups (12 ounces) semisweet chocolate chips**
- **1/4 cup butter**
- **1 cup heavy whipping cream**
- **3 tablespoons strong brewed coffee**
- **1/8 teaspoon salt**
- **2 egg yolks, lightly beaten**
- **Cubed pound cake, sliced bananas and fresh strawberries and pineapple chunks**

In a heavy saucepan, melt the chocolate chips, butter, cream, coffee and salt. Stir 1/2 cup into egg yolks; return all to the pan. Cook and stir until mixture reaches 160°. Transfer to a fondue pot and keep warm. Serve with cake and fruit. **Yield:** 10 servings.

Sweet Shoppe Caramel Apples

Prep: 35 min. Cook: 1 hour + chilling

Mary Bilyeu, Ann Arbor, Michigan

I think these hand-dipped apples are as impressive as the ones you find at gourmet candy counters—only these are fresher, better-tasting and more economical!

- **6 large McIntosh apples**
- **6 Popsicle sticks**
- **2 cups sugar**
- **2 cups half-and-half cream**
- **1 cup light corn syrup**
- **1/2 cup butter, cubed**
- **1-1/4 cups English toffee bits *or* almond brickle chips**
- **1 cup semisweet chocolate chips**
- **1 cup white baking chips**

1. Line a baking sheet with waxed paper and grease the paper; set aside. Wash and thoroughly dry apples. Insert a Popsicle stick into each; place on prepared pan. Chill.

2. In a heavy 3-qt. saucepan, combine the sugar, half-and-half cream, corn syrup and butter; bring to a boil over medium-high heat. Cook and stir until a candy thermometer reads 245°, about 1 hour.

3. Remove from the heat. Working quickly, dip each apple into hot caramel mixture to completely coat, then dip the bottom into toffee bits, about 1/2 in. up the sides. Return to baking sheet; chill.

4. In a microwave, melt the chocolate chips; stir until smooth. Transfer to a small heavy-duty resealable plastic bag; cut a small hole in a corner of bag. Drizzle over apples.

5. Repeat with white chips. Chill until set. Remove apples from refrigerator 5 minutes before serving. **Yield:** 6 servings.

Editor's Note: We recommend that you test your candy thermometer before each use by bringing water to a boil; the thermometer should read 212°. Adjust your recipe temperature up or down based on your test.

Cinnamon Apple Cheesecake

Prep: 40 min. **Bake:** 40 min. + chilling

Emily Ann Young, Edmond, Oklahoma

With a topping of cinnamon-spiced apples and an oat-and-nut crust, this creamy cheesecake is a definite showstopper.

- 1/2 cup butter, softened
- 1/4 cup packed brown sugar
-   1 cup all-purpose flour
- 1/4 cup quick-cooking oats
- 1/4 cup finely chopped walnuts
- 1/2 teaspoon ground cinnamon

FILLING:

-   2 packages (8 ounces *each*) cream cheese, softened
-   1 can (14 ounces) sweetened condensed milk
- 1/2 cup thawed apple juice concentrate
-   3 eggs, lightly beaten

TOPPING:

-   2 medium tart apples, peeled and sliced
-   1 tablespoon butter
-   1 teaspoon cornstarch
- 1/4 teaspoon ground cinnamon
- 1/4 cup thawed apple juice concentrate

1. In a small bowl, cream the butter and brown sugar until light and fluffy. Gradually add the flour, oats, walnuts and cinnamon until well blended. Press onto the bottom and 1-1/2 in. up the sides of a greased 9-in. springform pan. Place on a baking sheet. Bake at 325° for 10 minutes or until set. Cool on a wire rack.

2. In a large bowl, beat cream cheese until fluffy. Beat in milk and juice concentrate until smooth. Add eggs; beat on low speed just until combined (batter will be thin). Pour into crust. Return pan to baking sheet.

3. Bake at 325° for 40-45 minutes or until the center is almost set. Cool on a wire rack for 10 minutes. Carefully run a knife around edge of pan to loosen; cool 1 hour longer. Refrigerate overnight.

4. In a large skillet, cook and stir apples in butter over medium heat until crisp-tender, about 5 minutes. Cool to room temperature. Arrange over cheesecake.

5. In a small saucepan, combine cornstarch, cinnamon and juice concentrate until smooth. Bring to a boil. Reduce the heat; cook and stir for 1 minute or until thickened. Immediately brush over apples. Refrigerate for 1 hour or until chilled. Refrigerate leftovers. **Yield:** 12 servings.

Hazelnut Cheesecake Parfaits

Prep: 25 min. + chilling

- 1/4 cup chopped hazelnuts
- 1/2 teaspoon sugar
- 1/3 cup semisweet chocolate chips
-   2 tablespoons half-and-half cream
-   2 tablespoons whipped cream cheese
-   2 teaspoons brown sugar
- 1/2 cup coffee yogurt
- 1/4 teaspoon vanilla extract
- 2/3 cup whipped topping
-   2 whole chocolate graham crackers, crushed

Chocolate curls and additional whipped topping, optional

1. In a small heavy skillet, cook and stir hazelnuts over medium heat until toasted, about 4 minutes. Sprinkle with sugar; cook and stir for 2-4 minutes or until sugar is melted. Spread on foil to cool.

2. In a small saucepan, melt the chocolate chips with the cream over low heat; stir until smooth. Remove from the heat; cool to room temperature.

3. In a small bowl, beat cream cheese and brown sugar until blended. Beat in yogurt and vanilla; fold in whipped topping.

4. In two parfait glasses, layer the graham crackers, yogurt mixture, chocolate mixture and hazelnuts. Refrigerate the parfaits until chilled. Garnish with chocolate curls and additional whipped topping if desired. **Yield:** 2 servings.

SHELLY PLATTEN AMHERST, WISCONSIN

These nutty, layered delights are as yummy as they are eye-catching. Your guests will be thrilled to see them on your dinner table…and will be sure to save room for dessert!

GRAND PRIZE WINNER

Peanut Butter Ice Cream

Prep: 15 min. + chilling
Process: 20 min./batch + freezing

Sigrid Guillot, Thibodaux, Louisiana

The inspiration for this delectable recipe came from, strangely enough, the ducks my husband and I used to raise. When we found ourselves with a surplus of their eggs, ice cream seemed like the perfect place to put them!

- 1 envelope unflavored gelatin
- 1/4 cup cold water
- 1-3/4 cups milk
- 1 cup sugar
- 1/4 teaspoon salt
- 3 egg yolks
- 3 packages (16 ounces *each*) peanut butter cups, crumbled
- 2 cups evaporated milk
- 1 tablespoon vanilla extract

1. In a small saucepan, sprinkle the gelatin over the cold water; let stand for 1 minute. Heat over low heat, stirring until the gelatin is completely dissolved; set aside.

2. In a large saucepan, heat milk to 175°; stir in sugar and salt until dissolved. Whisk a small amount of the hot mixture into the egg yolks. Return all to the pan, whisking constantly. Cook and stir over low heat until mixture reaches at least 160° and coats the back of a metal spoon. Remove from the heat. Add the peanut butter cups and softened gelatin; stir until melted.

3. Cool quickly by placing pan in a bowl of ice water; stir for 2 minutes. Stir in evaporated milk and vanilla. Press waxed paper onto surface of custard. Refrigerate for several hours or overnight.

4. Fill the cylinder of ice cream freezer two-thirds full; freeze according to the manufacturer's directions. Refrigerate remaining mixture until ready to freeze. When the ice cream is frozen, transfer to a freezer container; freeze for 2-4 hours before serving. **Yield:** about 1 quart.

Chocolate Panini

Prep/Total Time: 15 min.

Kayla Wilcoxson, Abilene, Texas

I created this treat for my husband when I was learning to use the panini maker we'd received as a wedding gift. Sometimes I'll use a different fruit in place of the strawberries.

- 2 teaspoons butter, softened
- 2 slices white bread
- 1/2 teaspoon sugar
- 1 tablespoon cream cheese, softened
- 1/2 milk chocolate candy bar (1.55 ounces)
- 1/2 cup sliced fresh strawberries
- 1/4 cup heavy whipping cream, whipped

Butter one side of each slice of bread; sprinkle with sugar. Spread cream cheese over the other side. Place candy bar on the cream cheese side of one slice; top with the other slice, butter side up. Cook on an indoor grill or panini maker for 2-3 minutes or until bread is browned and candy bar is melted. Cut in half; top with strawberries and whipped cream. **Yield:** 2 servings.

Black and Blue Cobbler

Prep: 15 min. **Cook:** 2 hours + standing

Martha Creveling, Orlando, Florida

It never occurred to me that I could bake a traditional cobbler in my slow cooker. Then I saw some recipes and decided to try my favorite. It took a little bit of experimenting, but the tongue-tingling results were "berry" worth it!

    1 **cup all-purpose flour**
1-1/2 **cups sugar,** *divided*
    1 **teaspoon baking powder**
 1/4 **teaspoon salt**
 1/4 **teaspoon ground cinnamon**
 1/4 **teaspoon ground nutmeg**
    2 **eggs, lightly beaten**
    2 **tablespoons milk**
    2 **tablespoons canola oil**
    2 **cups fresh** *or* **frozen blackberries**
    2 **cups fresh** *or* **frozen blueberries**
 3/4 **cup water**
    1 **teaspoon grated orange peel**
Whipped cream *or* **vanilla ice cream, optional**

1. In a large bowl, combine the flour, 3/4 cup sugar, baking powder, salt, cinnamon and nutmeg. Combine the eggs, milk and oil; stir into dry ingredients just

until moistened. Spread the batter evenly onto the bottom of a greased 5-qt. slow cooker.

2. In a large saucepan, combine berries, water, orange peel and remaining sugar; bring to a boil. Remove from the heat; immediately pour over batter. Cover and cook on high for 2 to 2-1/2 hours or until a toothpick inserted into the batter comes out clean.

3. Turn the slow cooker off. Uncover and let stand for 30 minutes before serving. Serve with whipped cream or ice cream if desired. **Yield:** 6 servings.

Nutty Cheesecake Squares

Prep: 20 min. **Bake:** 20 min. + cooling

Ruth Simon, Buffalo, New York

These rich, crumb-topped bars are easy enough to make for everyday occasions but special enough to serve company. They also travel well to potlucks and picnics.

    2 **cups all-purpose flour**
    1 **cup finely chopped walnuts**
 2/3 **cup packed brown sugar**
 1/2 **teaspoon salt**
 2/3 **cup cold butter**
FILLING:
    2 **packages (8 ounces** *each***) cream cheese, softened**
 1/2 **cup sugar**
    2 **eggs, lightly beaten**
 1/4 **cup milk**
    1 **teaspoon vanilla extract**

1. In a large bowl, combine the flour, walnuts, brown sugar and salt; cut in butter until the mixture resembles coarse crumbs. Set half aside; press remaining crumb mixture onto the bottom of a greased 13-in. x 9-in. baking pan. Bake at 350° for 10-15 minutes or until lightly browned.

2. In a large bowl, beat the filling ingredients until smooth; pour over the crust. Sprinkle with the reserved crumb mixture.

3. Bake at 350° for 20-25 minutes or until a knife inserted near the center comes out clean. Cool on a wire rack for 1 hour. Store in the refrigerator. **Yield:** 16-20 servings.

Peach Rhubarb Crisp

Prep: 20 min. **Bake:** 30 min.

Sandy Kimble, Salinas, California

When a trip to the farmers market left me with an abundance of quickly ripening peaches and rhubarb, I made this sweet-tart crisp. The two fruits really complement each other.

3/4 cup sugar
 3 tablespoons all-purpose flour
1/2 teaspoon ground nutmeg
1/2 teaspoon grated lemon peel
1/8 teaspoon salt
 3 cups sliced fresh *or* frozen rhubarb
2-1/2 cups chopped peeled fresh peaches *or* frozen unsweetened sliced peaches, thawed and chopped
TOPPING:
1/2 cup all-purpose flour
1/2 cup old-fashioned oats
1/2 cup packed brown sugar
3/4 teaspoon ground cinnamon
1/8 teaspoon salt
 5 tablespoons cold butter

1. In a large bowl, combine the sugar, flour, nutmeg, lemon peel, salt, rhubarb and peaches. Transfer to a greased 11-in. x 7-in. baking dish.

2. In a small bowl, combine flour, oats, brown sugar, cinnamon and salt. Cut in butter until the mixture resembles coarse crumbs; sprinkle over fruit. Bake at 375° for 30-35 minutes or until bubbly and fruit is tender. Serve warm or cold. **Yield:** 6-8 servings.

Editor's Note: If using frozen rhubarb, measure rhubarb while still frozen, then thaw completely. Drain in a colander, but do not press liquid out.

Old-Fashioned Pear Dessert

Prep: 20 min. **Bake:** 35 min. + cooling

2-1/4 cups all-purpose flour
 5 tablespoons sugar, *divided*
3/4 teaspoon salt
3/4 cup cold butter, cubed
 3 egg yolks
4-1/2 teaspoons lemon juice
FILLING:
1/2 cup sugar
 4 tablespoons cornstarch, *divided*
1/2 teaspoon salt
1/2 teaspoon ground cinnamon
3/4 cup water
 2 tablespoons plus 1-1/2 teaspoons lemon juice
 2 tablespoons butter
 1 teaspoon vanilla extract
 5 cups chopped peeled ripe pears

1. In a large bowl, combine the flour, 3 tablespoons sugar and salt; cut in the butter until crumbly. In a small bowl, whisk egg yolks and lemon juice; stir into dry ingredients with a fork. Remove 1 cup to another bowl; stir in the remaining sugar and set aside for the topping.

2. Press remaining crumb mixture onto the bottom and up the sides of a greased 8-in. square baking dish. Bake at 375° for 10-12 minutes or until edges are lightly browned.

3. Meanwhile, for the filling, combine the sugar, 2 tablespoons cornstarch, salt and cinnamon in a small saucepan; slowly stir in water and lemon juice until smooth. Bring to a boil over medium heat; cook and stir for 1 minute or until thickened. Remove from the heat; stir in butter and vanilla.

4. Toss pears with the remaining cornstarch; spoon over crust. Top with filling. Sprinkle with reserved topping. Bake for 35-40 minutes or until filling is bubbly and topping is lightly browned. Cool on a wire rack. **Yield:** 9 servings.

EILEEN UEBERROTH TOLEDO, OHIO

This never-fail pear recipe turns out moist and yummy every time. Some members of our family have even requested this dessert instead of cake for their birthdays!

GRAND
PRIZE
WINNER

Maple Mousse

Prep: 30 min. + chilling

Jane Fuller, Ivoryton, Connecticut

I love to prepare this using maple syrup produced in our area. A nice change of pace from heavier cakes and pies, the mousse makes a special finale to a holiday meal.

- 3/4 cup plus 6 teaspoons maple syrup, *divided*
- 3 egg yolks, lightly beaten
- 2 cups heavy whipping cream
- 2 tablespoons chopped hazelnuts, toasted

1. In a small saucepan over medium heat, heat 3/4 cup syrup just until it simmers. Reduce heat to low. Stir a small amount of hot syrup into egg yolks; return all to the pan, stirring constantly. Cook and stir until mixture is thickened and reaches 160°. Transfer to a large bowl; set bowl in ice water and stir for 2 minutes. Cool to room temperature.

2. In a large bowl, beat cream until stiff peaks form. Gently fold into the syrup mixture. Spoon into dessert dishes. Chill for at least 2 hours. Just before serving,

drizzle mousse with the remaining syrup and sprinkle with hazelnuts. **Yield:** 6 servings.

Ultimate Caramel Apples

Prep: 45 min. **Cook:** 25 min. + chilling

Clarissa Loyd, Mineral Wells, Texas

I have such a sweet tooth that I've been known to make a dessert just to satisfy my own craving! One day when I was in the mood for caramel, I came up with these fun treats.

- 6 medium Red Delicious apples
- 6 Popsicle sticks
- 1 cup sugar
- 1 cup light corn syrup
- 1/4 cup water
- Pinch baking soda
- 1/4 cup butter, cubed
- 1/4 cup heavy whipping cream
- 1/2 cup shelled pistachios, chopped, *divided*
- 3 ounces white baking chocolate, chopped
- 3 ounces semisweet chocolate, chopped

1. Line a baking sheet with waxed paper and grease the paper; set aside. Wash and thoroughly dry apples. Insert a Popsicle stick into each; place on the prepared pan. Chill.

2. In a large heavy saucepan, combine the sugar, corn syrup and water; bring to a boil over medium heat, stirring occasionally. Stir in the baking soda. Stir in the butter until melted; gradually add heavy whipping cream, stirring constantly. Cook and stir until a candy thermometer reads 242° (firm-ball stage). Remove from heat and cool to 200°.

3. Place 1/4 cup pistachios in a shallow dish. Dip the apples into caramel mixture until completely coated, then dip the bottom of each in pistachios. Return to baking sheet; chill.

4. In a microwave, melt white chocolate; stir until smooth. Transfer to a small heavy-duty resealable plastic bag; cut a small hole in a corner of bag. Drizzle over the apples. Repeat with semisweet chocolate. Sprinkle tops with remaining pistachios if desired. Chill until set. **Yield:** 6 servings.

Pomegranate Poached Pears

Prep: 20 min. **Cook:** 1 hour 25 min.

Bev Jones, Brunswick, Missouri

Your guests will love the subtle tastes that come from the wine, rosemary and fruit juices in these sophisticated pears. Soak them overnight in the poaching liquid in the fridge, and they'll pick up even more flavor and the pomegranate's ruby color.

- 3 cups dry red wine *or* red grape juice
- 1 bottle (16 ounces) pomegranate juice
- 1 cup water
- 1/2 cup sugar
- 1/4 cup orange juice
- 2 tablespoons grated orange peel
- 3 fresh rosemary sprigs (4 inches)
- 1 cinnamon stick (3 inches)
- 6 medium pears
- 6 orange slices
- 6 tablespoons Mascarpone cheese

1. In a Dutch oven, combine the first eight ingredients. Core pears from the bottom, leaving stems intact. Peel pears; place on their sides in the pan. Bring to a boil. Reduce heat; cover and simmer for 25-30 minutes or until pears are almost tender. Remove with a slotted spoon; cool.

2. Strain the poaching liquid and return to Dutch oven. Bring to a boil; cook until reduced to 1 cup, about 45 minutes. Discard rosemary and cinnamon. Place an orange slice on each serving plate; top with

1 tablespoon cheese and a pear. Drizzle with poaching liquid. **Yield:** 6 servings.

At the Core

An apple corer also works well for coring fresh pears. Insert the apple corer into the bottom of the pear to within 1 inch of the top. Twist the corer to cut around the core, then slowly pull the corer out of the pear to remove the core.

Pear Sorbet

Prep: 20 min. + freezing

Deirdre Dee Cox, Milwaukee, Wisconsin

With a touch of sweet white wine and a splash of citrus, this elegant sorbet is such a refreshing, tongue-tingling delight on a warm day. You can use canned fruit if fresh isn't available… or substitute lime juice for the lemon.

- 5 small pears, peeled and sliced
- 3/4 cup sweet white wine *or* apple juice
- 1/3 cup sugar
- 4-1/2 teaspoons lemon juice

1. In a large saucepan, combine all ingredients. Bring to a boil. Reduce heat; simmer, uncovered, for 8-10 minutes or until pears are tender. Cool slightly.

2. Pour into a food processor; cover and process for 1-2 minutes or until smooth. Transfer to a 13-in. x 9-in. dish. Cover and freeze for 4 hours or until firm.

3. Just before serving, process again in a food processor for 1-2 minutes or until smooth. Spoon into dessert dishes. **Yield:** 4 servings.

Hot Fudge Cake

Prep: 20 min. **Cook:** 4 hours

Marleen Adkins, Placentia, California

A cake baked in a slow cooker may sound unusual...but the smiles you'll see around the table will prove how yummy it is. When I'm in the mood for something a little bit different, I substitute butterscotch chips for the chocolate.

1-3/4 cups packed brown sugar, *divided*
   1 cup all-purpose flour
   6 tablespoons baking cocoa, *divided*
   2 teaspoons baking powder
1/2 teaspoon salt
1/2 cup 2% milk
   2 tablespoons butter, melted
1/2 teaspoon vanilla extract
1-1/2 cups semisweet chocolate chips
1-3/4 cups boiling water
Vanilla ice cream

1. In a small bowl, combine 1 cup brown sugar, flour, 3 tablespoons cocoa, baking powder and salt. In another bowl, combine the milk, butter and vanilla; stir into dry ingredients just until combined. Spread evenly into a 3-qt. slow cooker coated with cooking spray. Sprinkle with chocolate chips.

2. In another small bowl, combine the remaining brown sugar and cocoa; stir in boiling water. Pour over batter (do not stir). Cover and cook on high for 4 to 4-1/2 hours or until a toothpick inserted near the center of cake comes out clean. Serve warm with ice cream. **Yield:** 8 servings.

Editor's Note: This recipe does not use eggs.

Chocolate Crunch Ice Cream

Prep: 30 min. + chilling **Process:** 20 min./batch + freezing

1-1/2 cups milk
  3/4 cup sugar, *divided*
    4 egg yolks
2-1/2 teaspoons instant coffee granules
    2 cups 60% cocoa bittersweet chocolate baking chips, melted and cooled
1-1/2 cups heavy whipping cream
    1 teaspoon vanilla extract
  3/4 cup semisweet chocolate chips, melted
  3/4 cup slivered almonds, toasted
  1/3 cup milk chocolate toffee bits

1. In a large saucepan, heat the milk to 175°; stir in 1/2 cup sugar until dissolved. In a small bowl, whisk egg yolks and remaining sugar. Stir in coffee granules and bittersweet chocolate. Whisk in a small amount of hot milk mixture. Return all to the pan, whisking constantly.

2. Cook and stir over low heat until the mixture reaches at least 160° and coats the back of a metal spoon. Remove from the heat. Cool quickly by placing the pan in a bowl of ice water; let stand for 30 minutes, stirring frequently.

3. Transfer to a large bowl; stir in heavy whipping cream and vanilla. Press plastic wrap onto the surface of the custard. Refrigerate for several hours or overnight.

4. Line a baking sheet with waxed paper; spread melted semisweet chocolate to 1/8-in. thickness. Refrigerate for 20 minutes; chop coarsely.

5. Fill the cylinder of ice cream freezer two-thirds full with custard; freeze according to manufacturer's directions. Stir in some of the chopped chocolate, almonds and toffee bits. Refrigerate the remaining custard until ready to freeze. Stir in the remaining chopped chocolate, almonds and toffee bits. Allow ice cream to ripen in the ice cream freezer or firm up in the refrigerator freezer for 2-4 hours before serving. **Yield:** 1-1/2 quarts.

ROSALIE PETERS CALDWELL, TEXAS

Making this irresistible ice cream is even easier when you do some of the prep work in advance. I make the custard the day before and refrigerate it overnight. Plus, I toast the almonds ahead of time and separate my add-ins into labeled containers.

GRAND PRIZE WINNER

Chocolate Peanut Torte

Prep: 35 min. **Bake:** 30 min. + cooling

Crystal Christopher, Hustonville, Kentucky

With smooth peanut butter layers and a fudgy topping, this lightened-up but luscious torte is always a hit.

 This recipe includes Nutrition Facts & Diabetic Exchanges.

1-3/4 **cups all-purpose flour**
1 **cup sugar**
3/4 **cup baking cocoa**
1/3 **cup sugar blend**
1-1/2 **teaspoons baking powder**
1 **teaspoon salt**
1/4 **teaspoon baking soda**
1 **cup fat-free milk**
1/2 **cup egg substitute**
1/4 **cup canola oil**
2 **teaspoons vanilla extract**
1 **cup boiling water**
CREAMY PEANUT FILLING:
1-3/4 **cups plus 2 tablespoons cold fat-free milk,**
 divided
1 **package (1 ounce) sugar-free instant vanilla**
 pudding mix
3/4 **cup reduced-fat creamy peanut butter**
TOPPING:
1 **ounce unsweetened chocolate**
3 **tablespoons butter**
1/2 **cup confectioners' sugar**
2 **tablespoons fat-free milk**

1. Coat two 9-in. round baking pans with cooking spray; line with waxed paper. Coat the paper with cooking spray and sprinkle with flour; set aside.

2. In a large bowl, combine the first seven ingredients. In a small bowl, combine the milk, egg substitute, oil and vanilla; add to flour mixture. Beat for 2 minutes. Stir in water. Pour into prepared pans.

3. Bake at 350° for 30-35 minutes or until a toothpick inserted near the center comes out clean. Cool cakes for 10 minutes; remove from the pans to wire racks. Cool completely.

4. In a large bowl, whisk 1-3/4 cups milk and vanilla pudding mix for 2 minutes; let stand 2 minutes or until soft-set. In a small saucepan over low heat, stir peanut butter and remaining milk until smooth. Fold into vanilla pudding.

5. Place bottom cake layer on a serving plate; spread half of filling over layer; top with second layer and remaining filling. Chill for 1 hour or until serving.

6. For the topping, in a microwave, melt chocolate and butter; stir until smooth. Stir in confectioners' sugar and milk until smooth. Cool until spreadable. Spread frosting over top of cake. **Yield:** 16 servings.

Editor's Note: This recipe was tested with Splenda sugar blend.

Nutrition Facts: 1 piece equals 287 calories, 11 g fat (3 g saturated fat), 7 mg cholesterol, 407 mg sodium, 41 g carbohydrate, 2 g fiber, 8 g protein. **Diabetic Exchanges:** 2-1/2 starch, 2 fat.

Roasted Pears in Pecan Sauce

Prep: 20 min. **Bake:** 30 min.

Darlene King, Steven, Saskatchewan

Whenever I bring home fresh pears from the grocery store, my family begs me to use them for this recipe. Everyone loves the tender roasted fruit smothered in a rich sauce. Try serving it over scoops of vanilla ice cream or slices of cake.

  4 medium pears, peeled and cut into wedges
  3 tablespoons brown sugar
  3 tablespoons unsweetened apple juice
  3 tablespoons butter, melted
  1/4 cup chopped pecans
  3 tablespoons heavy whipping cream
Vanilla ice cream, optional

1. Place pears in an ungreased 13-in. x 9-in. baking dish. In a small bowl, combine the brown sugar, apple juice and butter; pour over pears. Bake, uncovered, at 400° for 20 minutes, basting occasionally.

2. Sprinkle with pecans. Bake 10-15 minutes longer or until the pears are tender. Transfer the pears to serving dishes.

3. Pour the cooking juices into a small bowl; whisk in the cream until blended. Drizzle over pears. Serve with ice cream if desired. **Yield:** 4 servings.

Apple Pizza

Prep: 40 min. **Bake:** 20 min.

Brenda Mowrey, Taylors, South Carolina

Pizza is a favorite food in our house, so when I had some apples to use up, I started searching for a dessert pizza recipe. I tailored this one to suit our tastes.

2-1/3 to 3 cups all-purpose flour
  3 tablespoons sugar
  1 package (1/4 ounce) active dry yeast
1/2 teaspoon salt
1/2 cup water
1/4 cup milk
1/4 cup butter, cubed
APPLE TOPPING:
  4 cups sliced peeled tart apples
  2 tablespoons butter
  1/2 cup sugar
  2 tablespoons all-purpose flour
  1 teaspoon ground cinnamon
CHEESE TOPPING:
  4 ounces cream cheese, softened
  1/4 cup packed brown sugar
  2 tablespoons caramel ice cream topping
STREUSEL:
  2/3 cup all-purpose flour
  1/3 cup sugar
  1/4 cup cold butter, cubed

1. In a large bowl, combine 1-1/2 cups flour, sugar, yeast and salt. In a saucepan, heat water, milk and butter to 120°-130°. Add to dry ingredients; beat for 2 minutes. Stir in enough remaining flour to form a firm dough. Turn onto a floured surface; cover and let rest for 15 minutes.

2. Meanwhile, in a large skillet, cook and stir apples in butter over medium heat for 2 minutes. Combine the sugar, flour and cinnamon; stir into the skillet. Cook 3 minutes longer. Reduce heat to low; cook, uncovered, for 4-6 minutes or until the apples are tender, stirring frequently.

3. In a small bowl, combine the topping ingredients. For streusel, in a small bowl, combine flour and sugar; cut in butter until crumbly.

4. Pat dough onto a greased 14-in. pizza pan, building up edges slightly. Spread with cheese topping, then apple topping. Sprinkle with streusel. Bake at 375° for 20-25 minutes or until crust is golden brown. Serve warm or cold. **Yield:** 10-12 servings.

No-Bake Lime Cheesecake

Prep: 30 min. + chilling

Robin Spires, Tampa, Florida

Being from the Sunshine State, I love any recipe containing citrus. This lime-flavored cheesecake is quick to whip up and disappears almost as fast. For a great variation, substitute the juice and zest of an orange instead of a lime.

  3 cups graham cracker crumbs
2/3 cup sugar
2/3 cup butter, melted

FILLING:
  2 envelopes unflavored gelatin
  1 cup lime juice
1/4 cup cold water
1-1/2 cups sugar
  5 eggs, lightly beaten
  2 teaspoons grated lime peel
  2 packages (8 ounces *each*) cream cheese, softened
1/2 cup butter, softened
1/2 cup heavy whipping cream

1. In a large bowl, combine graham cracker crumbs, sugar and butter. Press onto the bottom and 2 in. up the sides of a greased 9-in. springform pan. Cover and refrigerate for at least 30 minutes.

2. In a small saucepan, sprinkle gelatin over the lime juice and cold water; let stand for 1 minute. Stir in the sugar, eggs and peel. Cook and stir over medium heat until mixture reaches 160°. Remove from the heat.

3. In a large bowl, beat cream cheese and butter until fluffy. Gradually beat in gelatin mixture. Cover and refrigerate for 45 minutes or until partially set, stirring occasionally.

4. In a small bowl, beat heavy whipping cream until stiff peaks form; fold into lime mixture. Spoon into crust. Cover and refrigerate for 3-4 hours or until set. Just before serving, remove sides of pan. Refrigerate leftovers. **Yield:** 12 servings.

Tuxedo Cream Dessert

Prep: 40 min. + chilling

1-3/4 teaspoons unflavored gelatin
  2 tablespoons cold water
1-1/2 cups heavy whipping cream, *divided*
3/4 cup semisweet chocolate chips
VANILLA LAYER:
1-3/4 teaspoons unflavored gelatin
  2 tablespoons cold water
1-2/3 cups heavy whipping cream, *divided*
1/4 cup sugar
  2 teaspoons vanilla extract
STRAWBERRY SAUCE:
  2 cups sliced fresh strawberries
  2 to 3 tablespoons sugar

1. In a small bowl, sprinkle gelatin over cold water; let stand for 1 minute. In a small saucepan, bring 1 cup cream to a simmer. Stir 1/2 cup into gelatin mixture until gelatin is completely dissolved. Stir chips into remaining warm cream until melted. Stir in the gelatin mixture and remaining cream.

2. Transfer to an 8-in. x 4-in. loaf pan coated with cooking spray. Cover and refrigerate for 30 minutes or until firm.

3. For the vanilla layer, in a small bowl, sprinkle gelatin over cold water; let stand for 1 minute. In a small saucepan, bring 1 cup cream and sugar to a simmer. Stir in the gelatin mixture until gelatin is completely dissolved. Stir in vanilla and remaining cream. Carefully spoon over chocolate layer. Cover and refrigerate for at least 2 hours or until firm.

4. For the sauce, in a blender, puree the strawberries and sugar. Transfer to a bowl; cover and refrigerate until serving.

5. Just before serving, unmold the dessert and cut into slices. Serve with the strawberry sauce. **Yield:** 6-8 servings.

CAMILLA SAULSBURY NACOGDOCHES, TEXAS

This adaptation of my grandmother's signature dessert always gets oohs and aahs from guests. The two-tone treat is so pretty, especially with the strawberry sauce on top. Both Gran and I have considered it a favorite for entertaining because it can be made up to a day in advance.

GRAND
PRIZE
WINNER

Strawberry Cheesecake Minis

Prep: 15 min. **Bake:** 15 min. + cooling

Lori Lewis, St. Johns, Michigan

My daughter and I tried lightening up a recipe from a cooking show, and these yummy little cheesecakes were the result. No one suspects that they're lower in fat and calories.

 This recipe includes Nutrition Facts & Diabetic Exchanges.

> 2 packages (8 ounces *each*) reduced-fat cream cheese
> Sugar substitute equivalent to 1/2 cup sugar
> 1/2 cup sugar
> 1 teaspoon vanilla extract
> 1 egg, lightly beaten
> 1/4 cup egg substitute
> 12 reduced-fat vanilla wafers
> 1 can (12 ounces) strawberry cake and pastry filling

1. In a small bowl, beat cream cheese until smooth. Gradually beat in the sugar substitute and sugar. Beat in the vanilla. Add the egg and egg substitute; beat until blended.

2. Place each vanilla wafer flat side down in a foil-lined muffin cup. Fill with cream cheese mixture. Bake at 350° for 15-20 minutes or until puffed and set. Cool on a wire rack for 1 hour (centers will sink slightly).

3. Spoon the pastry filling into the center of each cheesecake. Store in the refrigerator. **Yield:** 1 dozen.

Editor's Note: This recipe was tested with Splenda No Calorie Sweetener and Solo brand cake and pastry filling. Look for both products in the baking aisle.

Nutrition Facts: 1 cheesecake equals 217 calories, 9 g fat (5 g saturated fat), 44 mg cholesterol, 209 mg sodium, 29 g carbohydrate, 1 g fiber, 5 g protein. **Diabetic Exchanges:** 2 starch, 2 fat.

Fancy Mousse Towers

Prep/Total Time: 15 min.

Christine Dohlmar, Valrico, Florida

You'll be amazed at how easy it is to assemble these creamy and crunchy chocolate "towers." They take only 15 minutes to fix, but guests will think you spent hours in the kitchen.

> 1/3 cup cold heavy whipping cream
> 2 tablespoons cold 2% milk
> 2 tablespoons instant chocolate fudge pudding mix
> 2 tablespoons chocolate syrup
> 6 chocolate wafers
> Whipped cream, chocolate garnish and fresh mint, optional

1. In a small bowl, beat the cream, milk and pudding mix until stiff peaks form. Transfer to a small resealable plastic bag; cut a small hole in the corner of the bag.

2. Drizzle two serving plates with chocolate syrup. Place a chocolate wafer in the center of each plate; pipe with some of the pudding mixture. Repeat layers twice. Garnish with whipped cream, chocolate and mint if desired. **Yield:** 2 servings.

Chocolate Almond Stacks

Prep: 30 min. **Bake:** 10 min. + chilling

Leah Lyon, Ada, Oklahoma

A delightful blend of sliced almonds, whipped cream and rich chocolate sauce goes into this showpiece dessert. If you prefer, lightly toast the nuts for extra flavor.

- 1 ounce bittersweet chocolate
- 3/4 cup heavy whipping cream, *divided*
- 1 egg
- 3 tablespoons sugar
- 1 teaspoon vanilla extract
- 2 tablespoons all-purpose flour
- 1/3 cup semisweet chocolate chips
- 1/2 cup sliced almonds
- 1/8 teaspoon almond extract

1. In a small saucepan, melt the chocolate with 1 tablespoon cream; stir until smooth. In a small bowl, beat egg, sugar and vanilla on high speed for 5 minutes or until thick and pale yellow. Fold in flour and melted chocolate. Pour into two 5-in. x 3-in. x 2-in. loaf pans coated with cooking spray.

2. Bake at 350° for 8-10 minutes or until cake springs back when lightly touched. Cool for 5 minutes before removing from the pans to wire racks. Cut cakes in half widthwise.

3. In a small saucepan, melt the chocolate chips with 3 tablespoons cream, stirring constantly. Spread over the top of cakes; sprinkle with almonds. Refrigerate for 15 minutes.

4. In a small bowl, beat the almond extract with the remaining cream until stiff peaks form. Spread half of whipped cream on top of two cake squares; top each with a remaining cake square and remaining whipped cream. **Yield:** 2 servings.

Dreamy Cream

For best results when whipping cream, start with cream that is cold. Choose a deep metal bowl, as the cream will double in volume. Place the bowl and beaters in the freezer for at least 15 minutes before using them.

Ice Cream Tacos

Prep/Total Time: 20 min.

Karen Oney, Fort Worth, Texas

Talk about a fun finale! These kid-pleasing treats look just like tacos—but they're stuffed with ice cream and topped with cherries and coconut instead of tomatoes and lettuce.

- 2 flour tortillas (6 inches)
- 1/8 teaspoon ground cinnamon
- 2 tablespoons canola oil
- 2 tablespoons chopped pecans
- 2 tablespoons flaked coconut
- 1 drop green food coloring
- 1 cup chocolate ice cream
- 1/4 cup whipped topping
- 6 maraschino cherries, halved

1. Sprinkle one side of each tortilla with cinnamon. In a large skillet, heat the tortillas, one at a time with cinnamon side up, in oil over medium heat. When tortilla starts to brown, fold into a taco shape; drain on paper towels.

2. In the same skillet, cook and stir the pecans for 2 minutes or until lightly toasted. Tint coconut with food coloring. Place two small scoops of ice cream in each tortilla shell; top with whipped topping, cherries, pecans and tinted coconut. **Yield:** 2 servings.

Caramel Apple Crisp

Prep: 20 min. **Bake:** 45 min.

Michelle Brooks, Clarkston, Michigan

When my children and I whip up this yummy, heartwarming crisp at home, we like to use different varieties of apples to give it a nice combination of flavors.

- 3 cups old-fashioned oats
- 2 cups all-purpose flour
- 1-1/2 cups packed brown sugar
- 1 teaspoon ground cinnamon
- 1 cup cold butter, cubed
- 8 cups thinly sliced peeled tart apples
- 1 package (14 ounces) caramels, halved
- 1 cup apple cider, *divided*

1. In a large bowl, combine the oats, flour, brown sugar and cinnamon; cut in the butter until crumbly. Press half of the mixture into a greased 13-in. x 9-in. baking dish. Layer with half of the apples, caramels and 1 cup oat mixture. Repeat layers. Pour 1/2 cup cider over the top.

2. Bake, uncovered, at 350° for 30 minutes. Drizzle with remaining cider; bake 15-20 minutes longer or until apples are tender. **Yield:** 12-14 servings.

Rhubarb Swirl Cheesecake

Prep: 40 min. **Bake:** 1 hour + chilling

- 2-1/2 cups thinly sliced fresh *or* frozen rhubarb
- 1/3 cup plus 1/2 cup sugar, *divided*
- 2 tablespoons orange juice
- 1-1/4 cups graham cracker crumbs
- 1/4 cup butter, melted
- 3 packages (8 ounces *each*) cream cheese, softened
- 2 cups (16 ounces) sour cream
- 8 ounces white baking chocolate, melted
- 1 tablespoon cornstarch
- 2 teaspoons vanilla extract
- 1/2 teaspoon salt
- 3 eggs, lightly beaten

1. In a large saucepan, bring the rhubarb, 1/3 cup sugar and orange juice to a boil. Reduce heat; cook and stir until thickened and rhubarb is tender. Set mixture aside.

2. In a small bowl, combine the cracker crumbs and butter. Press onto the bottom of a greased 9-in. springform pan. Place on a baking sheet. Bake at 350° for 7-9 minutes or until lightly browned. Cool on a wire rack.

3. In a large bowl, beat cream cheese and remaining sugar until smooth. Beat in the sour cream, white chocolate, cornstarch, vanilla and salt until smooth. Add eggs; beat just until combined.

4. Pour half of the filling into crust. Top with half of the rhubarb sauce; cut through batter with a knife to gently swirl rhubarb. Layer with remaining filling and rhubarb sauce; cut through top layers with a knife to gently swirl rhubarb.

5. Place pan on a double thickness of heavy-duty foil (about 16 in. square). Securely wrap foil around pan. Place in a large baking pan; add 1 in. of hot water to larger pan. Bake at 350° for 60-70 minutes or until center is almost set.

6. Cool on a wire rack for 10 minutes. Carefully run a knife around the edge of pan to loosen; cool 1 hour longer. Cover and chill overnight. Refrigerate leftovers. **Yield:** 12-14 servings.

Editor's Note: If using frozen rhubarb, measure rhubarb while still frozen, then thaw completely. Drain in a colander, but do not press liquid out.

CAROL WITCZAK TINLEY PARK, ILLINOIS

*I love cheesecake and my husband loves chocolate, so this is one of our favorite ways to indulge.
The rhubarb adds a tartness that complements the dessert's sweetness.*

GRAND
PRIZE
WINNER

GENERAL RECIPE INDEX

This handy index lists every recipe by food category, major ingredient and/or cooking method, so you can easily locate recipes to suit your needs.

✓ RECIPE INCLUDES NUTRITION FACTS AND DIABETIC EXCHANGES

ALPHABETICAL RECIPE INDEX

This handy index lists every recipe in alphabetical order,
so you can easily find your favorite recipes.

✓ RECIPE INCLUDES NUTRITION FACTS AND DIABETIC EXCHANGES